## Also by John Martel

*Partners*

*Conflicts of Interest*

*The Alternate*

*Billy Strobe*

*The American Lawyer*

# DRIVEN

Investigating Nine Decades of Stop-at-Nothing Ambition

## JOHN MARTEL

Christmas Lake Press

Published by Christmas Lake Press 2024
www.christmaslakecreative.com
Copyright © 2024 by John Martel
ISBN 978-1-960865-23-6

Interior layout by Daiana Marchesi

# DRIVEN

Nor will any man's reputation endure very long
For what men say dies with them
And is blotted out with the forgetfulness of posterity.
All that will remain of us is what is written down.
—Robert Harris, *Dictator*

# Contents

Acknowledgments .................................................................................. xiii

Author's Note ...................................................................................... xv

Prologue: Looking for Answers ............................................................ xvii

Chapter 1.  No, the Butler Didn't Do It ................................................. 1

Chapter 2.  Alice Laverna Martel, Devoted Mother .............................. 11

Chapter 3.  "Birth: The First and Direst of All Disasters" ..................... 15

Chapter 4.  Early Influences: Friends, Cars, and Movies ...................... 19

Chapter 5.  High School and College .................................................... 25

Chapter 6.  The Military ....................................................................... 35

Chapter 7.  In Pursuit of the Silver Wings ........................................... 39

Chapter 8.  On Second Chances and First Arrests ............................... 47

Chapter 9.  Learning to Drive a Superfortress ..................................... 53

Chapter 10. On Marriage, Becoming a Lawyer, and Other Odd Jobs ..... 65

Chapter 11. Bigger Fish ......................................................................... 81

Chapter 12. Children and the Dissolution ............................................. 95

Chapter 13. Esalen Institute, Big Sur ................................................... 105

Chapter 14.  Taking on a Corporate Giant...................................................109

Chapter 15.  Answering the Call—My Life in Music..................................123

Chapter 16.  Back to My Future: The Mondavi Case...............................141

Chapter 17.  Mondavi, Act Two: The Trial .................................................157

Chapter 18.  The San Francisco Newspaper Case: *Pacific Sun v. The Chronicle, The Examiner* and The Hearst Corporation........195

Chapter 19.  The Menendez Brothers and O. J. Simpson: Murder, Inc....213

Chapter 20.  Other Trials and Tribulations .................................................227

Chapter 21.  Closing Argument—My Life as a Trial Lawyer.....................257

Chapter 22.  After Law and Music, a Third Calling: My Life as a Writer....265

Chapter 23.  Women in My Life: In Search of *The One* ..........................289

Chapter 24.  Finding *The One* at Last—Bonnie Laird Martel.................313

Chapter 25.  Travels with Bonnie ................................................................325

Chapter 26.  Another Hurdle—A Senior Citizen Returns to the Cinders ....331

Chapter 27.  Three's a Crowd: Living with Dr. Parkinson ........................341

Chapter 28.  Mystery Solved.......................................................................345

Epilogue ........................................................................................................349

Appendix: Observations on Our Justice System.......................................351

# Acknowledgments

My thanks to the many friends and family who persuaded me to write a book about my life and then for refreshing my memory on important details. And to Christine Wolf who brilliantly showed me how to write a memoir. Special thanks to son Jay Martel and dear friend Jim Haydel for their advice and encouragement as I clawed my way through the early drafts, inspired, as usual, by my beloved wife, photographer, and copy editor, Bonnie Martel. I am grateful to Bonnie for her commitment to detail and her unfailing patience and support.

Thanks again to Christine Wolf, this time for showering me with her wisdom, connections, and experience by introducing me to the brilliant Thomas Fiffer, Publisher at Christmas Lake Press. Tom made sure from the very beginning that I was happy with the progress of the book every step of the way. Among other things, he assigned the skilled copyeditor, Erika Rundle, to the project. I will be forever grateful for Tom's sensitivity and competence.

Finally, thanks to Douglas R. Young, senior partner at Farella, Braun + Martel and Past President of the American College of Trial Lawyers, for encouraging and refreshing me on details of both organizations.

# Author's Note

The epigraphs that introduce each chapter consist of lines borrowed from over a hundred songs I wrote and performed in the 1970s. I would eventually present many of them at the Troubadour in Los Angeles, where Elton John made his US debut, and also at North Hollywood's Palomino Club, where I once opened for the great Hoyt Axton. The Joe Silverhound Band (Joe Silverhound was my stage name) also played in California clubs as diverse as Eddie & Jerry's Blue Crystal Club in San Francisco, the Sleeping Lady Café in Fairfax, and Marshall Tavern on Tomales Bay.

Logical subtitles for this memoir might be *He Ran for His Life* or *Schizophrenia*, for while my alter ego Joe was performing at night at various clubs around the state, my other persona performed during the daylight hours in various courtrooms around the country. My legal performance was in service to stalwart members of the establishment such as the Bank of America, the Hearst Corporation, and other buttoned-down clients, who apparently found my work adequate because they put up with my shoulder-length hair.

## Prologue

## Looking for Answers

> Ain't you glad you never had
> All the things you always thought you'd always need?
> Keep your fantasies
> And keep something new to read
> For when you're on your own
> All alone, alone, all alone.
> —"Stoned and Alone" (1977)

**DON'T WORRY ABOUT OLD AGE**; it doesn't last.

As I begin writing this book, I am eighty-eight years old. My mind won't accept it, sits sulking in silent denial, but the birth certificate attests, as does my body. So, it's settled: I'm old as dirt and in the winter of my life. But what do I do about a restless, implacable mind still unable to surrender its urgent need to achieve, to be acknowledged, to receive approval? A mind that even now is most at peace when it is at work, creating a song, an essay, anything.

Although I was diagnosed six years ago with Parkinson's disease, a progressive neurological disorder, it hasn't completely disabled me. Like all Parkinsonians, I have to deal with compromised coordination and balance, unpredictable bouts of fatigue, and the damn tremor that, like me, survived a brain surgery two years ago that was supposed to eliminate it.

I pump lightweight iron at my fitness center when I'm not thrashing my way around the golf course, and I suffer little pain. Still, I can't help but wonder how I got so old so fast. How is it that I'm a grandfather when just a year or two ago I was a kid? And why am I still that kid in my head?

Another question commonly asked by an older person looking back on his or her years is: Have I lived a purposeful life?

This is an important inquiry, one that should be asked by everybody, as a life without purpose is like going to Costco without a list. You wander aimlessly through the aisles hoping you'll be reminded of why you're there. This can happen in life, where distractions abound and one is caught up in frivolous activities, yielding to TV sports, news and entertainment, computer games, and social media platforms. A person can live life this way, and, I suppose, even be reasonably content. But there will be something lacking: the joy of incentive, an internal motivation, the satisfaction of accomplishment.

Sadly, many people these days don't even consider the importance of leading purposeful lives. There's simply too much foolish trivia competing for their time.

A purposeful life is essential, but the pages that follow attempt to answer different, even more personal and confounding questions, such as: What made me so compulsively driven to succeed, with nearly total disregard for the damaging consequences to my family and my own emotional wellbeing? Who or what can I blame for my unceasing restlessness? Could it be God, demonstrating that He or She has a cynical sense of humor? No. If there is a God—about which I have doubts—I don't think He or She would bother with such parlor tricks.

If not God, whose fault is it that even now this old man remains unrealistically ambitious, his restless brain overflowing with concepts, songs, books, and ideas that awaken him at dawn, pull him from his warm bed and loving wife to work on a novel that may never be finished, racing against the clock, the calendar, counting the meager grains of sand that pass through the hourglass, measuring one's remaining years. It's said that you can rent time, but you can't buy it. We all exist in fragile detente with time's inexorable haste.

Time is my unrelenting enemy. I am an insect on the head of its pin.

I could, of course, call my relentless drive "healthy ambition," but I'll be under oath here, like a witness in the courtroom, so let's be honest at the outset: my life has been marked by an insatiable, obsessive desire for success and recognition, shadowed closely by a fear of failure, with its attendant anxiety.

In short, I've been as neurotic as a lab rat in a maze.

I know I'm not alone. The great former number one tennis champion, Andre Agassi, wrote a book about his hatred of tennis, the emotional pain, the weekly torture of competition. I recently saw former San Francisco 49er star quarterback Steve Young interviewed on television, during which he confessed to a near-disabling performance anxiety. All those years we watched that cool guy winning the Super Bowl, setting records on the football field, unaware he was in constant psychic pain, often hating what he was doing so beautifully. The clutch in my throat as I listened wasn't just for Steve; of course, it was for myself.

As a courtroom lawyer, I tried nearly one hundred cases, winning all but four of them before I finally burned out and began to realize how much emotional trauma my job was inflicting on me, let alone the toll it had taken on my family. The string of victories was wonderful, of course, the rush of triumph stimulating and addictive, especially during a successful cross-examination or closing argument to the jury. But with every victory came yet another test, a bigger case sometimes commencing the very next day, with even more aggressive lawyers on the other side trying to notch their own wins. There was never enough time to prepare against all the things bound to go wrong and threaten my near perfect record.

The solution—my solution at least—was to abandon sleep, family activities, and anything else that stood between me and my frantic preparation for the next trial. What mystifies me to this day is why I never questioned my situation. To paraphrase Alfred, Lord Tennyson, mine was apparently not to reason why, mine was just to do and die.

Now, after fifty years of combat in the courtroom arena, I belatedly wonder why I was so driven that I continued, like Tennyson's Light Brigade, to ride into "the valley of Death" day after day, decade after decade, never once stopping to "reason why."

— — —

What caused this craving, this unrelenting drive that seduced me into embracing years of unremitting pressure, mainly as a trial lawyer, but also as an athlete, composer, and novelist? Viewed from the outside, my plight would surely not be seen as a curse by most observers, but rather as a healthy blessing, a natural hunger for attainment that I should be shot for complaining about. True, but what about the cost, the nearly disabling anxiety, the physical and emotional encumbrance of this constant pursuit of success and recognition?

I have days when my life is just a tent away from a three-ring circus.
—Anonymous

So back to the question: how did all this insane obsession with success and recognition come about, or, put more simply, how did I get this way?

Again, because I can't shrug off my affliction by calling it healthy ambition—an internal driver found in many people—I must attribute it to one or more external forces that drove me to succeed. Therefore I chose the title *Driven*. (Yet another subtitle might have been *Obsessed with Grand Achievement*.) No accountancy for me, no engineering, or dentistry, uh-uh. A quest to be worthy of my obsession must offer the potential for an olive wreath or at least fifteen minutes (or years) of fame.

I cannot recall when this preoccupation with recognition started, but certainly by my teens I had figured out that some accomplishments were more likely than others to gain the attention of people, particularly girls. So I quit the middle school marching band and began playing sports instead. Then later, with a war breaking out? Simple—become an Air Force pilot, complete with glamourous white scarf and goggles. Pick a vocation after the war? Become a trial lawyer. Still not challenging enough, insufficient recognition? Reinvent yourself as a rock and roll singer/songwriter. Forced to choose between music and law? Turn down Doug Weston's offer to record a *Live at the Troubadour* album featuring your voice and original songs, break up your band, return to San Francisco and go to trial in the nationally publicized *Mondavi v. Mondavi* case, an even bigger fish. And why not write a novel in your spare time while you're at it? Not a national bestseller? Write another one. Ah, good, check that one off, too. And so on.

One nice thing about egotists: they don't talk about other people.
—George Carlin

I realize there will be times in this book, like just now, when I come off as a braggart, a flaming egomaniac. I'm acutely aware of this, but want to assure the reader that, to the extent that truth is a defense, I have not exaggerated any of my achievements. I'm aware that my exploits will be read by people who are intimately familiar with them, people whose opinion of me I'm unwilling to jeopardize by mendacious boasting.

More importantly, I ask your tolerance and understanding, realizing that this isn't a book about my accomplishments per se, but rather an analysis of why I was driven at great personal cost to achieve them. I know of no way to analyze the "why" without first setting forth the "what." Moreover, much of what I have accomplished has been the result of a lucky break or due to the help of people wiser than I am. I have never claimed to be the smartest guy in the room. What I have been is the guy who was willing to work harder than anybody else, since failure was never an option.

Maybe some of my story will strike a chord with you. Perhaps you, too, are successful in much of what you do, yet derive little satisfaction from it. Or perhaps you feel you've wasted months or years on a job or project, or maybe given too much or too little of yourself to your children or to clients or customers or employers without the flood of self-satisfaction you feel you deserve and *should* feel.

Or maybe you feel the clock is ticking and you're not sure you're with the right person or in the right job or living in the right city. Or perhaps you're simply a person curious about how other people develop and mature . . . or fail to.

If any of these inquiries ring a bell with you, come along and seek answers with me. It'll be a trip back in time, during which I hope not to lose my way. In the process, I will candidly and truthfully examine how my successes were possible to achieve and how they might be possible for others to achieve, without having to suffer the associated discomfort I've described in this chapter. That's my secondary purpose in conducting this reflection—to spare others my pain.

I've often been categorized as a legal mystery writer, though I don't think of myself that way. I've never been much interested in writing whodunits, but rather in constructing a story in which the protagonist must discover things (usually already known to the reader) in time to avert chaos. So, I prefer the "suspense thriller" label, but why quibble? And why not write a story here—with a minimum of psychobabble— that seeks to solve the mystery of why a reasonably intelligent person like me cannot, even now, be sure of how he became who he turned out to be, or even what he really wants to do with what's left of his life? While I'm at it, I'll try to pin down who or what is primarily responsible for the way I turned out. I suspect that if I'm honest with the facts, the reader will have figured out the answer halfway through the book, an answer I'm not yet sure about myself.

All good mysteries involve a crime, a wrongdoing to be revealed and punished, a victim, and one or more potential wrongdoers. The usual suspects in a case like this are of course, the subject's parents. But isn't that too obvious? You know, like "the butler did it?"

Ladies and gentlemen of the jury, I submit it to you.

# Chapter 1

# No, the Butler Didn't Do It

Old friends, holding on, to fading visions
and decisions made so long ago.
Where did the fun and the music go?
Old friends, love has come and gone
There's nothing left to do
but love the one inside of you.
—"Old Friends" (1976)

I'LL START MY INVESTIGATION by looking first to genetics, which means an examination of the biological influences asserted by my parents, then move to a study of their environmental impact, specifically their child-rearing philosophies and techniques. Studies on childhood development show that a child's personality is created by an interaction of inherited genetics and parental environment.

My father, Henry Theodore Martel, was handsome, charming, and utterly French, by birth and in aspect. His brown eyes twinkled, promising wit and intelligence. His killer smile lifted the corners of his well-groomed mustache, yet rarely reached his eyes. He was a romantic, a faithful provider, and . . . an emotional tyrant.

I see my father as an unlikely candidate for having passed on a genetic predisposition for a healthy ambition. A lifetime dairy inspector for the State of California, Henry Martel had not a shred of discernable aspiration, despite a high native intelligence. Although he never attended college, I can recall listening to *Dr. I.Q.* on the radio with my parents and my father frequently knowing the correct answer to questions before the contestant could even open his or her mouth.

He could also be a bit of a charlatan in establishing his seeming brilliance. I vividly remember when I was about seven years old, during the one football game we ever attended together, he impressed me with his incredible prescience by accurately predicting when the team on offense was going to throw a pass instead of running, or go into a punt formation instead of running or passing. I left that game certain my father was a god. I was too young to understand that nearly all teams throw a pass on the third down when faced with long first-down yardage, just as they inevitably punt the ball on the fourth down when they're deep in their own territory. (This bit of chicanery didn't occur to me until well into adulthood.)

Much to his credit, my father did hold his job as a state dairy inspector throughout the Depression, work that kept us well-fed with a roof over our heads. He also assisted his out-of-work relatives in their times of need. As for his own genetically imbued ambition, what he may have lacked in drive he made up for with dependability.

He quit that job at sixty, the minute he qualified for his modest pension. He then hardly ever left the family home at 209 State Street in Modesto, content to play game after game of solitaire on the couch in our living room—"playing the Chinaman" he improperly called it—then proceeded to die of boredom within a year of retirement.

Chalk one up for the Chinaman.

At the age of sixty-one, with my younger brother and sister still in high school, and living at home, Henry Martel suffered a major stroke that would quickly prove fatal. I was twenty-nine and a new deputy district attorney in Oakland. Mom had summoned her sister, my Aunt Monie, and her husband, Uncle Lloyd, to Modesto, and Uncle Lloyd then summoned me. It was eleven o'clock at night and I was asleep in Oakland with Ann, my first wife.

"You'd better hurry, John," Uncle Lloyd said, "he's going fast."

I dressed quickly and exceeded the speed limit from Oakland to Modesto, a distance of less than one hundred miles. The bad news did not surprise me. At Mom's request, I'd taken my father to the hospital after he'd suffered a minor stroke two weeks earlier, then picked him up again the following day. At that time, the doctor told me, "You might as well keep him home."

I drove fast that night not because I was distressed I was about to lose my father, but because it seemed important to say goodbye to him while he was still alive. I arrived in time and was taken immediately by Uncle Lloyd past my teary-eyed mother and siblings into Pop's bedroom and then left there alone with him.

He was marginally conscious, but I can't say he recognized me. That didn't matter. What mattered was that I was able to say goodbye to a suddenly gentle man, pale and vulnerable, who seemed to know his time was up. He didn't ask my forgiveness for the way he had always berated me, but in my heart, I gave it to him anyway.

— — —

Returning to the issue of my father as suspect, his employment record does not bespeak ambition or drive. But wait. Although he wasn't himself ambitious, might his ancestral genetics, bestowed upon him by *his* father, have leapfrogged Henry's DNA and moved directly into the chromosomes of his progeny, your memoirist?

My grandfather, John Baptiste Martel, born in Québec on June 6, 1861, was known for his gambling spirit. He demonstrated not only ambition, but courage and initiative when he packed up his wife and three children (young Henry among them) and emigrated from Québec into the state of Washington. Once settled, he quickly founded a lumber mill that blossomed into a lucrative, fast-growing "company town." Moving an entire family into a new country, followed by his business success once there, would suggest a healthy ambition. Family legend, incidentally, is that he lost everything—his wealth, the lumber mill, and the entire company town—in an all-night poker game.

I can only remember two occasions when I actually saw my paternal grandfather. (I never knew my grandmother at all.) This was because Henry Martel hated his father for reasons never explained to me, but likely because John Baptiste was as crappy a father to Henry as Henry turned out to be to me. Grandfather John Baptiste probably also hated his own father, Luise Damase Martel (born 1834, in Québec), and Luise probably hated his father, Luise Isaie (born 1796, in St. Croix), who probably hated his daddy, Paul Joseph Martel (born 1759, in St. Croix), too, and so on, all the way back to Charles Martel ("The Hammer") who was too busy defeating the Saracens at Tours in 732 to have been a good father to his son, King Pepin (born 714) or to even take the time to play with his grandson, Charlemagne (born circa 742), the first Holy Roman emperor. (The three Frankish Kings were claimed by my father to be direct French forebears, but always with that twinkle in his eye. The others listed are true ancestors.)

I conclude that it's difficult for a man to be a good father without a role model. And where does that put *me* as a father, I wonder? Was I just another link in a dysfunctional paternal chain?

Let's take a closer look at Henry. After attending high school in Washington, my father became Corporal Henry Martel, serving in the US Army as an officer's driver during the First World War. When the armistice was declared, Henry ventured south into California and secured a job as a dairy inspector, based in Stockton. Soon after his arrival there, he wandered into a dance hall in the nearby small town of

Oakdale, where his gaze fell on the beautiful, blue-eyed, eighteen-year-old Alice Laverna Hallinan.

What a dashing figure he must have cut amongst the local yokels. It was love at first sight for both of them, and Henry, the romantic French Canadian, promptly proposed marriage. They were wed on October 19, 1929, just as the Great Depression loomed. If Alice's parents, Thomas and Mary Ann Hallinan, were put off by Henry's age—thirty-six—they were probably consoled to learn he was employed *and* a practicing Catholic. What my smitten mother had the good sense not to mention to her religious parents was that Henry, eighteen years her senior, was also the divorced father of a son named Stuart Martel, and had thereby been excommunicated from the One True Faith.

> The way we talk to our children becomes their inner voice.
> —Peggy O'Mara

Since it appears doubtful the DNA I inherited from Henry Martel is the source of my ambition, what about his "environmental impact," i.e., his parenting? Regrettably, I must testify that as a parent, he not only failed to encourage me to achieve success, he even seemed bent on inhibiting it.

He did try to "make a man out of me" when I was approximately three years old by pitting me in a fight against an equally young, frightened, and reluctant boy, the son of one of my father's acquaintances. This is one of my earliest memories. The two "adults" had apparently decided it was never too early to breed some violence into their male heirs. It ended badly, neither of us willing to hit the other despite being repeatedly pushed against one another by our fathers.

Henry, probably humiliated and obviously infuriated by my cowardice, called me a "sissy kisser," his favorite insult whenever I wavered from his standard of nascent manhood.

The occasional cruelty of my father was somewhat offset by loving aunts and an adoring mother who constantly reminded me I was "beautiful" and sent me to ballet school at the age of four. I might, under the now-discredited view of homosexual causation, have grown up to be gay. Instead, I became Exhibit A in support of the LGBTQA community's contention that homosexuality is a product of a genetic/constitutional predisposition rather than environmental-developmental-choice factors.

The dancing school experience, incidentally, did not turn out well. I rebelled during my second or third group lesson, sneaked out of the building, and miraculously found my way home, several miles in all, without getting kidnapped, lost, or hit by a car. My parents were so amazed by the feat that I wasn't punished. Nor was I sent back to the dancing academy, thus ending my mother's dream that her son would be the next Rudolph Nureyev.

I should clarify here that Henry was never physically abusive in his fathering, except for the "nubbin"—an uncomfortable snapping on my wrist or forearm from the sudden release of his coiled thumb and middle finger. It was rarely used. I was raised in the era of "children are to be seen, not heard," and if I were misbehaving, all I had to see, sometimes across a crowded room, was his hand raised, thumb and middle finger touching, the threat of a "nubbin." Such was my fear of his disapproval.

Probably for the better, I had little quality time with my father growing up. In fact, I can remember only five situations in which we did anything alone together:

1. Accompanying him to the post office to pick up the mail.
2. Taking me at a young age to the aforementioned Modesto Junior College football game.
3. Taking me to one Modesto Reds baseball game.

4. Taking me to a movie of his choice when my mother was hosting her sewing club.
5. Taking me to the train station once when I was four years old and lifting me up on his shoulders so I could see his political hero—the Republican presidential candidate Wendell Willkie—speak from the caboose of a train, the way they did in those days.

Spoiler alert: Roosevelt won in a landslide.

— — —

In 1951, I was twenty and on my first leave from the Air Force, still a private awaiting my cadet class appointment, proudly wearing my uniform and the most valuable material possession I had ever owned, a fine wristwatch I purchased at a substantial discount at the base commissary. My father and I stood together in the living room in Modesto, and, as I had hoped, he noticed the watch and complimented me on it. On an impulse, without even thinking about it, I removed it from my wrist and offered it to him. He accepted it without hesitation or thanks. I had conflicting reactions: pride, coupled with a sense of loss. I loved that watch and he seemed to take my gift for granted. Henry Martel remains—to this day—essentially a stranger to me, yet I never stopped striving for his love.

I now realize that, for a variety of reasons—not the least of which is that he never experienced love from his own father—he didn't know how to give me the love I needed. I also learned, from scraps of conversation as I grew up, that my birth had nearly killed my mother. My father always referred to her subsequent hospitalizations as "a problem with her leg." This helps explain the twelve-year hiatus before they dared to risk procreation again, producing my sister Mary, and then two years later, my brother Lloyd. I speculate that the pain and damage my birth caused my mother was something my father unconsciously blamed me for and could never entirely forgive.

Yet another complication in our relationship was my mother's unceasing and deep devotion to me. My father undoubtedly envied the dedication of time, energy, and unconditional love my mother showered upon me. My achievements as I grew older only exacerbated the situation and may have heightened the competition. Why else was he so dismissive of even my minor accomplishments? For example, when I made the first-string varsity basketball team in my senior year of high school, his response was, "You need basketball like you need water in your shoes."

I think he felt the same way about my becoming a pilot in the Air Force and then a lawyer, having not been an officer himself and having never attended college.

I wouldn't blame my Freudian readers for thinking of Oedipus, and how he had unwittingly killed his father, Laius, and married his mother, Jocasta. This would be wrong, however, as I was more than secure in my mother's love, and she worshiped my father. What I desperately desired was the love of my father, something he was incapable of giving.

Perhaps that's why, like Oedipus, I tried one night to kill him.

It was the spring of 1968 and drugs were rampant. My friend Jack Hawkinson had acquired some LSD and offered to share. I had recently been to the Esalen Institute where I'd met Timothy Leary, one of the godfathers of LSD, and was intrigued.

Jack had taken a summer rental near the Seascape Golf Club in Aptos, California. He and his buddy planned on taking the drug and attending *2001: A Space Odyssey.* I considered the idea of combining such a personal experience with a movie to be frivolous and opted to hang back.

"Do you think it wise," Jack asked, "being ripped on LSD for the first time here all by yourself?"

"No problem," I said, "you guys enjoy the show."

My recollections of the experience are surprisingly lucid, and here are two of them: The first thing I did after Jack and his friend left for San Jose was to put on some music by Cream. Soon thereafter, I was shocked to notice flames shooting out of two speakers mounted on the ceiling on each side of the living room.

I went out the back door, and to my immediate right noticed a small tree with a trunk about ten inches in diameter. Then, to my amazement, I recognized the clear face of my father imbedded in the trunk, staring at me with disapproval. I somehow had the presence of mind to find a saw in the toolshed and earnestly began to cut down the tree.

"I'm sorry I have to kill you," I said to my father, "but it's time for you to go."

My father had been dead for years, so I was speaking metaphorically. The tree, however, had been very much alive before my attack, and I had to confess to Jack the next day that although I had failed to cut it to the ground, I had probably succeeded in killing it. Indeed, an arborist pronounced it near death a few days later and took it away. The landlord settled for $200.

## Chapter 2

# Alice Laverna Martel, Devoted Mother

Young Joanna, untried but true
When she married my father, she was the first girl I knew.
She taught me that women were stronger than men
But I learned how to view them, to woo and pursue them
By the time I was ten.
—"Teachers" (1972)

ANOTHER LOGICAL SUSPECT WHO may have inspired my relentless drive, Alice Hallinan Martel, was born in Coulterville, California on June 26, 1908. A national census taken two years later listed Coulterville's population at 201, attesting to the town's relative insignificance. But Coulterville would always be famous in my mind, not because it was my mother's birthplace, but because it was an occasional hideout for California's most famous bandido, Joaquin Murrieta, known as the Robin Hood of the West.

Murrieta had been a California gold rush miner working in nearby Sonora when he and his brother were falsely accused of stealing a mule. Bigoted white miners hanged Murrieta's brother and horsewhipped Joaquin, but that wasn't the end of it. Joaquin's young wife was gang raped and died in his arms. Joaquin vowed revenge and achieved justice in his mind by killing every participant in his wife's murder. His violent life of vengeance and crime came to an end only after the State of California offered a $5,000 reward for his capture, "dead or alive." Although killed in 1853, rumors persisted one hundred years later that he survived.

I was a very young child visiting my mother's birthplace with my parents and grandparents when I was told the Murrieta story by my grandfather, Thomas Hallinan, who was also born in Coulterville. I remember being haunted by the thought that the bloodthirsty Mexican bandido might still be alive, lurking in the area, seeking more revenge.

Alice, highly intelligent, was nevertheless a victim of both her era and a paternalistic and overprotective husband. She had been editor of the Oakdale High School newspaper and the school yearbook and was headed for college to become a nurse (like her two older sisters), but she fell in love with and married the dashing French Canadian Henry Martel instead. She was eighteen, beautiful, five foot two, eyes of blue, and pure Irish.

While she may have been deprived of the opportunity to pursue ambitious goals, I have no doubt she had dreams. Whatever they were, they soon withered in the face of my father's dominance, to which she willingly succumbed (it was the 1930s after all). Moreover, she loved and trusted her husband. The problem with this dependence arose when he died. She was only in her late forties and sadly unskilled, a widow who had never written a check and who would die without ever having learned to drive a car. She never held a real job, though she once made a good faith, albeit unsuccessful, attempt at door-to-door sales, peddling a Fuller Brush cosmetic line.

Alice did have an acquisitive streak, though, when it came to her residence. She was the ambitious force behind every move we made, always to a slightly improved home. Our last house at 209 State Street in Modesto, after smaller homes on Walden and James Streets, seemed more than adequate to everyone but Mom. Even after the move, my siblings and I recall frequent trips across Dry Creek into the upscale homes district. Henry was able to hold the line at State Street, however, arguing the reality of his relatively modest salary as a state employee. Accordingly, 209 State was Mom's last home—at least until we enrolled her at the Casa de Modesto, where she lived several years before her death at eighty-nine, protesting all the while that she was "surrounded by old people."

Alice loved and protected me—a shy, introverted boy—with the intensity of a mother bear, tolerating no criticism of her eldest cub. The only heated arguments I remember her having (other than with my father) were with her two older sisters, both of whom were childless. When either my beloved Aunt Monie or the glamorous Aunt Lorna were so bold as to offer what they considered constructive criticism about her precious offspring, Alice would almost always perceive the comment as cutting (an attack on me or herself or both) and a vigorous argument would ensue, the decibel level in direct proportion to the amount of alcohol previously consumed. Both Monie and Lorna were registered nurses and unable to have children, but viewed themselves as my surrogate mothers, and enviously saw their younger sister as too immature to be raising a child. Faults and all, in my mother's adoring blue eyes I was a sacred cow—above criticism, even after my siblings Mary and Lloyd joined the family.

Although I never felt pushed by my mother to succeed, I'm certain she was entirely responsible for the original sin of having me skip kindergarten at the age of four. She was convinced I was a genius and told everybody who would listen about how I would look over her shoulder and read aloud from her book.

Alas, skipping kindergarten didn't work out for me. Everyone in the first grade class at Capitol Elementary School had attended kindergarten together with the same teacher and I was the only new kid, the interloper, not only incredibly shy, but also hopelessly confused. For example, when the teacher led the class in alternating (skipping) notes up and down the major scale, using her hand as a guide ("do-mi-re-fa . . ."), I believed all the other students possessed magic, a gift that had somehow eluded me, as I was used to a simple "do-re-mi-fa . . ." I did my best to bluff my way through those moments (early preparation for my life as a trial lawyer), but knew I was doomed without the supernatural powers enjoyed by my classmates.

Regrettably, teachers weren't as sensitive as they generally are now, and I was left in the dark, the new kid in town, living a daily nightmare that first year that undoubtedly influenced the rest of my life. I'm only guessing here, but I think that confused young kid must have vowed to do whatever it took, be whatever he had to be, to avoid future repetitions of his daily humiliating existence. Mom undoubtedly meant well, but for allowing me to skip kindergarten, I'll put her down as a person of interest in my investigation.

My mother had a wonderful sense of humor. When I was around twelve, I came into possession of a realistic rubber mouse. One night when she was steaming some artichokes, I placed the little gray mouse on top of one of the chokes and replaced the pot lid. Needless to say, the gambit elicited the desired scream, followed by relieved and infectious laughter. That gray mouse became well-traveled as it was passed back and forth between two pranksters—Mom and me. When I received a package at an Air Force base, for instance, I was careful when opening the contents because I knew the gray mouse was lurking in there. When Mom died, the family held a small graveside memorial service at her open casket. When I completed my own tribute, I placed the gray mouse near her hands, and the casket was sealed.

# Chapter 3

# "Birth: The First and Direst of All Disasters"

—Ambrose Bierce
Calliopes announce yet conceal your cause
As you try to climb up, beyond their applause.
But instead of looking down you listen inside
To the voice of a child you thought had died.
—"On and On" (1972)

MY LIFE BEGAN ON a dark and stormy night in Stockton, California, when I was cast from my mother's womb during the early hours of the year 1931 into a fragmented world, the economic black hole that became known as the Great Depression.

I was the first baby born that year in Stockton, and as mentioned earlier, childbirth hadn't been easy for my mother. The precise nature of the complications in her labor and delivery were never revealed to me, but I know she suffered greatly from the event, and I wasn't a healthy baby. Indeed, I soon developed a combination of whooping cough and pneumonia that almost claimed my life. Although the first antibiotic, penicillin, was discovered by Alexander Fleming three years before my birth, it wasn't used in Stockton until the 1940s.

I recovered, and the following year we moved from Stockton to a modest home on Boden Street in Modesto, twenty-eight miles away, probably to be closer to the young bride's parents, who lived in nearby Oakdale.

With no siblings or even cousins to play with, my alienation was aggravated by my mother deciding I would skip kindergarten. Consequently, I entered the first grade with neither experience nor ability in the art of socialization. Bereft of playmates, I learned to play by myself. At the age of seven, for example, I often morphed into Batman, complete with mask and cape, terrorizing imagined criminals near our two-bedroom wooden home, then at 617 James Street. I recall only once succumbing to the forces of evil, when Jimmie Pickthall, the neighborhood bully, laid me out with a single punch. After that encounter, Batman decided it would be prudent to limit his protection to those citizens living much closer to his home.

My early education is a blank, not so much because I have forgotten events but because there were so few memorable ones. I have only the vaguest recollections of being bored by teachers and harassed by bullies. I remember my mother showing me a report card when I was about seven years old, on which my home teacher noted, "John is academically advanced but socially deficient." Sadly, but truly, it was only in the seventh grade at Roosevelt Junior High that I finally emerged from my shell, alas not like a butterfly emerging from its chrysalis, but rather more like a drunken sailor on shore leave being tossed out of a bar. I was clumsily discovering the opposite sex, smoking cigarettes, playing second trumpet in the junior high school band, forging close friendships with other horny boys, and running for student body vice president. (I lost.)

Our family had little disposable income, so from middle school to high school, I worked part-time during the year at the Home Market and the Owl Drugstore. My paychecks were turned over to my father, who returned part of my earnings as my allowance after I completed household chores such as mowing the lawn. I learned early in life that there was "no such thing as a free lunch."

Later during the school year, as teenagers, my friends Ed Rotticci, Bob Jones, and I hitchhiked everywhere without fear, often to Pinecrest Lake, seventy-seven miles away, where we each experienced our first summer romances—and a syrupy bourbon whiskey called Southern Comfort.

We Martels were an insular and austere family. This austerity was partly a product of the Depression, but other kids I knew often went out to dinner. I recall only one occasion in twenty years when we went out to dinner. When I was about ten, we drove across town to a restaurant called Over the Waves. I ate tamales.

My favorite entertainment as a preteen was watching films, sometimes alone—about places I knew I would never go, and starring actors I would never know—at the Strand, Princess, or Lyric movie theaters.

Weekends growing up were spent either with my Uncle Lloyd and Aunt Monie in Lodi or with my mother's parents, Tom and Mary, in Oakdale. When in Oakdale, I would sleep in my khakis and T-shirt on the living room couch, lovingly wrapped in a blanket by Grandma, close enough to my grandparents' bedroom that I would fall asleep listening to the calming drone of them reciting the Catholic Rosary. Disproving the advertiser's creed that repetition breeds internalization, the Catholic faith never stuck with me.

I loved my grandfather, Thomas Hallinan, my widowed grandmother's second husband and my mother's father. Born in 1871 in Coulterville, California, he'd been both a cowboy and a butcher. His father, John Joseph Hallinan (my surname was preordained with forefathers on both sides of the family named John) was born in 1832 in Westport, Ireland, County Mayo, Province of Connacht, and came to America during the Irish potato famine, then travelled west, herding cattle with the famous American frontiersman, Kit Carson.

When I was nine, we moved to a house with a basketball hoop mounted to a patio above our short driveway. I spent many hours shooting baskets and competing against the taller and stronger Hancock, an imaginary hoops opponent whom I somehow always managed to defeat. What does it say about me that I never had an imaginary friend as a child, but did have an imaginary enemy? It tells me that the sad-faced lonely little boy I have seen in photographs, who knew little about making friends, couldn't even imagine one.

A year after we moved in, I was outside on a crisp winter day I will never forget, giving Hancock a good drubbing. It was December 7, 1941, and I clearly recall hearing an explosion of shouting from inside the house. Running up the porch stairs and through the front door, I heard my father yell, "The Japs have bombed Pearl Harbor! The Japs have bombed Pearl Harbor!"

## Chapter 4

# Early Influences: Friends, Cars, and Movies

> The old screen door slams shut in my face
> Your exits were always dramatic.
> Just like a movie, lacking only suspense
> The ending predictably tragic.
> —"Forget Me Not" (1980)

MOVIES, ESPECIALLY WAR MOVIES, played an important role in my education during the 1940s and should qualify as an entity of interest in the investigation of who or what was responsible for my driven nature. Having rejected my father as a role model by the time I was in junior high school, I looked to the screen heroes of the time—John Wayne, then later, Gregory Peck and Humphrey Bogart, as examples of ideal manhood. I was Wayne in *Flying Tigers,* Peck in *Duel in the Sun,* and Bogart in *Casablanca.* What I learned from these men was the importance of saying little but meaning a lot, simply by the force of one's presence. These and other cinematic role models, typically strong and handsome, dependably defeated evil and—equally important—always ended up getting the girl.

The problem was that at eleven, I felt neither strong nor handsome. Moreover, as a kid, I didn't distinguish between the characters the men were playing and the actors themselves. I later learned, for example, that my childhood idol, John Wayne, wasn't a war hero at all, but rather a right-wing reactionary and major supporter of the Hollywood Blacklist. Wayne fought his courageous battles only on a movie set and never served a day as an authentic military man. When I learned the truth in my early adulthood, I felt duped by Hollywood and formed an unreasonable dislike for Wayne that I maintain to this day.

Automobiles also played an important role in my youth, particularly during the high school years. Cars meant status to Modesto High School boys, and the louder the better. Every cent we got our hands on went into cars. The first one I owned, in partnership with a classmate, was a classic Duesenberg, the kind the despised Hitler rode in during parades, although ours didn't even run. Accordingly, it cost us only thirty-five dollars, but if I had put the car up on blocks and held on to it, I could sell it now for a fortune. After fixing it up a bit, we sold it for ninety dollars. I next owned a 1928 Ford Model T before going up-market in my junior year of high school to a 1931 Ford Model B with a Mercury eight-cylinder engine under the hood. The car was loud and fast and I felt hot behind the wheel, my status elevated.

## Backstory: My Extended Family

On balance, but for my abusive father, I enjoyed a relatively normal childhood, though neither I nor my much younger siblings suspected at the time that our parents, and our Irish aunts and uncles, were probably all social alcoholics. Henry, Alice, Uncle Leo Hallinan, and my mother's other older sister, Lorna McKay, were that form of alcoholic who drank little during the week (Jekyll), but turned into another person (Hyde) on weekends. You didn't want to be in the same time zone when my family got together with Early Times flowing, especially when the topic of politics came up. I believe the medical term for people like the members of my maternal Irish family is "functional alcoholic."

Little to no drinking took place during the week, but both Mom and Dad were argumentative, sometimes pugnacious, when drinking on weekends, so I gave them a wide berth. As an eight-to-ten-year-old, I recall coming out of my bedroom in the morning and more than once observing a packed suitcase by the front door. I never asked why it was there or why it would magically disappear soon after my parents woke up. (I later concluded that Henry's resolve to bolt would burn out from the effort of packing his bag and having to contemplate where the hell he might go if he really left us.) At one point, however, he apparently made it out the door, and was gone for several weeks. My mother assured me he was attending a state convention in Sacramento, and at six or seven, I was young enough to buy the story. I realize now that it must have been a trial separation.

Raised Catholic, I particularly disliked catechism class every Sunday. I see now the early signs of my budding insecurity. Though I often knew the answers to the nun's questions, I was so fearful of the humiliating consequences I'd face if I were wrong that I couldn't raise my hand. And then, when another kid inevitably gave the answer I knew to be correct and he or she was praised, I hated that kid almost as much as my own cowardice. I was apparently well-taught by my father that I had better never be wrong if I didn't want a painful "nubbin."

## Boys Will Be Boys

Q. It is the most abused and neglected part of your body.
What is it?
A. Mine may be abused, but it certainly isn't neglected.
—Paul Lynde, *Hollywood Squares*

I fainted twice at the communion rail while growing up, such was my unconscious discomfort with the whole Roman process. Weekly confession, in order to qualify for the holy sacrament of Communion, was another nightmare, particularly when, at an early age (ten or eleven), I became a blue-ribbon wanker, making Philip Roth's Portnoy look like a celibate. How was I to know that *all* boys whacked off—or "abused themselves sexually" as the priest instructed me to describe it. I was sure I was the only one guilty of this mortal sin—at least the only one who flogged the dog several times a day. I grew to hate Saturdays following confession, because I had to "remain in a state of grace" until receiving Holy Communion the next morning. Back home after church on Sunday, I couldn't wait to lock myself in the bathroom.

## The Martel Dark Secret

I wasn't the only one in the family with a secret. My devout mother's marriage in the Catholic Church to a divorced Catholic man in those days constituted grounds for her immediate and permanent excommunication, my father having already been given the boot by the Pope for divorcing his first wife—something they kept from almost everyone. Mom's parents went to their graves without knowing the family's Dark Secret, and I might never have become aware of it myself but for the fact that at the age of fifteen, I fortuitously came home early one day and was introduced to our visitor, a young man who bore an uncanny resemblance to my father, with identical eyes and coloring, right down to the mustache. I recall being stunned by the similarity, but it wasn't until the following Sunday that my father confessed that the young man, Stuart Martel, was my half-brother and the issue of a former marriage—of which I had also been unaware. I eventually became friends with Stuart before he died from a Parkinson's-induced fall at ninety-two years, an age I'm rapidly approaching.

At fifteen, I didn't consider the ecclesiastical consequences of this revelation for my devout Catholic mother and was too young and naïve to realize when I first met Stuart that I was shaking hands with a living manifestation of the Dark Secret. My mother's hypocrisy was quite pronounced when she later refused to acknowledge my first marriage solely on the grounds that my new wife was a Protestant. As my non-devout father had to live with my mother, I suppose he had no choice but to take up arms against me as well, though he seemed to relish the task. In fact, everybody in the family was angry with me, even my beloved Aunt Monie, and all of them boycotted not only the wedding but our young, married existence as well. Only the birth of our first son softened my family's position.

# Chapter 5

# High School and College

> I know a thing or two about a lot of things
> A regular jack of all trades, but a master of none
> Except maybe one.
> —"Survivor" (1977)

**LET'S EXPAND THE LIST** of potential suspects.

High school was the venue for some of my best and worst memories. Here's an anecdote from my sophomore year that undoubtedly had a powerful impact on my psyche. Yes, I know Freud assures us that our unconscious minds are already well formed by the time we're six, but this event left an emotional scar worthy of mention.

I'd completed my pledge year as a member of a prestigious high school fraternity, the 36 Club, and was attending a joint social meeting with a popular sister sorority. When I chastened a new freshman pledge for failing to respectfully greet me in a corridor of the high school, an attractive senior girl named Carol Clapper uttered words I will never forget:

"You're so small," she sneered. "He probably didn't see you."

Her comment was followed by humiliating laughter from both boys and girls. I wasn't small for my age, but I was a year younger than most of my classmates. I summoned the presence of mind to invite Ms. Clapper to go fuck herself, but damage to my ego had been done, and I suspect my sophomore self unconsciously resolved to become the kind of person to whom this kind of public insult would never again be directed. There wasn't much I could do to increase my height in a hurry, but I could begin to compensate for my other shortcomings by working harder than anybody else to make sure I was never overlooked. I knew there'd be other Carol Clappers in my life, but dammit, I'd be ready for them. I would, at all costs, become . . . *significant.*

Add Carol Clapper to the growing list of suspects.

All things considered (teen confusion, pimple outbreaks, exploding hormones), high school was generally a positive experience, largely because of sports, friends, and a nearly cinematic coming-of-age event that happened to me in my senior year—a real-life fantasy.

Because of my smaller size, sports in my first three years in high school were limited to track-and-field. I gained some growth in my senior year at the age of seventeen, but little realized how much my life was about to change.

One day Mick Parsons, the varsity basketball coach, picked me out of an intramural game and recruited me on the spot for the varsity team, where I quickly became first-string, shocking nobody more than myself. One of my good friends, Bill Wetmore, was a star center on the team. Suddenly having him setting picks for me so I could drive to the basket for a layup? This was a dream come true. Halfway through the season, I was the third-highest scorer on the team, until injuries sidelined me.

My father was unimpressed, but I'm eternally grateful to coach Parsons for giving me the opportunity to achieve what every boy dreams of growing up. I was suddenly popular, and my life seemed to come alive.

## Early Jobs

My first paying jobs were typical for young boys during that era: bicycle delivery boy for weekly shopping periodicals at eleven, the produce department of the Home Market at twelve, and busboy at the Owl Drug-store's soda fountain at thirteen.

My summer jobs meant working side-by-side with progeny of Steinbeck's dust bowl Okies, often in blistering heat in the agricultural industry of Stanislaus County. I started young, helping my mother at her job cutting peaches into halves for preparation into dried fruit, and then, once I was in high school, laying out the halved fruit in trays and loading them into sulfur bins. (I inhaled a good deal of sulfur and other toxins in those early summers of my life, and statistics have established a higher-than normal incidence of Parkinson's for residents of the agricultural Central Valley.)

At seventeen, between high school and junior college, I finally achieved a major growth hike to five feet eleven inches and 160 pounds, and with the connivance of an older friend, Ray Pope, I lied that I was eighteen and secured a job at the railroad refrigeration plant. The job involved pulling 300-pound slabs of ice off a conveyor chain that ran down the middle of a deck, fifty yards in length. This deck was constructed to stand at the height of adjoining refrigerated railway cars, into which the ice was to be directed. This was in 1948, when the only refrigeration available for transporting perishables by rail consisted of multiple fifty-pound "ice cubes" jammed into the end of freight cars. Getting these blocks of ice into the tops of the cars was a formidable challenge.

The process began when the conveyor chain transported the ice slabs out of the "galley" where they'd been frozen into rectangular blocks standing approximately three feet high, four feet in length and about one foot wide. Equipped with a six-foot wooden handle with a bayonet-like spike at the end adjacent to a curved hook, our job was to jerk the slab off the conveyor with the hook end, then keep the slab sliding across the deck onto an eight-foot long, two-foot wide "sled" that straddled the deck and the open hatch of the freight car. As the 300-pound slab slid past the worker on the narrow sled bridging the deck and the freight car, barely missing his steel-clad toes, the challenge was to use stabbing motions with the spike end, breaking the block into six (not five, not seven, *exactly six!*) fifty-pound pieces, and then guiding each block into and through the open hatch located at the end of the refrigerated freight car.

This process took less than ten seconds and was repeated over and over until either the boxcar was topped off, the galley blessedly ran out of ice, or the worker suffered heatstroke—which I once did. Camus' imagery in *The Myth of Sisyphus* comes to mind. Workers frequently fell onto the deck in exhaustion and others fainted from the heat, which was frequently over 105 degrees, sometimes reaching 110. Never far from our minds was rule number one: No ice blocks over the side onto the ground below. Violation of this rule constituted grounds for immediate termination. And, like a guard in a high security prison, a heartless foreman strode up and down the fifty-yard-long deck, looking for mistakes or for somebody lagging behind.

Cries of "corner off" and "round bottom" could be heard throughout the day as a warning to fellow workers further down the line that a slab heading their way was defective. One did not want a 300-pound block of ice falling on one's leg.

Working at the Modesto Ice Plant was the most physically demanding job I would ever have, but it paid well and I was glad to have it.

Looking back, I'm grateful for these jobs, though I didn't always appreciate it at the time. It's not altogether the fault of young people today that jobs aren't readily available, although some of the blame falls on over-protective parents. How are kids these days supposed to develop a work ethic when there are so few opportunities available, or they're spared the opportunity to work by their parents?

I believe that, to the extent any of my ambition was forged in a healthy way, it was because of my good fortune in growing up at a time when the obligation to contribute financially to the family was understood, if not always appreciated.

## Going "Away" to College

I graduated from high school and "went away" to college—Modesto Junior College—a mile or two from my home. I had received no scholarship offers and I couldn't afford to actually go away to college, so I did the next best thing. The education I received at MJC was fine, but the proximity wasn't, and it quickly became clear that I needed to get away from home to secure a sense of independence. I was tired of living with my parents, and they were clearly tired of putting up with me. Caught up in the tension between us were my two young siblings, Mary, then six, and Lloyd, five. Both were adorable kids who grew up to be straight A high school students (which I was not), and then public school teachers. To my regret, I had no time for them when they were young, though as adults, we have become best friends.

## My Sister Mary

I was twelve in 1942 when I finally scored a sibling, too late to arrest my growing narcissism as the center of the entire family's attention. Mary Celanese Martel was a beautiful baby, my father's dream come true, a daughter at last. Our father was teased about the twelve-year lapse in impregnating my mother (with Mary) after my birth, and then doing it again a year later, leading to Lloyd, to which I often heard him respond, "I forgot how to start and then I forgot how to stop."

Preteens growing up in my era didn't want to stand out or be perceived as "different," but with two sometimes noisy babies in the house, that's exactly how I felt. Moreover, I was also suddenly no longer the sole center of interest in the family. As an alternative to fratricide, I chose to pretty much ignore my siblings as I immersed myself in high school life. How could I have known that these loud, bothersome little kids would one day become some of my favorite people?

Mary, whom I call Mimi, Mims, or Sis, is in fact second only to my wife Bonnie as my closest friend and confidante, and proudly possesses the Martel sense of humor: a blend of camp and pure silliness. One of us can always lift the other's spirits no matter how low they might be. Now in her seventies, Mary has suffered the greatest part of her mature life with Epstein-Barr virus (Chronic Fatigue Syndrome) and frequently battles depression, yet she can always "get it up" when called upon. I suppose I'm the patriarch of the family now, but Mimi is the spiritual soul and a best friend forever.

Growing up, Mary was a recipient of the American Legion's Outstanding Student award at Roosevelt Junior High School. She matriculated at Holy Names University, then went on to become an outstanding grade school teacher. She married another fine teacher, Donald Eggleston, and they gave birth to two gorgeous daughters, Amy and Nicole, who upon graduation also became—you guessed it—outstanding teachers.


## My Brother Lloyd

Lloyd was known growing up as "The Good Boy," an accurate nickname, for he's one of the most lovable persons I've ever known. Lloyd is also a consummate family man. He and his lovely wife, Jill, raised two beautiful daughters, Lisa and Jenny, who are themselves wonderful parents. Like swallows returning to Capistrano, Lisa and Jenny, together with their husbands Todd and Josh and their children, eventually returned to Lodi, California to be near their parents. Such is their connection with and devotion to the loving parents who raised them.

After Lloyd's graduation from the University of California at Davis with a degree in viticulture, he assumed the post of head winemaker at the highly respected Heitz Cellar in Napa Valley. He later became a teacher at San Joaquin Delta College and, ultimately, with the help of Jill, an honored winemaker of his own. Now in his seventies, initially wheelchair-bound by a stroke, Lloyd courageously continues to supervise his cabernet and merlot vineyards from a golf cart. Over the past year he has heroically learned to walk short distances and continues to improve three years after his stroke, contrary to medical orthodoxy. He still enjoys life and maintains his keen sense of humor, thanks largely to Jill's devotion. She's a lovable saint and a pillar of strength.

My brother and sister were both popular growing up (Lloyd was elected president of Roosevelt Middle School) but suffered greatly when our father died in 1958, when they were fifteen and sixteen, leaving behind little for them in the way of disposable income. My brother worked in a supermarket and both Mary and Lloyd worked in the fruit and cannery operations during the summer. I was just out of law school, earning $325 a month with a new wife and baby, squeezed into a 300-square-foot, Albany, California student housing apartment, and was of no help. Looking back, I wish I had tried harder to come up with some financial assistance.

Lloyd additionally suffered the fate of many young males who are forced to become the surrogate husband after the death of a father or the divorce of the parents. He is understandably bitter even now, scarred by the enforced mantle of man-of-the-house at the age of fifteen, yet frequently reminded that he was still just a kid, a terrible catch-22 for any youngster. To my eternal regret, my son, Jay, probably experienced a similar fate after I left the family home when he was ten.

## Junior College

I mentioned earlier that while Mary and Lloyd were in grade school, I spent two years at Modesto Junior College, trying to make the best of our crowded living situation. I had finally grown up (physically) and played defensive end for the Modesto J.C. Pirates football team, while also lettering in basketball and track. I found myself fully accepted into the company of the top athletes in school and had no trouble dating the prettiest girls. Get in line, Carol Clapper!

Unfortunately, I was also drinking too much. Way too much. I frequently consumed two six-packs of beer after football practice with several of my teammates. Fortunately, my bedroom was in the back of the family home and I could slip in late at night without being detected most of the time. I would often vomit as quietly as possible in the back yard before entering the house. When I made for the cold-water pitcher in the morning, my mother's sarcasm was evident.

"Thirsty?" she would say, "Didn't get enough to drink last night?"

But soon, the twinkle in her blue eyes disappeared along with the humorous jibes in the morning. Still, I was only vaguely aware that my parents were now united in their disapproval of my lifestyle. Neither of them spoke to me at dinner time and both appeared vitally disinterested in my success with the Modesto J.C. Pirates varsity football team. I typically ate quickly in silence, then raced ran off to join my friends and teammates for another night of revelry.

Then one morning, there it was: a note in my mother's handwriting Scotch-taped to the door of my bedroom while I was out. I had been too drunk to see it when I stumbled in the night before. It read as follows:

> Your father and I have had enough. The only time we
> see you is when you put your feet under the dining
> room table to eat. It's time for you to either rejoin the
> family or move out.

I was both angry and deeply hurt. Was my father behind this? No. My mother had also been distant lately. They were united against me. Knowing I had no money with which to live on my own, my father and, until now, my ever-indulgent mother, had threatened and humiliated me. I had no choice but to give in and give up my nightly carousing and "rejoin the family," but it took time for me to get over the sense of betrayal by a mother who had always been my protector. Sure, I was behaving badly, but didn't she realize I was dying here in Modesto? At my age, living with my parents and young siblings in a small home had become intolerable.

Deep down, I knew she was justified, but that did little to lessen the eighteen-year-old's mortification as he surrendered to her ultimatum.

Mom clearly has to be considered another suspect in my investigation.

— — —

In 1950, when I graduated from MJC, the question was, "Where to go?" The University of Oregon was known as the "Country Club of the West," an appellation earned in part by the fact that there were two beer halls right on campus: Taylor's Bar & Grill and the Side Bar. Another plus, it was also the leading track-and-field college in the United States.

Perfect.

With a suitcase in one hand, a basketball in the other, and a partial athletic scholarship waiting for me in Eugene, I was given a send-off at the train station by my impassive father and teary-eyed mother. Head coach John Warren wasn't impressed with me, however, and I sat on the bench and watched future NBA stars like "Moose" Loscutoff do things with a basketball I could only dream of. Never mind. Track-and-field was my strength, and that's where I would make my mark come spring.

Meanwhile, I joined the Kappa Sigma fraternity upon arriving at Oregon and continued to drink far too much and study too little. Tests in those days were mainly multiple-choice or true-false, and most fraternity houses—including ours—had files that contained tests from previous years. Final examination week consisted of staying wide-eyed and wired on Dexedrine and Benzedrine while memorizing the old exams. My only challenge during an actual final, after racing through and correctly answering the familiar questions, was how long I should stay in the examination room so as not to arouse suspicion.

At the end of my first quarter, after staying awake for six days and finishing finals, I hitchhiked sixteen hours home to Modesto, still so wired I couldn't get to sleep when I got there.

So it was that with little effort and no guilt, despite my Catholic upbringing, I cheated my way into Beta Gamma Sigma, a national business honor society. I had always hated cheaters; was I becoming one myself? Was my drive for success so great that I was willing to sacrifice my integrity in order to achieve it?

My all-too-brief time as an Oregon Duck was rudely interrupted by the Korean War. Young men my age were suddenly receiving draft notices, and fraternity houses were closing.

To avoid being drafted into the Army, my buddy from Modesto, Bob Jones, and I decided to seek the glamor of becoming US Air Force pilots. We took the preliminary physicals and both of us provisionally qualified, although I was warned that my eyes were questionable and that I might not pass the more rigorous testing that would come with my appointment to an aviation cadet class. My eyes had never troubled me, so I'd take my chances. I wanted to fly. Meanwhile, to avoid the draft while awaiting our cadet class appointments, we had to immediately leave school and join the regular Air Force as buck privates. Gone (hopefully just postponed) was my dream of achieving track-and-field fame under renowned Oregon coach Bill Bowerman.

Once again, my father drove us silently to the station and my tearful mother reluctantly put me on a train, this time bound for San Antonio and an uncertain future with the military. No basketball under my arm this time.

# Chapter 6

# The Military

> Corporal Steve could not believe his eyes
> They should have kept him down on the farm
> So he wouldn't now be, near gay Paree
> Lookin' down at what was left of his arm.
> —"Corporal Steve" (1976)

LIKE MOST EVERYBODY, I detest war. It represents a failure of leadership, is typically associated with geographical and financial greed, and is always edged in ego. It's also often initiated by trickery. Ironically, the individuals who foment war are hardly ever its victims. Politicians and generals send innocent young men and women to kill other innocent young men, women, and children who can't get out of their way. In 1951, it was the Korean War, and I was one of those young men.

Bob and I were ordered to report to boot camp at Lackland Air Force Base, San Antonio, in May 1951. Conditions there were deplorable, and it wasn't unusual to awaken at reveille to find that your shoes had floated out of the tent during the frequent nighttime storms. I was told nothing changed after we left until a recruit, who happened to be the son of a congressman, died of pneumonia.

My luck is so bad that if I bought a cemetery, people would stop dying.
—Rodney Dangerfield

I soon caught a cold that quickly turned into a severe case of pneumonia. But my father wasn't a congressman. I was finally admitted to the base hospital, close to death, after passing out in the chow line with a fever of 105. Subsequently, I was confined to the hospital, and thereby "redlined" for five weeks. During that time, my buddy Bob Jones was transferred ahead to a pilot training class without me—boot camp being a temporary assignment—resulting in our first extended separation since meeting at the age of eleven. Our parting at the Lackland hospital was incredibly difficult for both of us and did little to hasten my recovery.

Once I recovered from pneumonia and finished boot camp, I was transferred to Perrin Air Force Base, located in the Sherman-Denison area of Texas, just south of the Oklahoma border, where several of us were classified as "awaiting cadets." My job there was polishing office floors during the night shift. This wasn't hard duty, just boring—except for the ever-present fear of being called to begin cadet flight training and flunking the more intensive eye examination. My naïve solution, and a source of amusement to my fellow awaiting cadets, was to eat at least one carrot a day. Though my eyesight remained normal, I continued to obsess about it.

Meanwhile, ever restless, I decided to take advantage of my free days and enrolled in Austin College—which is not located in Austin, Texas. The school was near Perrin, and the administration there welcomed me as an undergraduate student. But polishing floors at night and attending classes in the daytime was still not enough activity for your driven memoirist, so I also went out for the school basketball team. The Austin varsity greeted me with open arms.

Oddly, I played some of my best basketball in the service. When I eventually ended up in the Strategic Air Command (SAC), with headquarters in

Omaha, Nebraska, I captained the Forbes Air Force Base basketball team and helped lead us to Omaha where we played in the annual SAC basketball championship tournament. We didn't win, but it was great fun.

One of the stars of our team, Russell Jones, was inherently unreliable. Our first game in the SAC tournament was scheduled for nine o'clock in the morning and Russell, with swollen red eyes, didn't show up until the second half. As ranking officer and team captain, it was my task to discipline him after the game. It went like this:

> "You let the team down, Russell. You were late this morning and you were obviously up late last night."
>
> "You're right about both those things, Lieutenant."
>
> "That just makes it even more difficult to understand or forgive," I said. "We're not in New York or San Francisco or Chicago. We're in a cultural desert called Omaha, for God's sake." My temper and my voice were rising. "I doubt they even have a bowling alley in this godforsaken excuse for a city! Certainly nothing to keep you up past ten o'clock at night."
>
> Russell flashed me a smug smile and a dismissive shake of his head. "All I can tell you, Lieutenant," he said, "is that if you was Black just one night, you'd never wanna be white again."

I have since forgotten how far we got in the tournament, but I never forgot Russell's explanation that morning.

Arriving back at Perrin after attending morning classes at Austin College one day, I was met with the exciting news from friends that our cadet appointments had arrived at last. I was happy, of course, but anxious as well. I would now have to endure the eye examination I'd been dreading for months.

The day of the physical, I stood in line with other cadet candidates, all naked except for a towel wrapped around the waist. We were instructed to walk down a hallway that had small stations on either side, one for heart, another for hearing, yet another for hand-eye coordination. Our eyes would be dilated, and the testing equipment was state-of-the-art. My heart pounded as I approached the door. What could I do? Was my quest for the pilot's silver wings about to crash before getting off the ground?

Then it hit me—risky but worth a try. When my turn came to enter the small eye exam room in which the testing was done, I eased past the door, skipped the examination altogether, then copied the results of a willing cadet candidate who came out the door in front of me, transferring them on my exam sheet.

I got away with it. I had survived the physical and was assigned to Aviation Cadet Class 52-H, starting in two months in Moultrie, Georgia, December 1951.

Clearly this wasn't just cheating on a college exam, which I had done in my fraternity, and which lots of people were doing. This was cheating my way behind the controls of a powerful and expensive military aircraft that could kill me—and innumerable others. This was major league cheating, and inexcusable. What troubles me now is that I felt little guilt or remorse at the time. In my driven nature I saw a roadblock to an important goal and had simply brushed it aside. To be sure, I'd previously passed qualifying eye tests for my automobile license, had never needed glasses, and had proven my superior hand-eye coordination many times on the basketball court. Still, I didn't turn to those rationalizations. The opportunity to cheat presented itself, and I went for it—without thinking. I now see the danger I was creating and deeply regret the irresponsible action I took that morning. But when I hear a voice from afar saying, "You need silver wings like you need water in your shoes," I somehow feel justified.

## Chapter 7

# In Pursuit of the Silver Wings

> I'm a shipwrecked sailor
> Alone and lost in cold northern seas.
> I don't mind being cold and lonely
> It's the being lost that's troubling me.
> —"Shipwrecked Sailor" (1971)

THESE ARE THE OPENING lines to one of the first songs I wrote, and the very first one I recorded. "Shipwrecked Sailor" was no doubt inspired by the events of the day I'm about to describe. Although I later wrote many songs (some good, some not-so), this one best captures the cold fear and isolation I experienced on a day in 1951 when I attempted my first solo landing in a United States Air Force (USAF) North American T-6 aircraft near Moultrie, Georgia. It also marked the beginning of my lifelong relationship with challenge and fear.

I was now a twenty-year-old USAF aviation cadet, desperate to win the silver wings of an Air Force pilot. I knew that approximately 50 percent of cadets washed out—having failed to prove to their instructors that they were capable of soloing—so when my instructor, P. L. Wiggins, a former hero in the Battle of Britain, hopped out of the rear cockpit of our T-6 trainer and said, "You're ready, son," my first reaction was incredible relief that I was finally about to get my chance. As soon as he was clear of the wing, I throttled the plane forward toward the runway before he could change his mind.

*You're ready, son.* But suddenly I wasn't so sure, and as I taxied into position for takeoff, my sense of relief gave way to a surreal sense of dread. I felt disassociated from my body, as if watching myself from a safe distance. Was this *me* doing this? *Alone?* I wasn't afraid of dying, but of a worse fate: the possibility of failure. I was about to have good reason to fear both outcomes, and my life would never be the same.

Your future self is watching you right now through your memories.
—Aubrey de Grey

The eerily silent auxiliary landing strip where I would attempt my first solo was two miles from the village of Tifton, Georgia, and twenty-seven miles from Moultrie, where the main training base was located. I glanced again through my cockpit window over to where instructor Wiggins stood, but remained careful not to meet his eyes lest he motion me back and deprive me of my chance to win the glory that would come with the silver wings.

Nobody else was around except for the driver of a permanent standby emergency vehicle. Bruised afternoon thunderclouds loomed above us, and the air at ground level was so thick and humid it threatened to clog my nostrils despite a wind that gusted hard.

*Wind.*

It is said that horses hate wind, and I'm with them. The wind that day at Tifton was blustery, and I'd been painfully aware on our first two landings of my instructor's subtle but reassuring corrections made from his duplicate set of controls in the T-6's rear cockpit. It had seemed especially gusty coming down toward the runway on our last approach, but I wasn't about to question his decision to let me have my shot at becoming an Air Force pilot.

We would learn later why nobody else was shooting landings at the Tifton auxiliary field that day: the landing strip had been closed earlier due to occasional high crosswinds, with gusts of over forty miles per hour. Unfortunately, no one had notified my instructor.

My first solo takeoff was unremarkable, though I was surprised at how the aircraft was pushed to the right even before I was airborne. This told me the wind had shifted into a ninety-degree crosswind. Memo to self: take care coming down on final approach.

Upon reaching altitude, I flew the basic rectangular pattern as instructed, left onto the crosswind leg, then left again onto the longer downwind leg, and then another left turn onto the base leg. I was painfully aware of the absence of P. L.'s assistance. I also realized I'd stopped breathing.

On the positive side, I'd begun to feel more connected to myself, finally aware of the simple reality that I was truly alone—if I didn't control the plane, nobody else would. I made the last, steep left turn from base leg onto final approach, careful to keep my airspeed up to avoid stalling out while achieving alignment with the runway. This always-touchy maneuver would be the death of my friend, Bob Jones, who would stall and crash while turning onto final approach one year later in Korea.

Blood pounded in my temples as I tried to line up with the runway, but as soon as I completed the turn onto final approach, I was immediately blown off course to the right, completely out of alignment. *Holy shit!* I pushed hard on the left rudder and tried to angle the plane back into line, but heat spread throughout my body as I realized I was failing. The crosswind and sudden gusts felt like a giant hand manipulating my aircraft as if it were a toy. My own hands were wet on the control stick, and sweat dampened my face and dripped out of my helmet.

I fought off a wave of panic and gave my head a shake, trying to clear my thoughts. Everything was at stake—including my life—as the runway fast approached. The relentless crosswind kept sliding me off line no matter what I did. What the hell was happening? I had no radio contact with my instructor and wondered what he was thinking. What would he do in this situation?

I was now fewer than two hundred feet from touchdown, still drifting to the right of the landing strip. Crabbing the aircraft into the wind with left rudder was also causing a longitudinal misalignment with the runway of about thirty degrees. I was coming in slanted. In desperation, I switched to the sideslip—or wing-low—method, in which I employed the left aileron to drop the wing into the wind, then applied the opposite rudder to hold the aircraft on a straight alignment with the landing strip.

A new problem: I had lowered my left wing to compensate for the high wind, which led to my concern that it was so low it might strike the ground before the wheels. Sweat stung my eyes, partially blinding me.

Now, less than a hundred feet from the runway rushing up to meet me, my training and instincts told me the best I could hope for, given the conditions, was a ground loop—a high-speed horizontal spin on the runway that could risk collapsing the landing gear or even taking out a wing—and would also take me out of the cadet program. This was an unacceptable result. I'd have to take the bird around for another try. I jammed the throttle forward and waited for the powerful Pratt & Whitney 600 horsepower engine to respond, but the aircraft only shuddered as it struggled to overcome its inertia. I realized I had waited too long to apply power. The T-6 had already reached the optimum stall speed for landing, but landing was the last thing I wanted.

When it became clear I'd avoid hitting the tarmac, I managed to catch my breath, but my troubles had just begun. I was slowly regaining altitude—too slowly, perhaps two hundred to three hundred feet—but I couldn't reclaim a safe airspeed. The bird continued to shudder, warning me it was about to stall out and crash. To make matters worse, I was hit with vertigo, suddenly unsure of either the aircraft's altitude or attitude, whether I was level, sideways, or upside down. Since I couldn't see the ground, only sky, I deduced that I was probably in a dangerous nose-up position. The engine groaned, its protest drowning out the sound of my pounding heart. I was on the very verge of stalling, and wasn't there a stand of tall eucalyptus trees close to the airstrip? If I hit one of those, nothing could save me.

Despite my disorientation, I sensed I was about to either hit the trees and crash in flames or stall out and fly the plane straight into the ground. Either way, death felt certain. Survival was now my sole objective, and acting solely on instinct, I jerked the throttle back and thrust the stick forward. The engine died, the nose dropped, and suddenly, everything went silent as a graveyard. Below, I got a glimpse of land, rapidly reaching up to claim me. Fear gave way to grim resignation. This would end badly—the end of my short-lived career as an Air Force pilot; probably the end of my life.

Spoiler alert: I didn't die.

I've been thinking a lot about fear lately; about the various forms it takes, the masks it wears. There's healthy fear, of course, the kind that triggers a heavy infusion of adrenaline and urges us to run like hell from that saber-toothed tiger coming up behind us. I'm usually more concerned with the other kind of fear, the kind that dogs us at work and at play, the kind that makes our palms sweat as we stand up to speak to an audience, that plagues us as we approach the boss with a request for a raise, that paralyzes the lover about to pop the question.

There are also at least two types of people to whom fear must adapt itself in order to achieve its raison d'être, which is to destroy its chief enemy: peace of mind. I base this conclusion on a highly scientific sample of two people, both well-known to me.

Take, for example, my wife Bonnie's fear of nature and the potential for bodily injury. She's certain one of the many giant redwoods that surround our property has her name on it, that it will fall and crash through our house and kill us both in our sleep, or, worse yet, while we're awake. No amount of information—such as the fact that redwoods survive to gain their great height because of their unique and protective water-absorbent bark formation, plus a horizontal root structure that runs so far it interlocks with the roots of other redwoods, creating a grid that makes *semipervious* essentially impervious to wind—will alter her perception. *No matter*, assumes Bonnie. *We're going to die.* Partly to avoid this fate, our last sixteen winters have been spent in the desert.

I, on the other hand, possess an irrational fearlessness—not to be confused with bravery—where bodily injury is concerned. I don't spend ten seconds a month fretting about the panoply of natural tragedies that could befall me, even when I recently confronted a six-hour brain surgery to address my Parkinson's disease. My fears are not of death or injury, but that I might do something stupid and fail—that I might look bad, be exposed, be "found out."

I know I'm not alone in this. Take the plight of many successful trial lawyers as they mature in their careers. At the beginning, the rookie trial lawyer is given a small case on which to "cut his teeth," and is closely supervised. It's like diving into a swimming pool off a low platform. This is fun. With each success, however, the cases get bigger, the adversaries get tougher, and the stakes get higher—and so does the platform. If the lawyer continues to be successful, he or she eventually realizes the future of an entire corporation—or even the freedom of a human being—is at stake. The pressure becomes intense and the lawyer feels he or she now stands on a narrow platform high in the air, about to dive into a small bucket of water. At this stage, you can become a victim of your own success, but success is an aphrodisiac, so there's no turning back. At least, there wasn't for me.

Meanwhile, back to Georgia and my first solo landing—and the first and only time in my life when I confronted the contemporaneous terror associated with a high probability of death *and* the humiliating fear of failure.

I crashed. But through sheer luck or intuition, I didn't quite reach the tall stand of trees—toward which I'd been directly headed. My instructor told me later that he and the emergency vehicle driver watched in horror as the plane, at two hundred feet above ground, moved dangerously toward a grove of trees, and if I hadn't instinctively pulled back the throttle when I did, I would have been toast! But with the prop suddenly silenced, the bird fell nose down toward earth, apparently at a speed sufficient to allow for a modicum of control so when I luckily pulled back on the stick, the aircraft crashed into the ground in a general three-point landing attitude.

Harrison Ford is fond of quoting a World War II test pilot named Bob Hoover who once said, "Fly the airplane as far into the crash as possible." Unconsciously, that's apparently what I had been trying to do—and luckily what happened.

But it wasn't over, for although on the ground, I was barely conscious, and the aircraft was still powering forward toward what appeared to be a deep ravine—and an uncertain future. The wounded bird sped through a forest of smaller trees, its wings noisily decapitating them on our way to . . . what?

As I neared the ravine, a sudden peace embraced me. I remember thinking, *I'm going to live, but it's gonna be ugly.* Standing on the brakes got me nowhere, but I recall calmly tightening up my shoulder harness in preparation for the impact that was inevitable once I reached the end of the level surface and shot down into the shallow ravine. My fate was now out of my hands.

At the end of level ground, the aircraft went briefly airborne again, then dropped into the ravine and stopped with a severe jolt that pitched me forward and ripped at my shoulders. But the harness held and it seemed like only minutes before my instructor and the emergency vehicle driver were helping me out of the cockpit. I told them, with an assurance I didn't feel, that I wasn't seriously injured. As they assisted my unsteady progress toward the vehicle, I looked back over my shoulder and saw to my dismay that my plane hadn't fared as well.

## Chapter 8

## On Second Chances and First Arrests

> I keep thinking, where did I go wrong?
> I can't sleep, I just keep drinking
> and writing this sad song.
> —"Stoned and Alone" (1972)

**IN THE AIR FORCE** van back to the base at Moultrie, I confronted the reality that I was about to join the just under 50 percent washout rate for aviation cadets in 1952, a thought that momentarily—I was young, after all—made me wonder if I would have been better off dying in the crash. I was aware some washouts were offered desk jobs, while others were sent to navigator or bombardier training, a commissioned but subordinate, second-best role akin to a descent from the executive penthouse to the basement mailroom. How would I face everyone back home? Everybody knew I had made it into pilot training, and soon everybody would also know I lacked the right stuff to make it to the end. I'd read about suicides following washouts, and though I didn't come close to considering that grim prospect, I did realize that failure, to me, was itself a form of death.

I see now that this was not a normal reaction.

Once it was clear I wasn't seriously injured, I was required to suffer the final, traditional indignity that evening in the mess hall, in front of both upper and lower classmen, dutifully standing up on my chair, slapping my arms haplessly in the air, loudly declaring my failure as a pilot. My failure as a person. I tried to make eye contact with a couple of my fellow cadets, but they quickly looked away, not wanting to add to my embarrassment. I was dead in their eyes. And in my own.

I slept little that night, if at all. My worst fear was realized the next morning when my instructor solemnly told me to report to the Base Commander, "Scotty" Fitzgerald. I hadn't met him, of course, and was surprised I'd be given the shoe by the Big Dog with the Brass Collar himself. If offered the chance, I'd plead for mercy, but I knew it would do no good.

To my astonishment, Scotty Fitzgerald immediately grasped my hand and, before I could say a word, apologized for the "major breakdown in communication" and my instructor's failure to be informed that the Tifton auxiliary airfield had been closed for hours owing to high crosswinds and "treacherous gusts." He congratulated me for not killing myself, and I shrugged it off with the best aw-shucks smile I could muster.

"Follow me, cadet," Fitzgerald ordered, and within the hour I was back in a T-6 with no less than the Base Commander himself riding shotgun in the rear cockpit.

"Go ahead and land this bird," he said, and I proceeded to implement two near-perfect landings. After the first landing, I never felt his hand on the rear stick. Then, before my third effort, he stepped out of the aircraft and said, "Go for it."

My next two landings were solid and I was back in the program after having soloed—this time—without destroying a single airplane. In fact, months later in advanced training, I won the base competition for spot landings—putting the wheels down closest to a mark laid out on the landing strip.

Looking back, I think I was too young and stupid to draw any clear lessons from my close call with the grim reaper that day in Tifton, and certainly too naïve to recognize the first signs of a ruthlessly striving personality that, if not controlled, might never let me rest. I wasn't much into self-analysis as a young man. I simply felt relieved I had survived my first major failure in life—thanks to the understanding of another human being. No man is an island, and Scotty Fitzgerald's generosity and sense of fairness taught me I wasn't alone. So, although I had much to discover about my own neurotic personality, I had at least learned to be grateful for the kindness of others.

That crash, however, presented yet another challenge. Even though I had aced my solo the next day, the USAF regulations required all pilots who suffered a crash be checked for depth perception. My heart sank, as I knew I would be by myself this time and couldn't cheat my way through another eye exam—all the more frustrating because I felt sure I could be a good pilot, maybe a great one.

I entered the examination room and saw that instead of the more sophisticated testing equipment I'd dodged at the Texas clinic, this depth perception equipment involved a rather primitive narrow wooden table, much like a barroom shuffleboard game, that ran approximately twenty-five feet long and about eighteen inches wide. From where I was told to stand, two eight-inch sticks lay at the opposite end of this board. I was instructed to use two cords, one in each hand, to bring the two sticks into a vertical position exactly side-by-side.

It didn't take long to demonstrate that healthy depth perception was required to successfully align the sticks at a twenty-five-foot distance. My first effort was a dismal failure. I was so far off that the sergeant in charge of the testing thought I was fucking with him.

"Do me a favor, Sergeant?" I said, "I'm still a little woozy from a long weekend. Would you just align the sticks together for a second so I can see what it is you want me to do, then go ahead and mess them up and I'll try again."

I did this because I'd noticed that when properly positioned, the sticks created a unique shadow juxtaposition on the side walls of the test board. I took note of where the shadows fell when the sticks were aligned. All I then had to do was pull on the lines until the interrelationship of the shadows matched what they had looked like when the sergeant had aligned the test sticks properly.

"Perfect!" he announced, "But I'll have to ask you to do it twice more."

I had no trouble, of course, and was once again back in the aviation cadet program, only vaguely aware that I had cheated *again*.

— — —

The program was bifurcated into two six-month segments: basic single-engine T-6 instruction and advanced B-25 multi-engine training. Cadets who survived the first segment usually had a choice between a single-engine fighter or a multi-engine bomber.

When it was time to register our preference in mid-1952, my new buddy, Dave Amis, urged me to give up my fighter pilot fantasy and join him in Enid, Oklahoma, just north of his family home in Oklahoma City, where the base for advanced multi-engine training was located. Dave seemed surprised when I didn't immediately reject the idea, but my first solo crash and the knowledge that I had successfully cheated Moultrie's somewhat primitive and easily-foiled depth perception test, suddenly made the slower moving, multi-engine aircraft appealing. In addition, once in Enid, Dave guaranteed weekends at his father's luxurious Oklahoma City country club, chasing college girls around the pool and drinking his father's fine single malt Scotch whisky. All signs pointed to Enid and the possibility of flying the famous B-29 Superfortress.

I learned that the military is an institution where you quickly make close friends from whom you can then be suddenly separated. I never thought, however, that the Labor Day party of 1952 would be the last time I would ever see my longtime best friend, Bob Jones. Several of us, including Bob, had put together a weekend reunion of friends from the cadet program who had been scattered to different bases after completion of basic training. We also contacted Ed Rotticci, the third member of our Modesto middle school and high school triumvirate, who was currently in the Army, stationed at Fort Sill in Lawton, Oklahoma.

Our meeting place was Mac's College Inn on Mockingbird Lane in Dallas, which in those days required that you bring your own liquor and purchase ice and drink mix at the bar. By six o'clock, we were all roaring drunk and out of booze. Bob Jones, Pete Mohler, and I were deputized to walk up the street to a liquor store. We did so, then decided to stop at a bar on the way back called the Zombie (which should have been our first clue) and have a quick drink.

We immediately got into an altercation with some University of Texas college boys who obviously resented servicemen invading their local hangout. After some pushing and shoving, the bartender achieved order by separating the three of us out from the melee and offering to provide us with free setups. Order was restored, but at a terrible price. None of us suspected we were actually being mickeyed by the bartender. (A Mickey Finn is a drink laced with a psychoactive drug, often chloral hydrate, for the purpose of incapacitating an out-of-control patron.) We greedily gulped our drinks and left the Zombie but had only taken a few steps when the three of us spontaneously decided we needed to rest. We sat side by side on the curb, our feet in the gutter.

My next memory was being jostled around in the back of a police van, probably summoned by the bartender, with the three of us headed for the Dallas City Jail. Upon arrival, I displayed my promise as a future lawyer by demanding my one phone call. I was granted my wish but was so drunk I wasted my opportunity by having Ed Rotticci paged at Mac's College Inn. He commiserated with our situation but neither one of us had a clue about what could be done, especially since the three of us had been arrested for being admittedly drunk in public after creating a disturbance in an adjacent bar.

My night spent in the Dallas City Jail will be long-remembered. Despite the alcohol and mickey hangover, I was unable to sleep a single minute. The noise and beatings of drunk prisoners by jailhouse guards, together with my severe nausea, led to such a state of misery that at one point I tried to knock myself out on the prison bars behind my steel pallet, a brilliant maneuver that failed to do anything but exacerbate my headache and raise a lump on my skull. We were released the next morning after serving twelve hours of incarceration, the worst night of my life at that point.

The desk sergeant had contacted my commanding officer in Enid (thank goodness not my parents, who never learned about this), and I was ordered via the Sheriff's Department to report to my base by noon where further punishment would be adjudicated. The problem was that none of us had any money or means of transportation, and it was already eight o'clock. I told Ed Rotticci I had no choice but to start hitchhiking north in the hope I might make it by noon. Good friend that he was, Ed offered to hitchhike with me and, if possible, serve as a witness as I pleaded my case for leniency to my CO.

The next problem was that neither Ed nor I was thinking clearly and our jubilation at successfully hitching our first ride in the back of a pickup truck was diminished several hours later when we realized we had taken I-30 northeast to Tennessee rather than I-35 north to Oklahoma.

The outlaws were in Arkansas.

I eventually made it to Enid by late afternoon and spent the next several weekends confined to the base, walking punishment tours. Fortunately, the incident ended there, and I was assured my silver wings were not in jeopardy.

# Chapter 9

## Learning to Drive a Superfortress

I've lost sight of the sun, and I've begun to fall behind.
I find lately that my life is stalled on a railroad track
And a train's coming down the line.
—"Take Your Time" (1975)

UPON GRADUATION AND WINNING my wings and lieutenant bars, I returned to San Antonio, this time not as a buck private at Lackland's boot training camp, but rather at nearby Randolph Field as an Air Force officer, living in a comfortable room in the bachelor officer's quarters, with time to myself, and eating excellent food in the officers' mess. I knew it wouldn't last— this was the military, after all, and my duty status was labeled "pipeline Korea." Sure enough, I was soon "crewed-up" as first pilot on an eleven-man crew, including an aircraft commander, navigator, bombardier, engineer, and gunners. Together, we began intense B-29 bomber training.

Months of boredom punctuated by moments of sheer terror.
—Tom McElvoy

No words can better describe flying a B-29 in 1952. The once-formidable WWII Superfortress was growing old by the time I started learning to fly it, and losing an engine while on a long flight was de rigueur. During a typical ten-hour training mission in which we conducted mock bombing runs at targets around the US and Canada (most of the time fighting drowsiness and flying on automatic pilot) we'd be shocked out of our torpor and into action by the loss of an engine, sending us into an urgent search for the nearest landing strip. (This also happened once on our way to Alaska, and we spent three marvelous days during repairs in Edmonton, Canada, the country of my father's birth.)

It was soon clear that our training missions were not without risk. While at Randolph in 1953, a crew of close friends from our small training squadron was wiped out in a fiery crash of their aging bird. The lone survivor was a first pilot like me, a drinking buddy named Dick, a former professional singer in civilian life who successfully bailed out just in time to save himself, only to be subsequently court-martialed for cowardice. Like a sea captain, we pilots were not to abandon ship until the crew had bailed out. I'm certain many of us suffered a dark night of the soul as we tried to put ourselves in Dick's position, wondering how we might react under similar circumstances: engines on fire, losing altitude, controls freezing up.

There is nothing safer than flying—it's crashing that is dangerous.
—Theo Cowan

Landing a B-29 with one dead engine became routine in those days and hardly considered a serious problem in a four-engine aircraft. One late night, however, my own crew was faced with the loss of a second engine in the middle of a deadly thunderstorm. Our navigator located an Air Force base within range of our dwindling fuel supply, and despite the tower's warning, we had no choice but to bring the bird down through swirling winds and violent drafts that tossed the huge plane up and then down again, like a feather—more than three-hundred feet in two seconds.

Both the aircraft commander and I as first pilot had to use all the strength we could muster to keep the plane from flipping over during our final approach to landing. Fortunately, we'd flown together long enough that our efforts were well-coordinated and we somehow managed the emergency landing (the crew called it a "controlled crash") without serious injury. Robbie, a World War II veteran, admitted he'd never suffered a closer call. We were relieved and delighted to see that the bar was still open at the officer's club.

After several months of military bombardier training, my crew was transferred to the 90th Strategic Reconnaissance Wing at Forbes Air Force Base in Topeka, Kansas, for final "Pipeline Korea" advanced photoreconnaissance training. I think we were all eager to get away from Randolph Field and the haunting memory of Dick and his doomed crew dogging our every flight.

Topeka was close to Lawrence, home of the University of Kansas, where one of my fellow cadets from Moultrie, Pete Wynn, was a graduate. Through Pete, I met several of his fellow fraternity brothers at the Phi Delt house, and friendships made there would endure for decades. I achieved minor celebrity status at KU by buzzing the university at a prearranged time in a twin-engine C-45 at an illegally low altitude. Looking down, it seemed that half the campus, including my new sorority girlfriend, Rhonda Maxwell, was gathered to wave up at me.

> If at first you don't succeed, aerobatics is not for you.
> —Anonymous

I had learned low-altitude buzzing techniques while in basic training at Moultrie. Dave Amis and I had two favorite stunts. One was to fly barely over the heads of duck hunters with the goal of getting them to jump out of their blinds and hopefully into the water. It was great sport and the birds appreciated our efforts. The other stunt (so vicious I never executed it myself) was to fly at night barely above the ground toward a freight train, then lower the plane's landing lights at the last minute to create the impression that it was an oncoming train. This conduct, while reprehensible, seems almost conservative compared with Pete Wynn's caper, which I can now reveal because he is deceased.

> Q. If you're going to make a parachute jump, at least
> how high should you be?
> A. Three days of steady drinking should do it.
> —Cliff Arquette in his Charley Weaver role

Pete continually complained that parachute training wasn't included in the aviation cadet program. Flying alone one day, his frustration overcame him and he set the trim tabs of his T-6 aircraft so it wouldn't crash in a populated area, then bailed out. He later claimed to investigators that the engine had failed, and they bought it—partly because Pete was an excellent pilot they didn't want to lose, and partly because the $225,000 plane crashed in an open field, harming no one except the American taxpayer. Moreover, with the engine destroyed, there was no way to prove he wasn't telling the truth. Pete had committed the perfect crime.

Looking back, all this behavior—including my own—is about what you'd expect when you put a twenty- or twenty-one-year-old kid in the cockpit of a high-horsepower, fully aerobatic aircraft without constant adult supervision. It may be rationalization, but it occurs to me that given the times and behavior of my fellow Korea-bound buddies, my occasional cheating to achieve success wasn't much out of the ordinary.

## The Stead Survival School

Part of my three years of "Pipeline Korea" preparation was the Stead Air Force Base eighteen-day survival school training course, located in the

Plumas National Forest in the Sierra Nevada. It was deemed perfect as a place to train airmen how to survive if it became necessary to bail out over Korea.

The program was unbelievably rigorous. After a few hours of ground school training, my crew of eleven was thrown into the back of a totally enshrouded truck that took us deep into the rugged mountains. Several hours later, the truck stopped and, without words, we were dumped out with no idea where we were, and with nothing but our parachutes, a limited supply of raw meat, some nuts, and one compass. As second in command, I immediately took on the responsibility of smoking the raw meat, turning it into pemmican (beef jerky) to avoid spoilage. I first constructed a tent and a rack using cloth and metal from one of our parachutes as I had been taught to do in ground school. I then built a fire inside the tent and waited for the transmutation of raw meat to pemmican to magically occur. The problem was that I had forgotten one of the important elements of the process: creating an opening at the top of the tent for the more intense heat to dissipate while smoking occurred. As a consequence, a good portion of our precious meat was burnt almost into charcoal.

Like any good officer, I deflected attention from my negligence by ordering half of the crewmen to turn their parachute shrouds into slingshots for hunting and the other half of the crew to try their luck at fishing. Regrettably, we soon learned that the stream had been fished-out, but my sharp-shooting gunners came through beautifully with an assortment of squirrels, rabbits, and one porcupine.

Porcupines turned out to be easy prey and I eventually learned the secret of how to cook them, which I will now reveal. First, fill a pot with water and boil the porcupine for thirty minutes. Throw out the water, put in fresh water and cook for another thirty minutes. Throw out the water again, put in fresh water, and cook it one last time for an additional thirty minutes. Then throw out the porcupine and drink the water.

We all survived the eighteen-day ordeal by eating small animals, catching the odd fish, and primarily by learning to identify edible roots like wild ginger, camas, chickweed, bracken, and bitterroot. I have never been a fat person, and didn't really need to lose twenty-eight pounds, but I did anyway. I could teach Jenny Craig a thing or two.

We were given the first night back at the base to relax, but the next night we were once again thrown into the back of the hooded truck. It felt like a much shorter distance this time before we were dropped off at various locations, this time in pairs, and told we had to find our way back and return to the base by ten the following morning. We were warned we would be traveling the last 200 yards over essentially bare ground, referred to as "no-man's-land," where we would be hunted by "enemy soldiers" armed with binoculars, rifles, and searchlights. If captured, we were advised that we would be subjected to North Korean interrogation techniques, including having our hands attached to electrodes and suffering a shock if we were suspected of lying or if we failed to reveal our names and the names of all our fellow crewmen when asked. We had been taught that the new survival protocol when taken prisoner was no longer the stoic "name, rank, and serial number," with which I was familiar from World War II movies, but rather to appear cooperative with captors while actually providing them with disinformation. Eventually, however, we would be tortured, if necessary, to acquire the information our captors wanted from us. To say we were motivated to avoid detection in this exercise would be an understatement, particularly in our exhausted physical and emotional state.

I was paired for this final test with my tail gunner, an unlucky draw, as he was the only crew member I had experienced any issues with during the just-completed ordeal, but I was determined to make the best of it. He kept up with me for about five hours until we reached the edge of no-man's-land, still in darkness, where he broke down, both physically and emotionally. He was immobilized by fear and exhaustion, and in my own deep anxiety, I had no choice eventually but to leave him behind to surrender to "the enemy."

I then began inching my way across the open ground, my heart pounding, crawling most of the time on my stomach, never moving until the spotlight and attention was on some other area. It took at least four hours to make it safely across a distance of two football fields of exposed territory. My shower and hard bunk had never felt better.

The men who were captured were indeed interrogated and tortured with mild but painful electrical shocks. They also suffered various forms of emotional humiliation, being stripped naked and subjected to lurid remarks about photographs of actual wives or girlfriends taken from each airmen's wallet.

At the end of the eighteen days at Stead survival school, we were dismissed and allowed to meet with family. I was happy to see that Aunt Monie and Uncle Lloyd had joined my parents. They—including my father—were an eager, appreciative audience for my tales of survival.

## To Russia with Love

In 1955, with only several months left in my tour of duty, my elite crew was selected to conduct the first aerial reconnaissance over the Soviet Union. This secret mission was scheduled to take place five years before Francis Gary Powers was famously captured after his U-2 aircraft was shot down over Russia by an S-75 Dvina surface-to-air missile over Sverdlovsk. Powers was piloting a U-2 capable of flying at 70,000 feet, an altitude our US intelligence erroneously estimated to be well above the reach of Soviet air defenses.

My crew was ecstatic. We would all be granted a spot promotion of one grade. In my case, I would be immediately elevated to the rank of captain. We were told that the mission would involve high risk, was strictly voluntary, and each crew member would have to individually sign on. We could not see five years ahead into Powers' dark future, and naïvely viewed the mission as an opportunity for heroism.

I was still young, and the adventure was highly compelling, as was the fact that the final training for the top-secret mission was to be at Castle Field in Merced, California, a stone's throw from Modesto, my hometown.

But I had a dilemma. I was scheduled to be discharged in seven months after nearly five years of service. To participate in the mission would require me to reenlist for an additional three years. For the past two years I had been counting the days, looking for my exit ramp, eagerly awaiting the opportunity to finish college and get on with my life.

Tempting as the mission was, wisdom prevailed and, with mixed emotions and a heavy heart, I declined the offer and was replaced. The rest of the crewmembers signed on. I wasn't told, but I assume that the B-29's Wright R-3350, 2200 horsepower engines were replaced by the B-50's more powerful Pratt & Whitney R-4360, 3500 horsepower engines. Despite this upgrade, I learned later that the specially equipped B-29, loaded down with camera equipment, auxiliary fuel tanks, and extra gunnery protection, had been unable to achieve even one thousand feet of altitude after its maiden takeoff from Castle Field, and the entire mission was scrapped.

This, of course, was a blessing for the naïve volunteers who all would have died or been captured by the Russians as Powers was. The service ceiling of the B-29 was only 31,850 feet as opposed to the U-2's still-insufficient 70,000 feet. I never learned whether the crewmembers' spot promotions that the mission would have granted were withdrawn.

The Strategic Air Command began retiring the venerable B-29 even as I was training to fly one of them to Korea. Later, in 1955, I piloted the very last 90th Strategic Reconnaissance Wing B-29 to the aircraft's burial grounds—the "boneyard"—in Arizona at Davis-Monthan Air Force Base. The final leg of the trip required us to travel along a temporarily-closed freeway lane, and I took pleasure in waving out my window to gaping motorists paused in the opposite line of traffic.

Having turned down the mission over Russia, I was left with seven months of time before my discharge. I was transferred to Eielson Air Force Base near Fairbanks, Alaska, for three months TDY (temporary duty) during the late summer of 1955, where I had the unique pleasure of watching a baseball game played at midnight with no artificial lights.

I was assigned to head a supply unit in Fairbanks, which placed few demands on my time. My only other duty was flying airmen—who'd earned the trip through good behavior—into a fishing lake accessible only by air. The aircraft was a C-47 (the same as a commercial DC-3), affectionately known as the "gooney bird." The lake was packed with great northern pike, a good fighter, so aggressive in fact that all you had to do was cast a hook into the water and the pike eagerly took it on. While serving in Alaska, I also had the frequent opportunity to fish for better-tasting grayling, similar to our domestic brown trout.

I enjoyed my time in Fairbanks but missed having any feminine companionship. I had to settle for a fantasy romance with a beautiful girl on the cover of a *Pageant* magazine left in my quarters by my predecessor.

In early August of '55, when I returned from Alaska, Colonel Crane announced I had been enrolled in the three-month Squadron Officer School (SOS) in Montgomery, Alabama. The SOC was the precursor to today's Air Force Academy in Colorado Springs, reserved for career officers. I reminded the colonel I'd be returning to civilian life in four months.

"That's why I'm sending you. I don't have anyone else I can spare that long."

*And because you, Lieutenant, are the only useless short-timer I have available.*

I didn't argue, aware that mine was not to reason why, but I was about to learn another lesson in "going with the flow." Most people who reach the age I am now can think of two or three major events that were life-altering flukes. This was one for me.

I reported for duty in Montgomery, and, together with my classmates, was soon immersed in politics, culture, and, of course, military strategy. Approximately two hundred officers were divided into squadrons of twelve to fifteen airmen, practically all male (it was, after all, the early 1950s). One of my most painful challenges was to stand up in front of the other officers every week and make a ten-minute speech on a given subject. In high school and college, I had suffered from a fear of speaking in public and had been able to avoid it, but this was the military, and I had no choice but to overcome my paralysis and get on my feet.

Within just one month, I had miraculously overcome my fear and was, in fact, nominated by my squad mates to represent the squadron in the all-school speech contest, where I would stand and deliver my ten-minute creation on an assigned subject. I tried to decline, but to no avail.

Old fears die slowly, and I suffered a night or two of lost sleep as the day of the contest approached. Once I began, however—and to my utter amazement—I found my way, week by week, into the quarterfinals, the semifinals and then . . . *the finals*! On that day, the nerves came back as I was matched against one other officer in front of a panel of high-ranking officers and an audience of over two hundred people. Miracle of miracles, I won the forensic base championship—and a trophy.

But I'd been given far more than a trophy that day. I gained self-confidence and comfort with standing on my feet and speaking in front of a group—abilities that would have a profound effect on my future.

I spent nearly five years in the Air Force—the price I had to pay in order to become a pilot—with a considerably longer tour of duty than most of my contemporaries. I've never regretted, however, the time spent in service to my country. In retrospect, my pneumonia and the boot camp separation from my friend Bob Jones had, perhaps, saved my life. Had I not become ill, Bob and I would have gone on to single-engine training together. From there it would have been straight to Korea, together as usual, where I could have suffered a fate similar to his.

Instead, meeting the persuasive Dave Amis and opting for a multi-engine aircraft led to three years of B-29 training, delaying the issuance of my own orders to Korea until the very day the truce was signed, ending the war. As a result, my orders were canceled the day I received them. (If further proof were needed that I was still immature at twenty-four, consider the fact that I was inconsolable upon learning the war had ended without my having a chance to fight in it.)

All things considered, however, I'm grateful for my military experience. I was one of the lucky ones, never shot at and never seriously injured. I was given the opportunity to grow up (something I had studiously avoided) and, later, to become a graduate student at government expense. Most importantly, I lived through it, unlike best friend Bob Jones and many thousands of others.

I was honorably discharged in December 1955, and immediately enrolled at UC Berkeley as a senior undergraduate. After five years, I was eager to join the race to success as a civilian.

But first, I had to locate the starting line.

**Chapter 10**

# On Marriage, Becoming a Lawyer, and Other Odd Jobs

> Listen to the gossip, you know how stories grow
> Half of what they're sayin' is twice what they really know.
> —"Gossip" (1975)

FOLLOWING MY DISCHARGE FROM the USAF, I'd chosen to attend the University of California at Berkeley, commonly known as Cal, instead of returning to the University of Oregon, because I learned I could graduate from Berkeley in just one semester and two summer sessions. Once I started there, however, I was told I couldn't graduate as planned because a required course for a BS degree in business administration wouldn't be offered until the fall semester of the following year— 1956—presenting an untimely financial hardship for me, despite minor support from the GI Bill.

Ironically, the course was called Finance and it sounded very much like one I had previously taken at the University of Oregon called Money and Banking. I scheduled a meeting with a department faculty member and requested that I be given credit for the Oregon course because it was practically identical to the required Berkeley course. The initial decision by the faculty member, however, was that I would have to return to Berkeley in 1956, just to take that one three-unit course—a huge waste of time and money. I had already lost nearly five years to military service and now the University Board of Trustees wanted me to attend school for an extra wasted year.

I was irate and developed a strategy. First, I went to the campus bookstore and purchased the Finance course textbook. Next, I memorized the table of contents and a few other salient features, which took only a few hours. I then went to the Dean of the Business School and appealed the earlier decision, claiming again that I should be given full credit for the course taken at the University of Oregon and not have to return in 1956 just to take a three-unit course I had essentially already completed.

"Tell me in some detail about the course at Oregon," he said, as I had hoped.

"Well, sir, it's been a while, but I'll do the best I can to remember its basic elements." I then proceeded to describe in some detail not the Oregon course but the Berkeley course. He conceded the courses sounded very similar, and I spent the next twenty minutes answering his questions, careful not to be so specific as to arouse suspicion.

"Well," he said, "you show an amazing recall considering how long it's been, and I have to admit it does in fact sound like your course at Oregon was practically identical to the one we offer here at UC Berkeley."

I was given full credit for the course and was able to graduate with a BS degree in 1956, at the end of the second summer session. Ready to receive my BS in business administration, I interviewed with all the major recruiters who came to Cal. The offer I was about to accept came from IBM, the most sought-after employer at that time. During the mating dance leading up to the offer, I was introduced to one of their early computers. Although it filled nearly an entire room, it probably had less power than my cell phone does today. It was the first computer I had seen, however, and I was impressed.

But I had a dilemma. IBM started its non-engineering hires in their marketing division, and I couldn't imagine myself being happy as a salesman. I had sold Cutco Cutlery door-to-door while working my way through Cal and was terrible at it. For example, one Cutco marketing technique we were taught would guarantee a sale was to ask the lady of the house for a slice of bread (in those days, it was always white, usually Langendorf), which I would then lay flat on a cutting board. With a flourish, I would pass a razor-sharp Cutco bread knife through the slice laterally, and then, with an endearing smile, I'd present the prospect a thin slice in each hand, saying, "Now, Mrs. Jones, you have *two* slices of bread." This (along with cutting a penny in half with a pair of Cutco scissors), always produced a gasp of amazement and ensured at least a small sale.

One night, however, I made an imperfect cut through the bread and into my hand. My prospect's face went pale as my blood blossomed into a deep red pattern across the white bread.

The next day I turned in my sales kit.

I also turned down IBM. Now what? I was a college graduate without a clue. The only thing I knew how to do well was work in agriculture, refrigerate boxcars, and fly a bomber—but I was done with those jobs. My dilemma was that I couldn't conceive of any job I would be good at that would justify someone paying me a salary I could live on. I had not a scintilla of skill, experience, or confidence, and no idea how to move my life forward.

I came to a decision: I would return to school! Instead of accepting the IBM offer, I went to the University Dean of Men and told him I had served five years in the U.S. Air Force and had three full years of the GI Bill coming to me.

He gave me a puzzled look.

"So, I need you to tell me," I continued, "what job or profession takes exactly three years of additional education?"

"Oh," he said, and after staring at me for a minute, apparently to gauge my sanity or lack thereof, decided to cooperate with my strange request instead of calling campus security. He picked up a catalog and began listing possibilities.

"Well, let's see now, a master's degree in business administration takes just one year. How about becoming a veterinarian? No. That takes four years. Ah! What about a law degree? It takes exactly three years!"

"Great," I said. "Where do I go to do that and when do I start?"

"You go right up the street. It's called Boalt Hall. It's considered one of the top five law schools in America. The new semester starts Monday," he added as I headed out the door. "You're lucky—starting next year they will require prospective law students to take the LSAT."

Having tentatively resolved my career path, things were looking up. I was ready to become a lawyer, get a job, fall in love, marry a beautiful, intelligent woman, and then set about the business of raising beautiful, intelligent children. I didn't consciously think about this in such organized terms, but having matured a bit during my five years in the service, I was prepared to take the steps laid down by centuries of social convention. Priding myself as a multitasker, I attacked most of these projects at once.

When I'd first arrived at UC Berkeley, I had asked a fellow Kappa Sigma to name the most beautiful girl on campus. (In retrospect, this is an embarrassing revelation about myself. Regrettably, there will be many more.)

He said, "That's a no-brainer. Anyone will tell you her name is Ann Moore."

"I'd like to meet her," I said.

He laughed. "She'll have nothing to do with you. For one thing, she's deeply religious. Besides, she may still be going with Bob Albo, the basketball star." He explained that Ann was a legend on campus. She reigned as the University's homecoming queen, Fresno's Maid of Cotton, and the Sweetheart of Sigma Chi, among other honors. In addition, she was immensely popular and a genuinely good person. On top of all that, she was also a successful face model and cover girl. The perfect package.

Undeterred by my Kappa Sig friend's pessimism, I learned that Ed Rotticci's girlfriend and future wife, Jane Ann, was a sorority sister of Ann Moore's at the Delta Gamma house. She undoubtedly shared my fraternity brother's opinion but agreed to introduce me. It took time, but I finally managed to score a movie date with the fabled young woman. I was apprehensive, though when we finally met, I had a strange feeling I had met her before. I began to realize why I felt this way. Remember my lonely stretch stationed in Alaska, when I fantasized about the cover girl on *Pageant* magazine? Well, that was actually Ann Moore. I was about to date my Alaskan fantasy dream girl! (Ann later confirmed she had indeed modeled for three *Pageant* covers in the early fifties.) I didn't tell her about this until much later, concerned she'd take me for a pervert.

I failed to impress her on that first date, but persisted, ultimately pursuing her to Hawaii during the summer break between my second and third year of law school. She was there teaching at Punahou Elementary School, an exclusive private college prep school in Honolulu. In sharp contrast, I had wangled a summer job in Honolulu at the Superior Mattress Company for $3.25 an hour. Making mattresses was hard, dirty work. The payoff, however, was that I had free nights and weekends. Eventually I wore Ann down, and with just a month to go before I had to return to Berkeley for my final year of law school, I persuaded her to marry me.

Before Hawaii, when we were first dating, I had driven to Oakdale to visit my beloved Aunt Monie to take her out to dinner. After we were seated, I shared the good news that I had finally found a girl I was very interested in, and she asked if I had a picture. When I describe what happened next, I'll be accused of writing fiction.

"No, Aunt Monie, I don't have a photo," I said, trying to keep a straight face, "but if you look out the restaurant window to your right, you'll see a very good likeness."

She adjusted her glasses and did as I had suggested. Across a major thoroughfare was a huge billboard featuring a giant picture of Ann, advertising Ivory Soap.

— — —

Our wedding took place at the Honolulu Presbyterian Church on August 11, 1957. My parents boycotted the ceremony, deeply offended that I was marrying outside the One True Church, from which I later discovered they had both preceded me in mortal sin and excommunication. I was beginning to learn how deep hypocrisy sometimes runs in religion. I was disappointed but not saddened by their absence. Unlike many children, I realize now that I wasn't driven to please my parents (which was impossible anyway with my father) nor to seek their approval. Rather, in my quest to woo and wed Ann, the powerful emotional drivers at work were raw sexual desire and the eagerness to go through life with a beautiful, intelligent woman at my side. I would have appreciated having my brother and sister there, but they were in school and short of funds, as were my friends back on the mainland. I also didn't want my siblings to clash with our parents over the religious issue. Grace Augusta Moore, Ann's mother, graciously relented at the last minute and flew over for the wedding. Ann's father stayed at home, remaining appalled by my Catholicism.

My best man at the wedding was Len Stohr, Ann's brother-in-law, stationed in Honolulu, whom I had met earlier that day. My only guest—I jokingly called him my usher—was my foreman at the mattress factory. Fortunately, the Reverend Bob Munger, Ann's pastor in Berkeley and soon to become mine, was on vacation in Hawaii and performed the service in an essentially empty chapel, formalizing my own excommunication from the Holy Roman Church. The church that hosted our marriage was not struck by lightning that day, and I've never had cause to regret being booted by the Pope.

The absence of my family did, however, cast a bit of a pall over the wedding service. Also missing was my one decent suit. I had forgotten to get my only suit from the cleaners and had to track down the owners on a Sunday morning and beg them to open up the shop. By this time, however, I realized I was going to be late for my own wedding, so I grabbed my suit and raced to the church. I got there with five minutes to spare, only to find that in my haste I had grabbed the wrong suit—it belonged to someone else and was two sizes too large. I had no choice but to wear it anyway, despite looking like Bozo the Clown.

My bank account, already fragile, gasped its last breath when I purchased two seats to Kauai on Hawaiian Airlines, and reserved a small honeymoon cottage—a humble but beautiful place.

Ann and I soon returned to the mainland together. She secured a teaching job, and I commenced my third and last year of law school. Ann almost immediately (and somewhat unexpectedly) caught a serious case of pregnancy and soon had to give up teaching because of related health complications. As a result, we had to move from a respectable ninety-five-dollars-a-month apartment into student housing at nearby Albany—a 300-square-foot hovel at thirty-five dollars a month.

Our son, Jay, was born little more than a year after our wedding, truly a love child. Ann was apparently as inexperienced at birth control techniques as she was at sex, and thank God for both those things!

It's ironic that, while parenting is one of the most challenging tasks people can undertake, procreation is so simple. I wasn't perfect at parenting, but fortunate in the latter, gifted later with two beautiful children.

I was not, however, financially prepared to start a family. I had no job and had been surviving on my GI Bill stipend of $110 per month, and by "hashing"—waiting tables for meals and a token hourly wage—at the Delta Gamma sorority house. A bonus with our new apartment was a small walk-in closet, just large enough to serve as baby Jay's bedroom when he was born on November 10, 1958. I shook my head, realizing that within a period of fifteen months, when I was freed from military service, I had gone from the life of a carefree college bachelor to an adult with the responsibilities of marriage and fatherhood.

When Ann had to give up her job, my anxiety level rocketed. Fortunately, I was able to secure a job at the Calfee law firm in Richmond as a law clerk for two dollars an hour, and now that I was married, my generous GI Bill payments soared from $110 a month to $130. We would be okay, but barely.

The hours at Calfee Westover & Calfee were demanding and took a toll on my law school GPA, but I learned a lot clerking at the firm, particularly from the venerable senior partner, Tsar Calfee. I was always amazed at the elderly gentleman's patience as he dealt with a constant line of people, all of them with petty complaints no other lawyer in the firm would entertain, showing respect for each one of them.

"How," I asked him one day, "do you keep smiling all day long listening to people and giving them your time, even though I know you're frustrated?"

"Once you agree to do something, John, always do it with a smile and a positive attitude. It doesn't cost you a nickel and makes the client feel appreciated."

I've always tried to remember that simple bit of advice. I enjoyed my experience clerking, but I was approaching graduation and realized I would soon need a full-time job.

In June 1959, I graduated from the UC Berkeley School of Law—just as my GI Bill payments ran out—and began studying for the toughest bar exam in the United States (my New York friends would argue the point), with a fail rate of 60 percent. Fortunately, I was given a free ride to the costly Wick's Bar Prep course, a traditional perquisite of having been elected senior class president. We couldn't afford it otherwise, and I was grateful for the help. Despite my nerves during the two-day ordeal and my growing pessimism while awaiting results, I passed the State Bar on the first try.

But now what? I couldn't see myself drafting wills for a living or even forming corporations. Too dull. I'd heard of a competition for a trial lawyer position at the Alameda County District Attorney's Office. They were going to engage in an experiment in which they would hire a raw recruit out of law school to be assigned directly to the Superior Court, trying felonies without the usual minimum two years in municipal court prosecuting minor offenses. This fast track to the courtroom struck me as an incredible opportunity. I agreed with Clarence Darrow, who famously said, "The only real lawyers are trial lawyers, and trial lawyers try cases to juries." I filed my application and entered the competition. I experienced the rigorous interviews and, for the first time, contemplated a career path as a trial lawyer.

This sudden, focused interest would have come as a shock to anyone who knew me in high school or college, when I was incredibly shy about speaking before any audience in excess of two people. But now that I was comfortable speaking in front of a group, thanks to the Air Force Squadron Officer School, it was clear that becoming a courtroom trial lawyer was what I wanted.

After a week or two, I finally heard back from the Alameda County District Attorney's Office. I'd been shortlisted for their experimental program and should contact the office for an oral interview with District Attorney J. Frank Coakley himself, nationally famous for having successfully prosecuted Burton Abbott for the kidnap-murder of fourteen-year-old Stephanie Bryan. That trial had captured the attention of the national press and made Coakley a celebrity. Abbott, convicted of first-degree murder, was executed in 1957. I was appropriately apprehensive about the interview but told Ann later that night that I thought it had gone well. Then, more waiting.

Finally, the suspense was over and the County announced I had won the job. I was, of course, thrilled, but suddenly I wasn't so sure how I'd get by on the going rate of $350 a month as a deputy district attorney—barely above the poverty level—with a wife and new baby to support. (To put my monthly salary in perspective, when I retired from the active practice of law, I was billing twice that amount for a single hour of my time.)

What was about to happen to me gives "fast track on-the-job training" new meaning. It started when Mr. Coakley told me to fly to LA so I could be sworn in as a lawyer immediately, two weeks before they were conducting the same ceremony in San Francisco for Northern California graduates, including my classmates at UC Berkeley School of Law.

"Yes, sir, but why?"

"Because you're trying a felony burglary case next week and you need to be a lawyer to do that."

I was apprehensive, actually scared shitless. Other than television and movies, I knew nothing about trying a case, let alone one involving a serious felony. I took comfort in the knowledge that the great trial lawyer D. Lowell Jensen, my new office mate and mentor, would be in the back of the courtroom during my baptism of fire and could take over if I froze up, had a stroke, or threw up on my shoes. None of those things happened, and before my classmates had even been sworn in as lawyers, I had won my first felony jury trial. The experiment was deemed a tentative success, and I was officially Deputy District Attorney John Martel, a trial lawyer.

During the next fifteen months, I would try about two cases a week. While the jury went out to deliberate on the two- or three-day trial I had started on Monday, I'd sometimes pick a new jury and start a second trial on Wednesday or Thursday. On a couple of occasions, I actually tried two jury trials and one nonjury trial in a single week. My learning curve was shooting straight up. In less than two years, I probably tried sixty-five cases, mostly jury trials, including co-trying two capital death cases (*People v. Hamilton* and *People v. Purvis*) with Frank Vukota, Alameda County's senior prosecutor. I also eventually tried a third, noncapital murder case on my own, and more burglary, robbery, fraud, and rape cases than I can count.

My first murder defendant, Raymond Hamilton, was a truly scary guy. One night, scarcely out of prison, he'd crept up to the home of Estella

Hamilton, his estranged wife, and peeked through her bedroom window. What he saw was Estella in bed with a man named Lorenzo Bernard. In a rage, Hamilton crashed through the bedroom window, seized his wife by the hair and then led her to the broken window on which he decapitated her. He killed her so quickly that he had time to turn and shoot Bernard to death as he tried to escape down the hallway. Hamilton was a killing machine, and if ever a man deserved capital punishment—to which, incidentally, I'm strongly opposed—it was Ray Hamilton. Without hesitation, the jury put him on death row.

But that's not the end of the story. About eight years later, when I had moved into private practice, I spotted a time entry by one of our young associates, E. Roy Eisenhardt, that read: "In re Raymond Hamilton," a pro bono case entry. I couldn't believe my eyes. Roy, my own associate, was trying to get a guy off death row whom I'd helped to put there! My frustration was tempered by my personal hatred of the death penalty and the realization that this enigma represented both the irony and beauty of our legal adversary system. There were indeed two sides to every story, and the adversary system ensured both parties would get a fair hearing before a fair and open-minded judge or jury, each side represented by a dedicated advocate and able to resolve their dispute absent gunfire, knife wielding, or even fisticuffs.

My time at the DA's office representing "the People" was an invaluable experience. For one thing, I was fortunate to be mentored by Jensen, the top deputy at the office and eventually district attorney of Alameda County, then later assistant attorney general of the United States, and still later, a US federal judge. I owe him much and we remain friends to this day.

I lost only two cases as a prosecutor in just under two years, but I learned a valuable lesson from each defeat.

My first loss ironically involved one of my most creative efforts in fifty years of practice. The case involved a knifing, but not the usual West Oakland drug-related crime that garnered little attention in the early sixties. The defendant in this case was a reputable man from Oakland who had taken his date out on San Francisco Bay for a "fishing trip" and allegedly attacked her sexually when they reached deep water. When she resisted, he cut her with a fishing knife in anger. This seemed clear, but the police couldn't produce the weapon, and it was a "he said, she said" case. Both the man and the woman were Black, but he was, as stated, a reputable Oakland businessman, and she was a sex worker. I knew I would need more than her word to keep my winning streak alive.

On direct examination at trial, she was able to describe the weapon as a typical fishing knife with a serrated edge, while the defendant denied ever owning such a knife. She seemed quite believable to me, and a hospital report confirmed her injury. Moreover, the defendant admitted taking her on a boating trip on the day in question, though steadfastly denied he had attacked her.

Lacking the alleged weapon, I had the victim draw on a large, mounted chart for the jury a replica of the knife she claimed was used in the attack. It indeed appeared to be a standard fishing knife with a serrated edge. The defendant, however, looked at the drawing and flatly denied ever having such a knife. Her word versus his.

My case was in trouble. Every day at the trial, the defendant showed up meticulously dressed in a suit and tie while the woman, despite my instruction, appeared dressed in the tools of her trade: a short skirt, a revealing blouse.

Feeling the case slipping away toward the end of day three, I engaged the defendant in a desultory conversation about fishing in the Bay, getting him to talk. I acted naïve, and once I had put him at ease in the role of teacher, I casually asked him where he bought his fishing equipment.

"I buy all my fishing gear at Simon's Hardware in Oakland," he replied.

After court recessed for the day, I raced to Simon's Hardware and was excited to find that the defendant indeed had an account there and that all purchases were routinely recorded on microfiche. I flashed my DA identification and asked to speak to the manager. Claiming confidentiality, he first refused to give me access without a subpoena.

"If that's the way you want to play it," I said, "I'll get a court order and bring a crew down here tomorrow. I can assure you, however, that they will be disruptive. Very slow-moving and *very* disruptive."

The manager instantly caved, and soon I was looking at the defendant's account and specifically item number "7-4623, knife, fishing." My heart was pounding. I asked the manager to show me item number 7-4623. It was, as I had hoped, a standard fishing knife with a serrated edge, *exactly as depicted by the victim in her drawing.*

Never have I looked forward to a cross-examination so much. I had already learned that before showing your ace in cross-examination, you should first close off any means of escape, so I asked the defendant again to deny ever having had a fishing knife with a serrated edge that resembled the one I'd had the victim draw. Having built a verbal wall around any escape possibility, I was ready to sink my hook.

"So, sir," I said, holding the knife I had purchased from Simon's Hardware behind my back, "It's your sworn testimony that you have never owned a knife"—I then dramatically thrust the knife in front of his face and added, "*like this?*"

He nearly fainted and, after recovering his composure, had no choice but to continue to deny that he had ever owned such a knife. I had him.

"Your honor," I said, turning to the judge. "I request permission to call a representative of Simon's Hardware out of order."

"For what purpose, Mr. Martel?"

"I will elicit from this new witness that the defendant purchased a knife identical to this one from Simon's Hardware which, the record will show, is a replica of the drawing by the victim marked Exhibit 1 in evidence."

The rest was easy, and I was sure I had won my case; my perfect record would be intact. But to my amazement, the verdict of the jury was "not guilty." How could this be? The hard but important lesson I learned—and ultimately used to great advantage—was this: Despite the fact that judges generally instruct juries to set aside their emotions and decide cases solely on the basis of the evidence brought forward at trial, juries routinely ignore both the facts and the law when the victim is either unlikable or fails to meet their standards of morality. This conundrum was confirmed when I interviewed a female juror after the trial who described the victim as a "common prostitute" who had probably "provoked the defendant."

I was crushed by the verdict and felt I had let the victim down. What must she have thought of a justice system that conveniently looked the other way when a victim was deemed socially unworthy? I learned a painful lesson that day that was corroborated many times over during the next forty-five years of practice: Jurors will bring about the result they want, even if it runs counter to the facts and the law. Years later, I carried this lesson into the O. J. Simpson case but couldn't convince Deputy DA Marcia Clark of its universal applicability.

My other loss as a deputy district attorney was a burglary case in which the defendant was a recently discharged soldier with a good record, and the victim a drug dealer, a similar case of social disparity that had beaten me in the fishing boat case. The evidence was clearly in support of the charge, but I don't I have to tell you what the result was.

In summary, a trial is all about people and their perceptions of each other. Jurors leave neither their past experiences nor their judgments at the door when they enter the courtroom. In considering the facts before them, they will align themselves with the individual who most conforms to their notion of a "good person," and will rationalize this choice as being "fair." Lawyers who offer evidence that contradicts jurors' values will create cognitive dissonance in their minds. This can make jurors impatient and sometimes even angry. A good trial lawyer must always be aware of this danger.

Another very important lesson I learned while trying cases at the District Attorney's Office came to me as a gift from the senior criminal department judge, James Agee. After I had tried and won several cases in front of Judge Agee, he called me into his chambers one day. It was late in the afternoon, and he took out a bottle of whisky and two glasses.

"You're a promising young trial lawyer," he said, after a bit of small talk about how I liked the new job, "but there's something you need to learn if you want to become a great trial lawyer."

I kept my hand steady as I reached for my glass, saying, "I would appreciate anything you could tell me, Your Honor."

He smiled at that, probably amused I could sit across from him with a drink in my hand and address him so formally. I certainly couldn't call him Jim, but I should have called him "Judge Agee" or simply "Judge" to acknowledge the informality of our meeting.

He took a sip from his glass, met my eyes, and said, "You only lack one thing, John." He then put the glass down, looked me dead in the eye, and said, "You've got to learn how to bleed."

I nodded my head, trying to process what he had said, but he saw that I didn't have a clue.

"I'm being metaphorical, perhaps obscure," he said. "I'm referring to how quick you are."

Now I was hopelessly confused. "Thank you?" I said warily.

"Well, being quick is a good trait in a trial lawyer. But you're sometimes a little too quick on the trigger when you feel your adversary has one-upped you. You're too quick with the cutting retort, meeting fire with fire." He paused, seeing I was still confused before adding, "Jurors don't admire that."

Now I knew what he was saying: I was overcompensating for my insecurity and lack of experience, trying to show the jurors I could hold my own with my veteran opponent. But Jim Agee was saying that juries want to see light, not fire, and they don't like bullies. They will admire the advocate who "bleeds," who suffers an insult in silence rather than one who becomes a more adept bully and bludgeons his opponent.

I have tried to internalize that lesson over the years and am grateful for the Judge's counsel. Jurors are influenced in their decision-making by how they feel about the lawyers in a trial nearly as much as how they feel about the parties. They admire intelligence and quickness, but not irascible behavior. It took me a few trials, but I eventually learned "how to bleed" and, in the process, capture the jurors' sympathy rather than their disdain.

I mentioned earlier that we won most of our cases, and I have perhaps taken undeserved credit for my string of victories. The truth is that the evidence was usually overwhelming in the prosecution's favor and it would have taken a genius to lose most of them. In addition, we could almost always count on a defendant lying on the stand—and jurors hate liars. It was in the DA's office that I absorbed yet another important lesson: in litigation, just about everybody lies, particularly a suspect facing the possibility of prison.

Here's an actual example: Two suspects were interrupted while burglarizing a grocery store and fled the scene. Both had been wearing socks on their hands, a common, low-budget technique to avoid leaving fingerprints. One of the suspects was arrested at the scene while the other escaped temporarily but was stopped walking along a sidewalk one hundred yards away. The officer noticed that the man had no socks on.

"Well, officer, I was just taking an evening stroll and suddenly realized my socks were dirty so I took them off and put them in my pocket. See?"

Looking back now at over a half-century of trial work, my first full-time legal job as a deputy district attorney was the most amazing (and exhausting) trial education I could have asked for.

## Chapter 11

# Bigger Fish

Looking for truth, searching for proof
Is a really nice way of wasting your time.
And when you're dying of thirst you do the last thing first
Until you find you're down to your last dime.
—"On and On" (1973)

IN 1962, AFTER FIFTEEN months in the District Attorney's Office, I realized I'd tried just about every kind of case I was going to see as a prosecutor, including three homicides. Only the names of the defendants seemed to change. The district attorney's "experiment" was deemed a success, both for the county and certainly for yours truly, the guinea pig. My growth curve had leveled off, however, and I was tempted to take on even bigger professional challenges.

Vernon Goodin, a senior partner at Bronson, Bronson, and McKinnon, the premier trial firm in San Francisco, had heard about my string of victories at the DA's office and invited me to lunch. I accepted the invitation, trying not to sound too eager. He picked me up on the appointed day in front of the county courthouse in his powder blue, top-down convertible and dazzled me with stories about his firm and what it could do for my career. When I summoned up the nerve to ask what I would earn, like any good trial lawyer, he turned the question back on me.

"What are they paying you here at the DA's office, John?"

I knew I was being out-negotiated and had no choice but to tell him.

"Three-hundred-and-fifty dollars a month," I admitted, fearful he might laugh.

But Vernon, who would later become my mentor at BB&M, wasn't finished negotiating. He managed a troubled look and replied, "Well, I'll have to talk to the partners."

After keeping me in suspense for three days, he called back and told me he had good news. "The partners are prepared to meet your present salary!"

I was stunned, but I kept my cool, telling myself it was time to show them I could negotiate, too. "I'm afraid that won't do it, Mr. Goodin. The new commute to San Francisco from Oakland will cost me an additional twenty-five dollars a month."

I wasn't bluffing. Ann, Jay, and I, and a lovely new addition to the family, baby Melissa, were about to move into a large fixer-upper on Contra Costa Road in Oakland, with a significant mortgage. (It would cost us all of $47,000!) We were barely making it on my salary of $350 a month, and I was feeling stressed. My beloved family was increasing in size and I was the sole provider, feeling at times like I was operating on a strange highway without a road map.

The Bronson partners ultimately approved my $375 per month request and my nearly two years at BB&M became a bittersweet time of high stress and self-medication with alcohol. Most of the partners were trial lawyers, and this was the early-sixties *Mad Men* era, so most of them were also heavy drinkers who viewed women as sexual objects. I'll never forget my first social event, two weeks after joining the firm. Upon entering senior partner Jim Morris's beautiful home, wife Ann was quickly pulled aside by Mrs. Morris and guided into a room composed entirely of the other wives, and I was directed into a separate room where the men were smoking cigars and listening to a peroration by the venerable Roy Bronson, BB&M's senior partner. He seemed to be railing against the current trend of fraternization between lawyers and secretarial staff. I vividly recall his conclusion.

"I've been a lawyer for forty years," he summed up, pontificating proudly, "*and I've only fucked three secretaries!*" What was most amazing to me was that nobody laughed. They didn't laugh because they knew he was bragging about his restraint, not joking. I could visualize the partners doing quick mental calculations now that the standard of sexual morality—about one secretary every thirteen years—had been clarified by the senior partner.

Incidentally, a typically heavy-drinking senior partner named Arthur Sugden, arguably the best trial lawyer in the firm and, like me, a graduate of the Alameda County District Attorney's Office, ran into a cement post on the way home from the party that night, killing himself and severely injuring his wife.

I had hoped the insane pace of the DA's office would slacken at my new job, but I could not have been more mistaken. My caseload soon grew to 120 active trial files, which meant I was taking depositions, appearing in court on motions, or trying cases before a jury five days a week, then preparing and catching up with case status reports on weekends or preparing for a frequent Monday morning trial. I barely slept and rarely saw my family. I felt no guilt at the time—that would come later. I was supporting my family and busy building a reputation. After I won my first ten cases in a row, my workload got worse: the senior trial partners began shoveling off their troublesome trial files to my desk, counting on me to bail them out, often at the last minute.

I had truly become a victim of my success, and so was my family. I could almost hear my father telling me I needed another trial victory like I needed water in my shoes, and maybe he was right for once.

Ann and I were still feeling alienated from my family so we mostly avoided Modesto, though I called my mother occasionally. She seemed to be recovering from the knowledge that her eldest son was doomed to eternal damnation, having been married outside the Church. I had rarely seen my father, though I felt it important for Jay to at least meet his grandparents on a couple of occasions. Though my own maternal grandparents were long-deceased, I still treasured the memory of getting to know them.

Meanwhile, work was stressful beyond comprehension. I would sometimes be given a serious case, involving severe injuries, as late as Thursday or Friday—with jury selection the following Monday. As a result, when I left the firm in early 1964, after less than two years, I had tried over thirty jury trials to conclusion, as well as many nonjury trials (following a jury waiver by the plaintiff), winning all of them. Most cases were fairly routine automobile accident matters—though many of them involved serious injuries, including quadriplegia—and with each victory, the dollars at stake grew larger. But instead of making me feel more secure, my undefeated streak only increased the pressure to keep winning, which was the only way to satisfy the partners' expectation that my string of victories be extended.

Looking back, I was unhappy, but didn't admit—even to myself—the depth of my growing despair. I rationalized that I was lucky to be given the opportunity to show the partners what I was capable of. I think that's when my excessive drinking began, but it seemed like the thing to do, and we were, after all, Mad Men. Were the senior partners surrogate fathers? Potential suspects in my investigation?

The three-martini lunch was de rigueur, and when a senior partner took me out, I was expected to keep up. Although relatively new to the firm, I was older than my classmates by virtue of my military service and considered a senior associate. Accordingly, despite being a rookie, I was welcomed into the firm's informal "subaltern society" by several male senior associates, all of whom—including myself—were incipient alcoholics and didn't know it or didn't care. I cared but continued to self-medicate my deepening anxiety. Fortunately, Ann wasn't much of a drinker and my need for medication abated when I got away from the courtroom and the influence of the senior Bronson partners.

Incidentally, in a fictional closing argument in my second novel, *Conflicts of Interest*, rookie defense lawyer Seth Cameron ridicules the injuries claimed by the plaintiff, who swallowed one of three potato bugs that allegedly contaminated a can of beans produced by the defendant. Cameron further ridicules the seriousness of the case by referring to the incriminating bugs as Huey, Dewey, and Louie in his closing argument. This tactic was based on an actual desperation stratagem, executed to perfection by fellow Bronson associate Bernie Kearns at the close of a Fresno County Superior Court jury trial. In *Conflicts*, Cameron— fighting revulsion and trying to appear calm after swallowing Exhibit 1A (Huey)—calmly tells the jury the snack wasn't bad but would have benefitted from a dollop of Dijon mustard. Bernie won his case in real life, and so did the fictional Seth Cameron.

Sadly, Bernie died young (though not from ingesting insects), and the pressure on me at the Bronson firm continued to build. The more cases I won, the more was expected of me. I was told by a senior partner that I was viewed as the "thoroughbred in their stable" of senior trial associates, and he acknowledged I was being "ridden hard and put away wet." I hardly ever saw Ann or the kids and I don't recall ever having a weekend of relaxation. When I occasionally did get home at a reasonable hour, I was usually too exhausted to play with Jay or Melissa or to carry on a decent conversation with Ann. When I did have a free weekend day, which was rare, it was spent repairing our old house—installing an irrigation system, stripping and wallpapering walls, dealing with plumbing problems, etc. I was burning out, but in denial, running too fast to notice.

When Frank Farella, a former senior business associate at BB&M, called me one day and proposed that I consider joining him at his new firm, I was vulnerable. My perfect track record at Bronson opened the door to several opportunities, so why did I choose Elke, Farella, & Braun, a new and relatively unknown three-man law firm? The answer is best summed up by what I told Ann when she asked the same question:

"If these guys were a corporation, I would buy all the stock in them I could afford."

All three of the EF&B partners were young and ambitious former honor students at Stanford Law, and when I met with them, they all expressed the same goal and philosophy: "To do good work at a price that's right." I liked that there was never any talk about making a lot of money or gaining high professional public profiles. When pressed, their true stated objectives were to perform superior legal work, maintain high ethical standards, and eventually be known as the best law firm in San Francisco. Of course, being the best interested me immediately, given my driven nature. If they maintained that focus, the remuneration and public recognition would take care of itself.

It has been declared by some military observers that soldiers walk into danger not necessarily for their country but for their fellow soldiers in battle. I believe this sort of band-of-brothers psychology motivates commercial partnerships in a similar fashion. I quickly learned, as the others already had, that failure by one impacted all—that the worst sin of all was to let down the team. Accordingly, my new partners became not only close friends, but three additional demanding fathers, possible prime suspects in my inquiry.

## Thomas Walter Elke

I knew Tom Elke slightly from ecumenical church activities in which we were both involved before I distanced myself from religion. He had a far higher profile in the Presbyterian church than I did, and I soon learned Elke had a high profile everywhere, whatever the activity. He graduated from Stanford University at the age of eighteen, when most aspirants were just beginning, notorious for such hijinks as running naked through the campus on a bet before getting busted in fully exposed stride by a faculty member.

Tom was indeed a character and the smartest man I would ever know: a true genius. He would also become one of my dearest friends. Our most interesting experience together wasn't in a courtroom, but in Spain.

Elke was trying to talk his way out of a lawsuit for having breached an agreement with a Spanish boot manufacturer. He had entered a contract with the manufacturer that promised to supply him with a number of crocodile skins from Africa that the Spaniard would make into designer-style boots. Tom had previously contracted with an African tribal leader to supply the manufacturer with a sufficient number of crocodile skins at a nominal cost.

The theoretical profits produced by Elke's business plan were astonishing. A West African villager would start the process by clubbing a crocodile to death, for which he would be paid twenty-five cents per skin. The villagers were ecstatic, for they were not only making money with which to feed their children but were also ridding their village of vicious creatures capable of eating those same children.

For another quarter, the alligator skin would be transported upstream to the tribal chief who would rake off another fifty cents per skin for collecting and delivering them to a sea port. From there, they'd be shipped to Alicante and fabricated by the Spanish company into boots that women would buy on Madison Avenue for over $500.

What could possibly go wrong?

You guessed it. An animal rights group got wind of the killing of Elke's crocodiles in West Africa and succeeded in getting the local government to ban the practice, leaving Tom without the material he had agreed to supply to the Alicante manufacturer. I'm an animal rights advocate, but the result of the group's well-meaning effort in this instance was that the villagers were deprived of needed income and the crocodiles went back to eating little children who wandered too close to the river. In addition, the Spanish manufacturer and his employees lost work and Tom lost his shirt settling with the manufacturer.

Elke's suggestion that I meet him in Alicante coincided with my first trip to Europe. By now, my marriage to Ann—which had been disintegrating under the strain of my intense workloads and the absence they created—had finally fallen apart and was fully dissolved. I was still paying significant child support, but Spain was a destination where I could stretch my meager disposable income. On the trip over, I prepared myself for the experience by reading James Michener's excellent book, *Iberia*, taking particular note of his chapter on Pamplona, where the famous Festival of San Fermín, including the storied running of the bulls, was about to take place.

According to Michener, the Festival commenced every year on July 6, and a glance at my calendar revealed it to be July 3. I saw this as the opportunity of a lifetime and resolved to go directly to Pamplona from Alicante, taking Elke with me if he was willing. He was, and two days later, we boarded a train for Pamplona, where we learned that every hotel, home, and hovel was fully booked and had been for several months. Fortunately, the weather was warm and we were able to sleep the first night on park benches until we were rousted in the morning by the local constabulary. We then went to the nearest bar-restaurant where we met newlyweds from UCLA and their best man, who'd apparently had so much fun at the wedding he decided to join the happy couple on their honeymoon. They were able to get us into a sleeping porch in their hotel, and we proceeded to enter into the spirit of the festival.

There's no way to adequately describe the twenty-four-hour-a-day adventure that is the Festival of San Fermín, although Michener, and Hemingway before him, have done excellent jobs. It's nonstop drinking, dancing, music, and instant companionship. And, of course, running with the bulls, a practice that involves running in front of typically a dozen bulls who have been let loose on a course of sectioned-off streets. The origin of this event derives from the need to transport the bulls from the off-site corrals where they've spent the night, to the bullring where they will probably soon be killed by a matador. The length of the run is 903 yards and goes through four streets of the old part of the city before entering the bullring. At least sixteen people have been killed in Pamplona running with the bulls. I couldn't persuade any of my compatriots to join me, but Tom got up early with me the next morning, promising to summon medical attention if things didn't go well.

It was a warm morning in 1977 when I jumped down into the street in front of our hotel and was soon surrounded by youthful Spaniards dressed in white T-shirts and trousers, red waistbands and neckerchiefs, and, of course, running shoes. Awaiting the arrival of the bulls, I have rarely felt so out of place, surrounded by these athletic-looking young men who looked at me as if I were some crazy person, especially when I kept saying "*Qué dirección?*" It was evident they resented the crazy *Americano* and were not about to help me, so I resolved to just start running with them in whatever direction they went. Among the things I didn't know about running with the bulls was that the previous day, bodies had piled up at the tunnel entrance to the stadium and at least one man had been killed.

I learned later that the average speed of the herd is fifteen miles per hour, which is faster than it sounds. The herd is composed of the six bulls to be fought in the afternoon and six steers who help guide them. When a cannon announced the bulls had been released, I showed those young bucks a thing or two about speed and made it into the *plaza de toros* about ten yards ahead of the first bulls. I then ducked off to the side and watched them thunder past my cowering body into their holding pen, where they would all sadly await their deaths during the *corrida de toros*.

I breathed a sigh of relief, prematurely it turned out—because it wasn't over. The arena was full of steers, seemingly bent on killing an American, and there was no runners' exit from the Plaza.

While you might think I'd feel relief in making it into the stadium, in reality, this was much scarier. The stadium was full of people in the stands wanting to see blood. Would-be matadors distracted most of the animals, giving me opportunities to try to escape into the grandstands. I leaped up several times, grabbed a rail, and began pulling myself up out of the arena, but each time I got a handhold, the young locals in the stands laughingly pounded on my fingers, sending me tumbling back down. This was obviously great sport for the locals, watching the stupid American dodging a bloodthirsty steer while looking for another place to try to save himself. The trouble was, my energy was waning and I didn't have many leaps left in me.

Luckily, the young matador wannabes continued to distract the steers still in the arena, enabling me finally to pull myself up into the stands just ahead of a horde of laughing young Spaniards running toward my new location but arriving too late to push me back. Far from anger or even disappointment, they all gave me a thumbs up, shook my hand, and I think said something complimentary about the *loco Americano*.

After three days of partying at the Festival, I put Tom on a train back to Barcelona and then joined the wedding trio on a trip to Biarritz, France. We traveled together for two more days, at which time the bride and groom belatedly decided they would like some privacy and the best man and I departed, going our separate ways.

## Frank E. Farella, Jr.

I had been a fellow associate with Frank Farella before he left Bronson, Bronson, and McKinnon to form Elke, Farella, and Braun. I knew him to be a brilliant, young commercial lawyer, a highly regarded attorney in a highly regarded firm. Because I was a rookie, and because Frank was on the "business side" of the office, dealing strictly in commercial work, our paths hardly crossed. Frank was a budding star at Bronson, and the partners never forgave him for leaving and taking some good clients with him.

Frank called me in early 1964, telling me he had a proposition he thought might interest me, and asking if I'd like to meet for lunch. He picked the Ritz Old Poodle Dog, San Francisco's first—and most notoriously haughty—French café, because nobody we knew would ever eat there, and because secrecy was crucial.

The offer presented to me was that I would come into the firm as an equal partner with my name added to the masthead after six months, assuming we were all still happy. I was mildly concerned that the three of them had been classmates and close friends at Stanford and that I'd always be regarded as a Berkeley Boalt Hall outsider. For that reason, I briefly considered another tempting offer I'd received from the offices of Farr and Horan in Carmel. Fred Farr was a popular state senator and I'd been close friends with Larry Horan at the District Attorney's Office when we were both deputies. I knew Larry to be an outstanding trial lawyer, but the prospect of moving my family to the Carmel Valley and leaving our Oakland home and our friends militated against the offer. All things considered, the reputations of the three partners at the Elke firm made their offer irresistible.

Frank and I had much in common: we were both from small towns with big aspirations and controlling personalities, both athletic and fiercely competitive. These similarities created significant friction over the years as Frank and I were capable of arguing over minutia like the weight of the stationery bond paper we should be using.

A more pertinent example involved the optimum rate of growth of our legal staff. I was an expansionist, arguing that we could leverage quality associate hours and dramatically increase our annual revenue. Moreover, I believed we needed to escape the small-firm boutique image in order to gain access to bigger clients and bigger trials. Frank argued for a conservative position of slow growth in order to ensure quality work. Both arguments had merit, and I believe we ended up with a good compromise over the years. Compromise didn't come easy, however, and although Frank and I came very close to blows once in his office, it never came to that. I may be rationalizing, but looking back, I believe the heat generated by our clashes more often than not produced light.

As we both mellowed over the years, we became very close friends and I can now freely admit that the firm would never have survived, let alone succeeded, without his brilliance as a transactional lawyer and law firm administrator.

His friendship and generosity of spirit in later years is confirmed by an email he sent to all lawyers on the occasion of our firm's fiftieth anniversary. Frank and Jerry Braun were honored as original founders, but Frank, as he had done before, wanted to set the record straight that he and Jerry also considered me to be a founder:

—Original Message—

From: Farella, Frank (28) x4411
Sent: Thursday, February 01, 2018 3:02 P.M.
To: Attorneys

I was late for a flight and did not finish our anniversary msg. John Martel joined us and sparked the great litigation practice he inspired when we **got him as our 4th founder**.

Thank you, Frank. You were the guy who might have suspected the great ship we were both aboard in the early sixties—the Bronson firm—was slowly sinking, and you returned in a lifeboat in time to save me. Yes, we've had our disagreements over the years, but out of our many conflicts we formed a superior law firm, and, eventually, an enduring friendship.

## Jerome I. Braun

I first knew Jerry Braun by his excellent reputation only, but I got to know him well in a hurry. We constituted the litigation side of the firm, while Tom and Frank made up the business-commercial side. The possibility for friction between us was obvious, as I would try to carve my niche in the firm's trial side. Fortunately, unlike my relationship with Frank, there was little or no tension, for Jerry quickly gravitated toward the appellate side of litigation, while I was more interested in trial work.

Jerry soon became known as the "balance wheel" of the partnership. As previously suggested, there was a great deal of tension during the early years of the firm, with Tom and Frank fighting over Tom's lack of administrative discipline and my frequent arguments with Frank about anything and everything. Jerry was always the calm "man in the middle."

He was also the closest thing we had to a truly distinguished attorney and he dressed the part, seldom showing up for work without a three-piece suit, complete with traditional pocket watch and fob chain. (I settled for off-the-rack two-piece suits, "tailored" at the point of purchase.)

Jerry's list of honors and accomplishments on behalf of the state and federal bench would fill a book. Amazingly, he's a recovering alcoholic, now sober for more than a decade. His reputation remains untarnished, and he is a past president of The Other Bar, a support group for alcoholic lawyers.

## A Gamble: Leaving Bronson

At the time I changed firms, Ann and I were still married, and I suspect she saw what the Bronson lifestyle was doing to me before I realized it myself. With her full agreement, the decision to join Tom, Frank, and Jerry was settled. It wasn't an easy decision for either of us, so thank you, Ann, for trusting me.

Telling the partners at BB&M was the hardest part. They were stunned when I announced I was leaving, and one at a time offered me the moon to stay. I was waiting for one of them to tell me I needed a small, four-man firm like I needed water in my shoes, but no one did. One senior partner, Edgar Rowe, told me I was the lawyer to whom they "planned to turn over the keys to the firm." I was flattered, but my decision had been made and I never looked back. There were simply too many fathers at BB&M, at least thirty senior partners. I was in my thirties and hungering for more control in my life and in my work. Reflecting on it now, I believe I had probably become a lawyer to achieve the control I never had while growing up and had then mistakenly joined the General Motors of law firms, where it would take years, if not decades, to have any measure of control over my career.

Incidentally, like many large prestigious San Francisco law firms, Bronson dissolved twenty-five years later, while Farella Braun + Martel is flourishing with 140 lawyers at present. Little did I know when I left the Bronson ship in 1964 that the dominant and venerable firm had already sprung a leak and would eventually sink. Proof once again that sometimes even a blind hog comes up with a truffle.

I'll always be grateful to Tom, Frank, and Jerry for inviting me to join them in what turned out to an unforgettable adventure. Our figurative blood oath to never let each other down, however, establishes all three of them as suspects in my investigation.

## Chapter 12

# Children and the Dissolution

> In hero movies you would steal every scene
> Although your dreams keep falling like a broken kite.
> Harlow, Garbo, Hepburn, too
> They played easy roles compared with you.
> —"Survivor" (1972)

I'VE BEEN BLESSED WITH two perfect children whom I adore beyond words. Ann agrees they are more than worth the pain of a failed marriage. Jay and Melissa are among the most loving, decent, and competent human beings I know, and I wake up each day with gratitude that I have been granted two such undeserved blessings.

Some of my happiest memories from those turbulent sixties are watching our babies grow and engaging in simple playtime activities such as the "pencil game," in which the two of them would attempt to get around the dreaded giant (me), all three of us sprawled across the living room carpet as the kids tried to capture a common pencil while I "tried" to stop them. I would allow one of them at a time to crawl past me and get within an inch or two of grasping the pencil before I would pull them back by one of their little legs, while holding the other one at bay, all of us laughing hysterically. The game ended when it was time for dinner and the giant allowed one or both children to crawl past him, followed by whoops of delight as they seized the pencil. The pencil game was fun for all and provided the kids an introduction to competition and teamwork.

Even though I was often an absentee father, I was always rewarded upon my return from business trips with shouts of joy. Jay recalls a time when he and his sister both enthusiastically leapt into my arms and Jay inadvertently (I think) kicked me in the balls.

I also encouraged fantasy and imagination. When we lived near Lake Temescal in Oakland, for example, we were often in a rented rowboat in search of "the Magic Duck of the Himalayas" (a.k.a. a common mallard).

Then there were the not-so-great experiences, such as the time when a well-meaning father took his two young children—approximately nine and seven—on an overnight river rafting trip on the American River near Sacramento in the middle of winter. Mom wisely stayed at home. I recount the adventure (which is what it turned out to be) here to illustrate what courageous and good sports both children were—and still are.

Our trip got off to a bad start on a freezing morning while entering the rafts. Melissa slipped through my hands and fell into the river. I was easily able to pull her out, but there was no way to dry her as the guides shoved the seven or eight rafts off from the shore. No matter, we were soon *all* soaking wet due to the freezing rain that persisted for the next day and a half.

Despite the conditions, I don't recall a single tear or complaint. Jay still remembers being so cold that when the guides would occasionally stop at a small beach, we would bury our bodies in the sand, wet clothing and all, to capture the minuscule residual warmth from the day before.

Our guides' efforts to start a fire were frustrated by the steadily falling, freezing rain. Eventually, we stopped to spend the night in hastily assembled tents, the three of us huddling together for warmth.

The guides were apologetic but ill-equipped to deal with the challenges created by the unforeseen weather. I felt terrible, too, guilty of parental malpractice, but both kids came through the disaster with courage, understanding, and appreciation for my bungling effort to be a good father. Miraculously, none of us became ill.

One of my chief regrets as I look back over my long life on the planet is not spending more time in search of that Magic Duck and/or rolling around on the living room floor playing the pencil game. For all the cases I won in court, these were precious opportunities lost.

## Jay

Jay was born on November 10, 1958, and was, practically from birth, a runaway creative locomotive. His creativity was accelerated in his middle school years when he transferred to an alternative education school called Safari, where he blossomed. He reentered the public school system at Skyline High School, starring in school plays and winning a national English award. As a thespian, he played roles that had previously been played by a classmate a year ahead of Jay at Skyline. That student was Tom Hanks.

More evidence of parental malpractice: When Jay was in his early teens, we took a three-day hiking and camping trip into the Sierras in violation of a mountain closure order (and common sense). I hadn't checked the weather (a major storm was imminent) and, to avoid disappointment, irresponsibly dodged forestry officers blocking access to the trailhead.

We both had heavy backpacks with plenty of food, a cassette player loaded with *The Best of Eagles*, a Coleman stove, and everything except what we needed most: a waterproof tent. Anticipating that we'd be sleeping under the stars in our sleeping bags, I brought only a tube tent that barely covered the two of us side by side through three days of continuous rain. Cold though it was, the trip represented another bonding experience for father and son, and neither of us is sorry we did it.

When Jay was sixteen, we took a far more successful trip together to Spain, Portugal, and England. In Portugal, I introduced Jay to expatriate friends I had made two years earlier, a delightful British couple, proprietors of the GB Bar.

When Jay was a few years older, he, Melissa, and I traveled to England and Ireland, where Jay and I had a terrible blowup over my leaving the family in 1969 and other parental shortcomings. It was a gut-wrenching, sometimes tearful, always emotional, outpouring on both our parts— including a discussion about my own lack of proficient fathering from my own dad, Henry Martel. Jay seemed further moved by my expressed belief that Henry's father had also suffered from inadequate fathering. My candor marked the beginning of true forgiveness on Jay's part and guilt resolution on mine. We embraced in tears of understanding. We owe much to that trip.

Jay and I played a lot of tennis together until my Parkinson's, and we loved attending the US Open in New York City. Our best tennis trip, however, was to France in 2007 to see Roland-Garros (the French Open), with my wife, Bonnie, Jay's wife Sarah Hemphill, and their new baby girl, Cleo.

After graduation from Stanford, Jay moved to New York, where he became a freelance writer working for *Mother Jones, Rolling Stone*, and other magazines. In his free time, he wrote, produced, and acted in plays performed at the West End Theatre in New York City, some of which I was lucky enough to attend. I was—and am—incredibly proud of him. He also worked as a writer, producer, and actor for several television shows, movies and Off-Broadway plays, such as *Kenny the Shark, Death in a Landslide, Escape from It's a Wonderful Life, Strangers with Candy, Halfway Home, Terrorists* (which he both wrote and directed), *TV Nation, The Awful Truth* (with Michael Moore), and *Red Nose Day*.

Following several successful and creative years in New York, Jay decided his heart was in the movie business, so he and his wife, a book publicist, moved to Los Angeles. There, he teamed up with writing partner Ian Roberts, writing comedy feature films (including *Get Hard*, which starred Will Ferrell and broke $33 million in ticket sales its opening weekend) and for television series such as *Teachers* and *Key & Peele*, the latter of which ran seven seasons, winning Jay an Emmy and a Peabody award. He continues to write for *The New Yorker* and has published two novels: *Channel Blue* and *The Present* (currently being adapted as a film starring Greg Kinnear and Isla Fisher).

After Cleo's birth fourteen years ago, Jay and Sarah were blessed with a son, Julian. Both are great kids. I count myself lucky to have lived long enough to enjoy my talented grandchildren.

## Melissa

Unlike the fortuitous accident that brought us Jay, our wonderful daughter, Melissa, was the result of a carefully planned and aggressively pursued campaign. We prayed for a daughter and we got a beauty. Melissa has become many things: a brilliant executive, a top international 1500 meter runner, a two-time US Olympic Trials qualifier, a fabulous mother, and a daughter who has never ceased to bring me joy.

Like many children, she went through a drifting period in her youth, seeking her passion, until she discovered horses. I helped her sponsor one named Sam for a monthly fee and a commitment to nurture the animal. I frequently drove her to the stables and sometimes rode along with her on a gigantic horse named Molière. One of my greatest joys has been watching Melissa compete, first as an equestrienne and later as a track athlete. Few things gave me greater pleasure than watching Melissa astride Sam, charging out of the gate in a barrel racing competition. Melissa's trademark confidence and aggressiveness made her instantly recognizable, even from a distance. These traits, first revealed as a middle schooler on horseback, have subsequently been reflected in all aspects of her life.

Melissa, like Jay, was a perfect travel companion. Her favorite place in the world was Hawaii, and we made several trips there together. We also traveled together to the world-famous hotel Villa d'Este on Lake Como, Italy, with my mother, and then later on the trip with Jay to England and Ireland. More recently, Melissa obtained two finish-line seats to the 2016 Olympic Trials and while there, we shared an apartment, all our meals, and a mutual appreciation of the greatest athletes in America.

After a distinguished high school career, she accepted an athletic scholarship to the University of California at Santa Barbara, where she set many track-and-field school records, some of which stood for several decades. What follows is a concise summary of her achievements there, which I proudly prepared for her nomination to UCSB's Hall of Fame.

> After high school, Melissa went on to run for UCSB (1979–1983) where she held long-standing school records in three events: the 800, 1500, and 3000 meters. Her UCSB record in the 1500 meter (4:24:04) stood the test of time for twenty-two years, until 2005. Somewhat similarly, her 1983 800 meter record of 2:08:84 stood until 1998. The longevity of these school records attests to her dominance at the time all three were established. Melissa also ran cross-country for three seasons, running the fastest 5 kilometer by any Gaucho at that time (16:59), on a hilly, wet course. I respectfully nominate my daughter for long overdue recognition for Track and Field and Cross Country. Incidentally, she continued to distinguish herself after graduation by setting four stadium records in Sweden, France, and Finland while competing internationally in the 1500 meter. She was a finalist in the 1500 meter at the 1989 USA Outdoor

Track and Field Championships, and a 1988 US Olympic Team Trials semifinalist in the 1500 meter.

In 2001, Melissa gave birth to a long-awaited daughter, Riley Martel-Phillips. Riley is a physical and emotional beauty, an avid reader, a star distance runner like her mother, and a straight A student. Riley is currently attending UC Santa Cruz, running distance races, and still getting straight As.

After graduating from UCSB, Melissa received a master's degree in natural resources from Humboldt State University in 1993, then served as a hazardous materials specialist at the Humboldt County Division of Environmental Health, soon becoming director of the entire division. Melissa frequently appeared on the front page of the local newspaper as she dealt with a variety of environmental hazards ranging from toxic agents in air and water to high-volume marijuana producers.

In 2020, Melissa faced the biggest career challenge of her lifetime: COVID-19. When it hit California, the Humboldt County Board of Supervisors declared an emergency and moved to create an Office of Emergency Services. The OES's mandate would include every conceivable aspect of citizen vulnerability, whether it be medical, public health, laboratory testing, contact tracing, health and welfare, homeless services, building infrastructure for hospital bed overflow, food for those in isolation or quarantine, epidemiology, and more. Somebody would have to oversee all branch directors, group supervisors, and team leaders, sixteen divisions in all, plus task forces as needed. The problem: finding one person capable of supervising and coordinating this entire, unwieldy structure. The answer: Melissa Martel, who, as operations section chief, juggled many plates without dropping a single one. She retired in March 2022, with the heartfelt thanks of the county.

— — —

My love for Jay and Melissa is endless, as is my admiration for the manner in which both have succeeded in their chosen professions and personal lives.

## The Dissolution

The dissolution of my marriage to Ann was painful for both of us, but the failure was primarily mine, and Ann suffered the most. Nobody's perfect, but she's a good woman who deserved better. I make no excuses and would like to avoid the old cliché, "We grew in different directions." But we did. Partly, my driven nature and the ubiquitous challenges in the courtroom made a normal home life impossible. A trial lawyer is only as good as his last victory, and to ensure I wouldn't lose a single case, I damaged myself *and* the marriage, all against the backdrop of the wild and crazy sixties. It was the era of *Mad Men* on Montgomery Street, the flower children and "free love" movement in San Francisco's Haight Ashbury, the reign of the Beat poets, Bob Dylan, and experimental drugs. Some suburban couples were even experimenting with open marriages. It was an unsettled decade, and unsettling for those who lived it. Creativity and joy were everywhere, and I felt like an overwhelmed factory worker, chained to his machine.

The bottom line is that, through no fault of Ann's or certainly the children's, my soul was shriveling in the marriage, and I was driven to leave it. The path that beckoned me had to be walked alone. Later—years later—a brilliant psychiatrist would tell me that if I had not acted out my destiny when I did, I could have made myself sick, very sick. Perhaps that's retrospective rationalization, but when my soul answered the siren call to find itself, I felt it necessary to change everything, including my address.

After twelve years of marriage, when the kids were ten and eight, I moved out of our beautiful home into an unfurnished, windowless basement studio apartment on Bush St. in San Francisco. I bought a plant at Cost Plus and slept on a mattress on the floor. A few days later, I purchased a guitar at a pawn shop for fifteen dollars, a table, and two chairs, and began trying to rebuild my life. I was on Bush Street for several months and nobody but my old childhood Modesto friend Gardner Smith ever saw the place. I hated that bleak studio apartment and had never felt so lonely. I suppose living there was a modern form of sackcloth and ashes.

For the record, there was no "other woman," only the "other life" I felt called to embrace. Okay, after we had been married for at least ten years, I did "cheat" with a couple of meaningless one-nighters, but I was never fully comfortable in the one-night stand game and eventually confessed my unfaithfulness to Ann. (Call it a residual Catholic hang-up.)

The major victims of any divorce are always the children, and our split-up was no exception. Many tears were shed. While in no way an excuse, I did try to be a better and more attentive father after the separation, truly cherishing our time together, even if just a telephone call or visit to my office. And for the first time when I was with my children on weekends, I was really *with* them, not out of a sense of duty, but out of pleasure in their company. Still, that's small consolation to preteens whose security in large part depended on the daily presence of a father—even a distant figure who'd always put work ahead of family, indeed ahead of *everything*, including his own health and happiness.

My guilt over the pain I caused my family will never completely cease to haunt me. Again, it's no excuse, but I was suffering, too, and lived for weekends when I could see my children. I'm immensely grateful for their efforts as adults to convince me of their forgiveness. It's been harder forgiving myself, but it has helped to have the kids' constant expressions of love for their father. I take comfort from the fact that although I was a divorced father, I was never emotionally absent from my children's lives in the way my father was absent from mine. In a way, he was more divorced from my life even though we were always in the same home.

Ann has been similarly gracious. Indeed, in a recent email to me, Ann took a kind, non-accusatory, and philosophical position in describing our split. She observed that the marriage ended because, and here I'm quoting her note to me, it had simply "run its course, and, in its way, was therefore complete." Wholly apart from the good times we shared in happier days, the fact that our union produced Jay and Melissa, two wonderful human beings, is sufficient proof that our marriage was, indeed, "complete." Thank you, Ann.

Marriage isn't easy, and the first marriage between young people is often challenging. Ann and I were young. Did we know what we wanted? Did we really know each other? Did we even really know ourselves? When Brad Pitt and Jennifer Aniston broke up, some blamed Aniston for not wanting to start a family, but Pitt said the following to *Vanity Fair* in June of 2004, six months before the breakup:

"Neither of us wants to be the spokesman for happy marriage . . . I'm not sure it really is in our [human] nature to be with someone for the rest of our lives, just because you made this pact."

But what would Brad say to wolves and the lowly coyote, who do mate for life, as do eagles and barn owls? If birds do it and bees do it, why can't we humans do it? Well, as will be seen later, I've now been happily mated for life for the past thirty years. I credit a blend of aging, having learned hard lessons, tiring of the game after more than twenty-five years engaging in serial monogamy, and the sheer luck (call it fate or destiny) of meeting the right person at the right time.

# Chapter 13

## Esalen Institute, Big Sur

> Growing up with her was like a Gray Line tour
> Of things important to see, yeah I wanted to be
> A halfback and a priest, a king at a feast
> Everything but me.
> —"Teachers" (Mother's verse) (1972)

IT IS SAID THAT people need a "bridge relationship" after a divorce, a person to ease the pain and facilitate the transition back into single life. My bridge relationship wasn't with a woman, but a place. Looking back, I still wonder how a lawyer from a small town came to embrace a wild-ass destination like the Esalen Institute on the scenic coast of Big Sur. The Institute was a new-wave retreat established in the sixties where one could join others searching for answers.

Before my separation from Ann, I'd been writing an essay called "Christ and Self-Actualization," which posited that Abraham Maslow, the founder of self-actualization, and Jesus Christ, the founder of Christianity, were in pursuit of precisely the same goals, only using different language. I never finished that essay, perhaps because, in the process of writing it, I lost my faith. When I heard, however, that Maslow would be lecturing at Esalen, I was all in, despite my anxiety concerning the esoteric mystique that surrounded the mere mention of the place.

On the appointed weekend, which I believe was in early 1969, I traveled to Big Sur and met the Great Man. I was thoroughly impressed with Maslow's erudition and persona, but what surprised—indeed, overwhelmed me—was Esalen itself. I loved the total ethos, attitude, and overall beauty of the Institute and its surroundings. I know now that a good part of my state of awe resulted from experiencing leisure time, a rarity in my life. I was also enthralled by the Esalen staff, including an amazing collection of eleven social psychologists known as the "Flying Circus," one of whom would eventually become a spiritual and sexual partner for a few weeks when I finally awakened to the need in my life for both.

Perched on the cliffs of Big Sur, overlooking the Pacific Ocean to the West and surrounded by lush trees and vegetation, with a Joan Baez album often playing in the distance, Esalen provided a verdant cafeteria of introspection and exploration for the seeker.

On that first of what would be numerous weekends at Esalen, I recklessly threw myself into all available opportunities, including the coed nude hot springs, the various exercises and programs, the celebrity lectures, even a brutal "structural reintegration" of the body called Rolfing (yes, I cried and begged for mercy, without success).

I also vividly remember some of the knowledge gained from my time with my idol Maslow, including how self-actualized people could achieve a "peak experience" that was unavailable to others. Years later, on the rare occasions I approached something close to self-actualization, I sometimes had a Maslowian peak experience during a closing argument to the jury. In these moments, I entered an out-of-body state in which I seemed to observe myself with approval as if from a distance as words more lucid than my normal capability flowed from my lips without thought or prejudice.

I will not soon forget meeting Maslow, or Fritz Perls, the father of gestalt therapy (who, like former president Trump, was uninhibited when it came to walking into female staff members' private quarters without warning or apology), or the Marin psychologist Jacqueline Doyle, or the many others who impacted my life during my "Year of Esalen Enlightenment."

Perls was particularly intimidating and was even said to have insulted the gentle Maslow. He was a large man with white hair and features concealed by a prodigious beard. When we were introduced, he enclosed my hand in a viselike grip and refused to release it for a matter of several seconds (which seemed like minutes) while his eyes burned into my soul. Such was his power. He made me feel like my father did when I was a child: small and inadequate. I smiled, wondering what my conservative father would think about me being in a place like this.

Gestalt therapy is based on the notion that the human mind and behavior must be looked at as a whole, and that we shouldn't be distracted by detail but rather see everything as part of a greater whole and as parts of a more complex unity. A special Saturday night entertainment often featured Fritz Perls analyzing dreams for volunteers. I always found a chair in the back of the room, having heard a story about a man who had been so demolished by one of Perls' dream sessions that he walked straight out from the room and leapt to his death from a cliff. Though staff members never admitted the truth of this event, neither did they deny it.

I also met Timothy Leary (the noted psychologist who promoted the benefit of LSD) one weekend, as well as Will Schutz who, with girlfriend Pamela Portugal, was co-writing a book on the perfect loving relationship—a project they had to put on hold when they broke up. There was never a dull moment at Esalen, and I'll be forever grateful for its healing presence in my life at the time when it was desperately needed. I was working too hard, living alone, and out of touch with my family. Weekends at Esalen provided a kind of surrogate family.

## Chapter 14

# Taking on a Corporate Giant

> I'm tired of walking down the same old street
> Smiling hard at everybody new I meet.
> But I'll keep playing the same old game
> 'Cause this nice country boy could use a little fame.
> —"Nice Country Boy" (1974)

WELL BEFORE MY SEPARATION from Ann, I had hardly settled into my new firm when I was paired with Tom Elke and thrust into an insane deposition and motion schedule on the East Coast. My new partners had made clear that this imminent trial was a material reason for bringing me into the firm. That was fine with me, although I suddenly found myself litigating against some of the top antitrust lawyers in the nation, and not a week went by when I didn't feel like a country boy a long way from Modesto, California.

Our little firm was taking on Smith-Corona Marchant, Inc. (SCM), a Fortune 500 company, in a plaintiff's antitrust case on a contingent fee basis. In other words, Tom, Frank, and Jerry had bet the ranch on their ability to defeat a well-funded corporate giant, and not just in one case. My crazy new partners had filed contingent fee lawsuits against SCM all across the nation, in Richmond, Virginia; Boston, Massachusetts; Peoria, Illinois; and Sacramento, California, with just the four of us covering all expenses, including court fees, expert witnesses, travel, and so on. What had I gotten myself into?

In 1969, the first of our cases against SCM came up for trial in Richmond. The case was designated *Virginia Impression Products Co. v. SCM Corp.*, Our client, the plaintiff Virginia Impression Products (VIP), was owned and operated by Donald Redman, a recently terminated SCM dealer. It was the circumstances of his termination that we claimed violated antitrust laws.

The preparation for trial was exhausting but exciting. Tom and I worked tirelessly. It wasn't unusual for us both to grind out a full day in the office until seven o'clock in the evening, then catch a red-eye to New York City—working and drinking most of the way—and arrive at our hotel room in the morning with just enough time to grab a shower before starting depositions or document inspections, which ran until five in the afternoon the following day. At lunch one day in a posh restaurant, hosting an important potential expert witness after we'd flown all night, fatigue caught up with Tom and he fell asleep at the table; worse, he went literally face down in his mashed potatoes. I can clearly remember the look on his face as his head snapped up and he blinked his eyes, needing only a carrot in his nose to resemble a snowman. We were too exhausted to be embarrassed, but the potential witness wanted nothing more to do with us.

Later, there were days when I raced up and down the East Coast between Virginia, New York City, and Boston, taking depositions and arguing motions against far more experienced antitrust lawyers. I once passed in and out of the Washington National Airport three separate times in a single day. I found myself constantly playing catch-up, bluffing witnesses, opponents, and even judges, generally succeeding and always hoping I wasn't betraying my inexperience—or worse, a whiff of desperation.

Despite the arduous schedule and a tight budget, Tom and I maintained a team esprit and a sense that we were trying to accomplish something worthwhile: righting a wrong that had been done to our client. Don Redman had worked hard to build his little business and he deserved all the justice we could win for him—and the contingent one-third fee that would accompany a big victory wouldn't be bad either. Our firm's line of credit was stretched thin. We had to get to trial before we went broke and we had to win when we got there. The pressure was building.

Notwithstanding the stress and long hours, I liked working with Tom. The man was a true genius and a conceptual giant. He was a virtual cafeteria of emotionally charged stratagems and arguments, some of which I have tried to incorporate into my own trial persona. Tom was, however, a bit lacking in self-control, his mouth often quicker than his brain. He was particularly offensive to people he considered not as bright as he was—which was everybody. But working with him taught me to speak my mind as he did, often with a confidence I didn't feel. I began to see that although Tom wasn't always right, his conviction was so intense it took tremendous courage to disagree with him.

Tom's main weakness as a trial lawyer was a difficulty communicating his brilliance to mere mortals. That's where I—a mere mortal—came in. The plan Tom and I eventually adopted was that when we got to trial, he would handle the arguments to the judge behind the scenes in chambers, while I would perform the jury trial work in the courtroom.

When the trial date was finally set, Tom and I got off to a bad start upon his arrival in Richmond, owing in part to our high anxiety. I had arrived early in order to handle some preliminary work, which included the shearing of my shoulder-length hair—hip and acceptable in San Francisco, but not so much in the South. When the somewhat hostile barber asked me what style I wanted, I told him, "Just cut it the way you would cut any local customer's hair." (He smirked and I was afraid he was reaching for a machete.)

I met Tom at the plane the night his flight landed, and, to my chagrin, he had not only failed to shave off his Leninesque beard (as we had discussed) but was wearing a Russian *ushanka* fur hat. All he needed was a red star on his lapel, a hammer in one hand, and sickle in the other. I hustled him out of the airport and into the rental car, whereupon we had the first of many passionate arguments. I advised him that we were in the heart of the Confederacy, about to try a jury trial before twelve conservative Richmond citizens, and that we owed it to our client to fit in and avoid the stigma of looking like West Coast hippies. Our heated arguments rarely produced any light, although I persisted in reminding him that we were working on a contingent fee basis and that the future of the firm rested on our success in Richmond.

Sure enough, soon after we'd been seated in a nice restaurant that first night, two conservatively-dressed local gentlemen coldly introduced themselves as city councilmen.

"May we inquire," began the tall one, "as to the nature of your business here in Richmond?" His question was delivered in the challenging tone of a clichéd Southerner from a bad movie.

I smiled deferentially into the speaker's gaze and said we were lawyers representing a local merchant who'd been treated badly by an out-of-state company. This seemed to satisfy them, and they left us in peace. Elke got the message from the encounter and dumped the hat that night, though he insisted on keeping the beard.

All five of our nationwide cases against Smith-Corona Marchant claimed essentially the same thing: the defendant was requiring independent dealers to sell only SCM copy paper and ink toner for use in SCM copy machines as a condition to continue as SCM copy machine retailers. Copy paper and toner represented a major profit center for the corporation, much like a company practically giving away a razor that could only use its own blades. Our position was that the defendant's conduct constituted an unlawful tying arrangement under Section 3 of the Clayton Act antitrust laws, restraining its retailers from selling competitive brands of paper and toner.

We'd heard that other dealers who'd refused to sell only SCM paper and toner for use in their machines (rather than a competitive paper and toner that was less costly and of equal quality) were not only shut out from access to the sought-after SCM copier but had also been terminated as dealers.

SCM's defense at trial would be to simply deny the practice of terminating dealers who sold competitive paper and toner, and, as a backup, claim that only their toner and copy paper worked properly in its machines, and that they were only asking that the machine be used in the manner for which it was designed and intended.

The five dealers we represented across the nation had all been caught violating the SCM policy, and all of them had been terminated as dealers. Because the Richmond case was the first of our five to go to trial, it captured the attention of the top executives of the Fortune 500 company. Accordingly, the defendant made a business decision to nip this first threat in the bud and to spare no expense in sending these young California upstarts home empty-handed.

SCM chose the well-known Richmond lawyer Milton Farley, a Fellow in the American College of Trial Lawyers, as their lead counsel for the Virginia trial. Farley was senior trial counsel at the biggest firm in Richmond, the same one in which Lewis Powell, a future Supreme Court Justice, was a named partner. We knew we were in for a battle. Worse, when I later began to select our jury, I recognized several of the people in the back of the courtroom as lawyers who represented SCM in other cases we had filed. I saw attorneys from Boston's Widett & Kruger, and New York's Sullivan & Cromwell, two of the largest and most prestigious law firms on the East Coast, if not the nation. Their obvious purpose was not only to monitor the Richmond case in order to gain advance knowledge of our strategy and skill level, but also to assist Farley in the Richmond case. Between Farley and his high-powered colleagues, Tom and I felt outgunned, outnumbered, and a long way from home, facing Goliath with nothing but a sling and a few small stones. Everybody's favorite movie at the time was *Butch Cassidy and the Sundance Kid,* and we began to see ourselves as Butch and Sundance, cornered by the Bolivian army. We were hoping for a happier ending.

Because we were not members of the local Bar Association, federal rules required us to retain local counsel, sometimes referred to as a "mail drop," and we settled on a little-known sole practitioner named Jack Ellis, partly because we didn't want somebody who would get in the way, and partly because the more prominent Richmond lawyers wanted nothing to do with us. Although Jack was not a heavyweight, he was a decent man for whom we soon gained a great affection. Jack's job was to sit next to us, stay out of the way, act like he liked us, and generally try to minimize the appearance that we were West Coast carpetbaggers.

I'd done my flight training in Georgia, so I wasn't immune to the vulgarities of racism, yet I never ceased to be amazed at the flagrant racism and insensitivity I occasionally saw in the South, even after the Civil Rights Act of 1964. Jack was not a racist, but he lived outside of Richmond in a hamlet actually called "Nigger Foot" (more recently changed to "Negro Foot," according to Google), located in Hanover County off VA Route 54 between the towns of Ashland and Montpelier. The sign I saw the first time Jack drove us to his home had not been updated, and read simply, "Nigger Foot." Tom and I exchanged a look but said nothing.

Our visit to Jack's home, during which we enjoyed a home-cooked meal and abundant quantities of Jack's fine sour mash bourbon, was marred by Tom falling down a flight of stairs and puncturing a lung, necessitating a race to the local emergency room.

Tom recovered quickly, but our mission got off to a further rocky start before the trial had even begun. We were ordered to a settlement conference with the senior federal district judge. This wasn't the judge assigned to the case for trial, but rather a theoretically neutral arbiter who could fairly and independently assess and encourage the possibility of achieving a settlement, thus avoiding a trial. The judge started out by affecting an avuncular style—*we're all friends here, let's just work this out and save a lot of time*—but it was soon obvious he expected us to walk away with a nuisance settlement and be grateful for it. It was also evident he wanted to clear his trial calendar of a complicated case (represented by troublemakers from the Left Coast) that might go on for months. When I resisted, making it clear we knew SCM was never going to offer a fair settlement, his mood hardened and his tone grew icy.

"I think I can get you something in the area of $7,500, *and you had better take it.*"

"Our client wouldn't take twenty times that amount, Your Honor," I said. "With all respect, we are wasting time here."

"I guarantee," he said, his irritation turning to anger, "that you will never get one dollar more than $7,500 out of a Richmond jury."

So much for the concept of a fair and independent arbiter.

"We'll have to take our chances, Your Honor," I said, and Tom nodded agreement. The judge shook his head in disgust and stormed out of the room. Not a good start.

"He doesn't know our case," said Butch to Sundance. "He doesn't know what he's talking about."

"I'll believe that if you will, Butch," said Sundance.

Both of us left the room drenched in perspiration and doubt.

— — —

With the trial scheduled to commence the following day, the reality of the task ahead hit me like a sledgehammer. I'd never tried an antitrust case, or even a business dispute. My experience was in prosecuting felonies and defending personal injury cases, sometimes difficult trials but without the complexity I would face in the weeks ahead. Late that night, through glassy, red-rimmed eyes, I stared at my notes for my opening statement to the jury. The words suddenly made no sense, and I knew I might as well try to get some sleep.

The next day, after some preliminary legal arguments in chambers ably handled by Tom, the trial finally began with my voir dire (French for "to speak the truth") questions to the jury panel. I could not help but be aware of the half-dozen big-firm lawyers watching my every move from the rear of the courtroom. But selecting a jury was something I knew how to do, and I began to calm down and even consider the possibility that I could do what was expected of me.

After several hours, I was satisfied with the jury—six women and six men—and so was Farley, SCM's lead counsel. The judge looked down at me. Although not a tall man, Judge Merhige's handsome features conveyed a sense of strength and power that discouraged disagreement. His courtroom was also very attractive, with an incredibly high ceiling and multiple rows of seating to handle a daily gallery of numerous onlookers attracted to a jury trial featuring not only their famous judge, but well-known top local trial attorneys battling lawyers from distant California bent on setting a record top-dollar jury verdict.

"You may make your opening statement, Mr. Martel."

A small shudder passed through me as I rose on fairly steady legs, hoping words would come when I opened my mouth. I ignored the lectern and walked up close to the jury, as I always did, an advantage afforded me by a good memory. I had never used notes in my opening statements and wasn't about to start now. Eye contact with jurors is crucial, and lawyers who are shackled to the lectern by their notes pay a price in terms of establishing trust. Scarcely thirty minutes into my opening, however, the Honorable Robert R. Merhige, Jr. began interrupting me with remarks like, "Are you nearly done, Counsel?" and "How much longer will you be taking, Mr. Martel?" The clear implication was that I was extending my statement unnecessarily and wasting everybody's time, including the jury's.

I glared at him but tried to stay cool. Everything was at stake, and I knew a bad beginning in a jury trial could result in a bad ending. Taking on the judge in front of the jury is always dangerous, particularly at the beginning of a trial, when jurors are keenly sensitive to what the judge thinks about the case. This was especially true here, with a nationally recognized figure as powerful as Judge Merhige, famous for his courage in having recently ordered the busing of schoolchildren in Richmond in accordance with *Brown v. Board of Education*, decided in 1954. Merhige's mandate had enraged a large segment of the Richmond population, to the extent that the judge's home had to be surrounded 24-7 by US Marshals for the protection of him and his family. For that, he had my respect, but not for the way he was interrupting—indeed insulting—me in front of the jury. My heart began to pound harder.

I took a deep breath and reminded myself I wasn't the only one under stress here. Even Judge Merhige must be feeling pressure. Word had traveled that a big case was starting in his courtroom, and the gallery had quickly filled with citizens and visiting lawyers watching every move of every actor in the drama, including his. I could only imagine the duress the cadre of silk-stockinged lawyers from Boston and New York, not to mention the SCM assistant in-house general counsel, put on Farley—all of them monitoring his performance. I understood they were monitoring me as well. Also on my shoulders was the knowledge that Tom and I carried the financial future of our firm. With this much tension in the courtroom, I felt a single spark could set off an explosion.

I continued with my planned opening statement until the judge interrupted me yet again, this time saying, "Are you just about finished, Counsel?"

The jury looked confused and distracted by the judge's comment. I was, too, but concealed my frustration. "I'm getting there, Your Honor."

But I was clearly not getting there fast enough for Judge Merhige, and with the next interruption, which followed soon thereafter, I took a deep breath and said, "Your Honor, I request a meeting in chambers." He surprised me by granting it, and I knew I was about to take a risk. I had concluded that if we were going to have a chance at victory against a popular hometown defense attorney, we could not also have a popular hometown trial judge obviously and vocally disdainful of our case. Before taking the bench, Judge Merhige had been a successful trial lawyer in his own right, and it was evident he was the kind of judge who liked to inject himself into the trial. I had to find a way to stop him. Tom and I followed Judge Merhige into his chambers.

"I assure Your Honor I'm trying to be as concise as possible," I said, "but this is a complicated matter."

"I've read the pleadings, Counselor," he said in a slightly sarcastic tone.

"I know you have, but by your interruptions, you're aiding the defense by creating the impression that I'm wasting everybody's time here—and worse, that you don't like our case and you don't like me. I respectfully request that you stop doing it before any further damage is done to the plaintiff's case."

Tom looked at me as if I'd lost my mind, but to our amazement, Judge Merhige seemed sincerely contrite, even surprised at the possibility that the jury would be influenced by his interruptions. The judge, who later became a good friend, actually apologized, and when the trial resumed, he stopped interrupting me. Resuming the trial in open court, I concluded my opening statement without incident. Farley then delivered his opening statement, and the first day of trial came to an end.

I felt a profound sense of relief that night. *I could do this!*

The second day of the trial opened in the typical manner, with the presentation of the plaintiff's case. Our key witness, on whom we placed great hope, was named Joe Lett. Mr. Lett had been an SCM district manager who'd first warned our client against selling non-SCM paper, then terminated him when Redman refused to stop making an equally good paper available to his customers at a lower price. Mr. Lett had been fired by SCM by the time our case was coming to trial, and Don told me he'd contacted Lett, as he and Don had been on friendly terms until their mutual terminations. Mr. Lett indicated he'd be willing to talk about the case and maybe even testify on behalf of the plaintiff. After my first meeting with Mr. Lett, I told Don I was surprised at the degree of his cooperation and hoped Don had not made any backdoor promises.

"Hell no," Don said, "I just told him there might be a bottle of liquor in it for him if it went well."

I later told Tom I didn't want to know what "a bottle of liquor" meant in Richmond, Virginia. In subsequent meetings with Mr. Lett, it was clear his motivation to help us arose in large part from bitterness at SCM for the manner in which he was fired. I would have to be sure that the extent of his anger didn't come out at trial and damage his credibility.

"I just want the truth to come out," he assured me.

It was evident that Lett was, indeed, going to be a key witness for the plaintiff. How best to use him? Standard trial tactical orthodoxy is to hold a key favorable witness like Mr. Lett until the end of one's case in order to make the most dramatic and lasting impression on the jury, but Tom and I decided to gamble and surprise the defense by calling Lett as our first witness. This decision proved successful beyond our wildest dreams.

Farley, lead counsel for the defense, wasn't expecting the unorthodox gambit and had no choice but to call upon his less experienced young associate and co-counsel, Bob Dolbeare—who'd been assigned to prepare Lett's cross-examination in anticipation of Farley's use of it when the time came—to conduct the cross-examination himself. This was a disaster for the defense, as the bright but inexperienced Dolbeare walked from one verbal trap into another.

When Mr. Lett's testimony was finished, a recess was called and we were ordered into chambers. I remember Judge Merhige's words to Dolbeare as he entered the room behind us: "Don't you be trackin' blood onto my new carpet, Mr. Dolbeare."

> How does Moses make tea? Hebrews it.
> —Anonymous

119

Judge Merhige, now deceased, had a wonderful sense of humor, but he was also the most intimidating judge I have ever been before. One day during the trial when the lawyers from both sides were at each other's throats in chambers, the judge lost patience and ordered us all to "go across the street to the White Tower, have a cup of coffee, and calm yourselves down." Tom noticed me sipping from a cup of coffee instead of my usual tea.

"What the hell are you doing, John?" he asked.

"When the judge tells me to go across the street and have a cup of coffee," I replied, smiling, "that's exactly what I do."

On another occasion, we had made demand on defense counsel to produce George Hall, the SCM general counsel, for testimony, but Farley announced that the general counsel was a "very busy man" and it would be difficult for him to come from New York to testify.

"Mr. Farley," Judge Merhige said, "you tell your Mr. George Hall to be here the day after tomorrow ready to testify or I'll see to it he spends the rest of his legal career searching titles in the recorder's office."

The general counsel did show up and proved to be a star witness for our side, largely because I had access to a very fine deposition Tom had taken months before I'd even joined the firm. Hall had no choice but to admit he was largely responsible for the SCM policies at issue, then try his best to defend them, including the tying of SCM toner ink at an exorbitant price to the sale of the copier machine. He even denied SCM was making a profit on the toner—and when he said that, I knew I had him. The night before Hall's testimony, we broke down the cost of every element that went into the SCM toner, and I knew I would be able to show through his own testimony that SCM was charging over twenty times what it cost them to manufacture the ink, and several times more than competitive toners of equal quality.

"We make little or no profit off the sale of toner," he repeated, and I was so confident in my response that I engaged in a bit of drama to ensure the jury was paying attention.

"Just so there is no misunderstanding, Mr. Hall," I began, "I am now about to show the jury that you have lied to them. I will then prove, through your own testimony, that you were in fact making a huge and indefensible profit on the toner ink you were requiring your dealers to force upon their customers." The gallery gasped at the challenge.

Working with a large chalkboard, I then took Hall through a step-by-step analysis of the true cost of the toner and when we were finished, it was obvious the jury didn't like the arrogant and evasive general counsel from New York—or his employer either. At one point, I was writing on the chalkboard so furiously that the chalk broke and a fragment shot off. Jim Haydel, a young, recently-hired associate, was in town to help with research, and he recalls that I reached out and snatched the piece of chalk out of the air without even looking at it or missing a beat in my questioning. Everybody was apparently impressed, but I went on writing and talking as if nothing had happened. I was evidently in the "zone," possibly having a Maslow peak experience.

After several weeks of testimony and closing arguments, the jury finally went out to deliberate. Frank and Jerry began phoning every hour, wanting an update we couldn't provide because the jury was locked up. On one memorable occasion, I told Frank to relax because the case could not have gone any better; Tom had brilliantly dealt with all their legal arguments, and the jury seemed to have been receptive to my closing argument. In keeping with our signature movie at the time— *Butch Cassidy and the Sundance kid*—I added that if we did lose, Tom and I would go to Bolivia.

"If you lose, John," Frank snapped back, "Bolivia won't be far enough."

Tom and I needed no reminding that our little firm would be broke. I confess to thinking somewhat wistfully of the secure position at the Bronson firm I had left.

We didn't lose. Indeed, the jury brought in the largest single plaintiff verdict in the history of the Commonwealth of Virginia. The case of *Virginia Impression Products Co. v. SCM Corp.* also made headlines in the *Wall Street Journal* and put our little firm of fewer than ten lawyers on the map for good. We were now a national law firm that had to be reckoned with, and we would never look back.

## Postscript

Several months later, our record-breaking Virginia verdict was reversed on appeal by the Fourth Circuit on a technical release issue unrelated to the merits of the case. We were consoled by the knowledge that we'd proven to the firms representing SCM in the other four cases pending in Illinois, Massachusetts, upstate New York, and California, that we knew how to beat them, and that there would be no release issues—which were applicable only to the Richmond case—to save them. Accordingly, they agreed to generous financial settlements of all the remaining SCM cases. In retrospect, I was glad lawyers from the other states had been monitoring the Richmond trial; they saw firsthand what we were capable of doing. The successful settlement of the subsequent cases alleviated the financial stress the Richmond trial had imposed.

On a personal level, the small-town kid had been given a taste of national fame and liked it. Those twelve Richmond jurors had done more than give my client a victory. They had given me belief in myself, a confidence that could never be taken from me now. I found myself wishing my father was still alive. I wanted to tell him he needed to question my ability like he needed water in *his* shoes.

But now what? How would I follow this act?

## Chapter 15

# Answering the Call—My Life in Music

> So come on in to the country dance
> Let yourself go and dance away all your gloom.
> Hang your mourner's coat on a music note
> And watch it fly right out of the room.
> —"Country Dance" (1973)

BEING BORN IN THE heart of California agriculture territory during the Great Depression had a profound effect on every aspect of my life, including my taste in music. My family moved from Stockton to Modesto soon after my birth, but as a high school kid, I frequently traveled the twenty-eight miles back to Stockton because the Arena was large enough to attract the biggest stars of the celebrated "big band" era of the late 1940s: Stan Kenton, Tommy Dorsey, Harry James, Benny Goodman, Buddy Rich, Glenn Miller, and Gene Krupa. They all came to Stockton, and I managed to see most of them.

Although none of us owned an automobile in our early high school years, my friends and I always found a way to get to the Arena, where we'd stand open-mouthed and awestruck before these musical giants. Unlike today, nobody sat down at those performances, and hardly anybody danced. We all just stood there mesmerized, letting the soothing big band sounds and delicious harmonies drown out the noise of the past week at work or school.

But another musical influence was affecting me even before high school. Modesto was a well-known destination for Steinbeck's dust bowl Okies, mainly decent people from Oklahoma and the Great Plains who brought their music with them. In the 1930s, these folks had been forced by drought and the Great Depression to pack up what remained of their belongings and migrate to California's Central Valley, hoping to find work in agriculture. By 1950, approximately four million people born in the Great Plains had moved outside the area, most of them headed west to California. Many of their sons and daughters were my age, and I have already mentioned working with them during the summer, mainly picking peaches.

Musically, this movement attracted country and rockabilly musicians like Woody Guthrie, Bob Wills, Buck Owens, Lefty Frizzell, and Merle Haggard, all presenting an earthy sound that fell somewhere between hillbilly and traditional Nashville country music. We didn't attract big bands to our small town, but as an underaged kid, I sometimes snuck through a rear window of the Uptown Ballroom in downtown Modesto to watch and listen to country artists, especially the Maddox Brothers and Rose. I'd hide among the crowd, hoping to avoid detection, spellbound by Rose's melancholy voice and natural beauty. In later years, I came to favor the big band sound at the Stockton Arena, but the seeds of my own musical development had already been sown in the Uptown Ballroom.

At the age of ten, I was exposed to yet another genre of music—jazz—played frequently by my parents on the family Victrola. Their favorites were Paul Whiteman and Henry Busse, a trumpet player born in the late nineteenth century, whose hits were "When Day Is Done" and "Hot Lips." I vividly remember hearing these two songs played over and over on the Vic by my father. Although neither of my parents played an instrument, they loved music and exposed me to popular music styles, from Whiteman to Kate Smith.

As I entered my teen years, my lung strength was still compromised due to my near-death experience at birth, when I'd contracted both pneumonia and whooping cough. As a result, I suffered shortness of breath and frequent bronchitis. What has this to do with music? Everything. My beloved Aunt Monie, a registered nurse, decided that playing a wind instrument would help build up my diseased lungs. She somehow came up with the money for music lessons—which she could ill afford at the time, and which my parents couldn't afford at all.

Always eager to impress and get the attention of my father (despite constantly failing), I of course chose the trumpet and even purchased the kind of mute that Busse employed to get his distinctive metallic sound. I began taking lessons with a local mini-celebrity named Carlisle Tourneau.

I soon monetized my growing musical ability by joining a five-piece combo. They paid me fifteen dollars a night—a lot of money for a high school sophomore in the forties—to sing and play the trumpet, mainly at Portuguese weddings and other weekend celebrations. I joined Modesto Local 652 of the American Federation of Musicians, and, though I had to pay dues, I earned additional money playing big band assignments, called "casuals," through my union membership.

Later, while attending Modesto Junior College, I helped form a far more sophisticated and progressive jazz combo with whom I enjoyed rehearsing, though we had trouble finding paying gigs. We were heavily influenced by bebop jazz musicians like Miles Davis, Charlie Parker, Thelonious Monk, and Stan Getz, but none of us possessed the technical skills to properly execute the kind of music we wanted to play. I continued my nascent singing career by imitating the voice of then-popular male vocalist Billy Eckstine.

My parents never managed to attend a performance of my five-piece combo. I didn't think it odd at the time, probably because they didn't go out at night, but I do think it strange that they were unsupportive of my musical achievements.

Modesto was a conservative valley town in the late 1940s, and although my close friends and I knew nothing about homosexuality, we were keenly aware of the preferred John Wayne "tough guy" masculine image. The lines of manly behavior were clearly drawn, and musicians—like tennis players—were vulnerable to being considered effeminate or referred to as "sensitive young men." We weren't sure why, but we didn't want any part of that.

I had already perceived that girls were more interested in athletes than musicians. As a consequence, our jazz combo took pains to ensure that everybody knew we were primarily athletes who were just fooling around with music. Our piano player, Bob Davis, was a javelin thrower on the track team, and Jerry Sanders, our tenor sax player, and I were both football players for the Modesto Junior College Pirates. Thank God those days are gone—due in part to the feminine adoration of a young crooner named Frank Sinatra and, of course, the emergence of the rock and roll era.

In 1949, our jazz group broke up and I sold my trumpet. The music world didn't mourn our absence, but I believe my lungs and pocketbook were better for my eight-year experience with the instrument.

— — —

By 1971, I was succeeding professionally as a lawyer but living with tension and becoming vaguely aware that a bit of my soul had grown cold, left behind in the rush for success and the pressure of raising a family. A spark remained, however, and was ignited into flame by the gritty protest songs of the late sixties, especially those written and performed by a young musical poet named Bob Dylan. I was captivated by his lyrics and heavily influenced by his music, as well as by the Eagles, The Band, Jackson Browne, and, of course, the Beatles.

I can remember exactly where I was—parked at a service station in Long Beach—when I first heard Bob Dylan sing *Like a Rolling Stone*. I think that song changed my life in a way I couldn't understand at the time, though I was increasingly becoming aware that I wasn't living the life of the person I was meant to be.

In the early seventies, with my marriage dissolved, I began to teach myself to play basic folk songs on my fifteen-dollar acoustic guitar. A few months later, Carl Faber, a friend from Berkeley who'd become a professor at UCLA and a guru of sorts, introduced me to Michael Franks, a professional musician who'd been playing and singing folk songs across Canada with his wife. Michael was scheduled to play a concert at UCLA in conjunction with a special lecture by Carl, and Michael asked me if I would like to back him on rhythm guitar. I was flabbergasted and confessed I was just getting started, but under Michael's generous guidance, I returned to the pawnshop, purchased a Guild electric guitar, and began practicing in earnest.

After two or three rehearsals, it was clear that our voices blended well, that I could sing a complementary harmony to his melody, and that I would probably not screw up too badly on the guitar—if I kept it simple.

Three weeks before the performance, and just as I was gaining a modicum of confidence, another challenge presented itself. One of the songs Michael wanted to sing was the Traffic tune "John Barleycorn," and Michael felt it was imperative we have a flute instrumental break. I agreed to provide it, even though I had never touched a flute.

I was able to rent one at Sherman Clay on Grant Avenue near my office, and I took a single lesson there to learn the embouchure (the mouth and lip configuration), which was totally different from the trumpet, as of course was the fingering. I also purchased a fingering chart and made several copies that I taped to my bathroom door and other spots throughout my small apartment. After two weeks of intense practice, I told Michael I would be ready.

I was appropriately nervous the night of the concert, as hundreds of people poured into the UCLA auditorium. What was I doing here? I had only recently returned from Virginia, having tried the SCM antitrust case, and was feeling like a juggler spinning too many plates in the air.

Carl addressed the UCLA audience for a half hour, then introduced "Michael and John," professional musicians from San Francisco. My heart was pounding and I wondered how foolish I looked in my mod-hip outfit that Sylvia, the girl I was living with at the time, had insisted I wear now that I was "about to become a rock star." What I felt (and probably looked) like was a nervous, middle-aged lawyer wondering how he'd ended up on this stage in front of all these people. Once we began playing, however, I got "into the music" and out of my self-consciousness.

I had begged Michael to allow me to sing a solo verse on "The Night They Drove Old Dixie Down," The Band's great tune, written by Robbie Robertson (ironically a Canadian) for drummer-vocalist Levon Helm, a true Southerner. I pulled off my verse and everything was going smoothly until it was time for "John Barleycorn." With trembling fingers, I removed the rental flute from its case. My part called for a simplistic trill and arpeggio, but when I blew into the flute, nothing came out but air. I tried to relax, not easy to do with over a thousand UCLA students, guests, and faculty members staring at me. Fortunately, sound began to emanate from the instrument and, judging by the applause when we finished the song, I think I got away with it, although any musicians in the audience would have known I'd done a mediocre job at best. I don't know why I thought—rightly or wrong—that I could master any discipline, no matter how little experience I had and how difficult the learning curve would be. This way of thinking seems to have been a theme in my life and bears further exploration.

Nonetheless, the performance was deemed a success, and I was hooked. Michael hinted that "Michael and John" could become a successful folk duo, a possibility I couldn't seriously consider given my responsibilities at the firm and my child support payments. Could I?

The dilemma was avoided as Michael soon succumbed to pressure from his wife to move back to Los Angeles where they had both been raised and where her parents still lived. I was disappointed, but Michael Franks went on to great success. He began recording for Warner Bros. Records, with backup by the Crusaders, and has enjoyed a successful career with many hits and several albums.

Meanwhile, buoyed by the success of our performance at UCLA, and hungry for more, I began thinking about forming my own band and started rehearsing popular covers by Dylan, Cat Stevens, James Taylor, and Van Morrison.

In the early seventies, on my first trip to Europe, I took a small acoustic guitar with me and played for drinks in several Paris coffeehouses. "Fire and Rain" was often good for a meal on the house. I was barely adequate, but I was an American, somewhat of a novelty, and it was a great experience.

When I returned home, I succeeded in forming my first serious band—with help from San Francisco bassist Brandt Larsen—which I called Joe Silverhound and His Magic Tooth. (My stage name, Joe Silverhound, came to me one night after too many tequila shooters.) Brandt's friend Garrett Morris played lead guitar, and a drummer filled out the quartet. We achieved a modicum of success playing small clubs in and around San Francisco, such as the Sleeping Lady Café and Marshall Tavern, and as an opening act at the Town & Country Lodge in Ben Lomond, where bands such as the Doobie Brothers, Elvin Bishop, and Charlie Musselwhite often played. I was particularly thrilled to play the Town & Country because when I was twelve years old, I had been allowed by a gracious bandleader to play "Stardust" on my trumpet with the Town & Country house band, probably the only time my parents saw me perform in public.

A musical turning point occurred when I began writing my own songs and inserting them into the Magic Tooth's playlist. My old Berkeley pal, Carl Faber, still teaching at UCLA, heard me singing an original tune,

"Orpheus Blues," and told me this song would fit in nicely with a new lecture he was about to give on a UCLA radio broadcast. He asked me to bring the band down to Los Angeles for a recording session of the song, to be used in the program. Although there was no compensation involved, the band thought it would be cool to hear ourselves on the radio and we eagerly drove down with our instruments.

Though I don't believe that "all good things come to an end," this one did. After a year of playing small clubs, my band was offered a gig at the Lion's Share in San Anselmo, a fairly major music venue. (This was the place where the Grateful Dead led an all-night party for fans gathered to say goodbye to Janis Joplin when she died.) We were all excited and began rehearsing in earnest for this important gig. By that time, we were known simply as the Joe Silverhound Band, since Brandt and the others had recently admitted they no longer wanted to be known as the Magic Tooth.

I rented a rehearsal hall on Geary Street and made it clear that the rehearsals would be serious business, closed to visitors. I mainly had in mind a troublesome rock and roll wannabe I will call Leroy, because I have blessedly forgotten his actual name. He was a friend of Brandt's who kept crashing our rehearsals and pleading with me to allow him to join the band. I found him incredibly annoying and told him repeatedly that we had no need for another guitar. I clashed with Leroy several times, but Brandt did nothing to discourage his persistence. To be sure there was no misunderstanding, I made it clear to Brandt and Leroy that I considered him to be a disruptive force and someone who would never join my band. He was specifically not to be admitted to rehearsals on Geary Street.

After having organized several bands, I have nothing but respect and admiration for the Beatles, The Band, and the Rolling Stones, not only for their talent, but for their longevity. Keeping a band together is a difficult thing. As leader, I had to be a mediator, diplomat, and provider of paying engagements. The band members were already stressed, mainly as a result of interference from Brandt's wife, Susan—our very own Yoko Ono—who insisted on reading astrological charts before any of us so much as purchased new guitar strings.

I was also fighting a great deal of external tension of my own at the time, working hard on other major cases at FB&M since returning from Richmond. As the Lion's Share gig approached, I wasn't totally satisfied with the progress we were making. Then, on the last night of rehearsal, I saw Leroy lurking in the shadows, his guitar case by his side. He had his usual smirk and negative comments about some of our songs and was going to give me "one last chance" to allow him to join the band.

I looked at Brandt, whose casual shrug told me he had revealed to Leroy when and where we were rehearsing, and something just snapped. I didn't even look at Leroy but told Brandt that Leroy could join the band . . . in my place. I walked out, called the Lion's Share, and canceled the gig. That was the end of the original Joe Silverhound Band and his not-so-magical tooth, but just the beginning of my own music adventure.

— — —

William A. Meyer was a friend and an important client of the firm whom I had invited to a rehearsal of the Joe Silverhound Band before its breakup. He was quite taken by my original songs and claimed there would be a market for my music. I knew he had done some major music management, and when he asked me if I had a manager, I said, "Maybe I do now?"

Bill was a world class entrepreneur who'd taken a little ice cream store in Pacific Heights called Swenson's and made it into a million-dollar international franchise. He then moved a tiny Mexican clothier called Aca Joe to Union Square in San Francisco, and with admittedly less success, turned it into a national franchise operation. He said he had once managed the popular horn band, Chicago, so when he announced that making me a star would be relatively easy, I believed him. Almost immediately, in 1972, he put his money where his mouth was by working with the blue-ribbon William Morris Agency in Los Angeles to set up an engagement at the famous Santa Anita Park, which hosted a summer weekend concert series for major bands. The Joe Silverhound Band was scheduled for the weekend following the Climax Blues Band.

I now apparently had a manager, an agent, and a big time Los Angeles gig that could make or break my music career; I was lacking only a band. What, me worry?

My hope was to rely upon Michael Franks, still recording with the Crusaders on the Warner Bros. label, to put some musicians together for me in Los Angeles and help me get through the gig alive and without embarrassing myself. I warned Michael that I was only going to play my original songs, no popular covers. He agreed to be involved.

I had a full book of solid original compositions and a decent voice with which to deliver them, but little confidence in my personal piano and guitar skills. I decided the best way to improve them and, in the process, gain confidence in a hurry, would be to challenge myself in a club atmosphere as a trio with nothing but drums and bass backing me up. I would alternate between piano and guitar and sing on every song.

With the help of my friend/roadie/sound man Jerry Scoggins (also my sister Mary's boyfriend), we canvassed the San Francisco nightclub scene with some of my better amateur recordings in hand, trying to line up a regular weekend gig for a trio that didn't even exist.

We were in our second weekend of searching in vain for a venue that might book me when we came upon a bar called Eddie & Jerry's Blue Crystal Club at Nineteenth Avenue and Taraval in San Francisco. It looked like a perfect setup for a trio, but the owner—though he liked the tape we played for him—was reluctant to commit, particularly when I admitted that I wouldn't be playing covers of popular tunes, only my original music.

We were about to leave when I observed that he had Pong, the video game. I challenged him to the best two out of three games of Pong. If he won, we would play free for the first weekend and fill the club with fans, but if I won, he would have to engage us for at least one long weekend at $150 a night. After that, it would be his decision whether to keep the Joe Silverhound Trio as a regular weekend band.

He was confident, and why not? After all, it was his game and his bar. But I had been playing a lot of Pong, too, and won the first game. I got nervous and blew the second game but managed to eke out a victory in the third. We had a gig. I just needed a trio, and I quickly signed a drummer and bass player—not difficult at seventy-five dollars a night (I never took any of the money).

We were a hit, and for the next two months played the Blue Crystal Club on Thursday, Friday, and Saturday nights, from nine at night to one in the morning. The regular patrons seemed to love us—which was surprising, as we only played my original songs, no covers. It was an exhausting time in my life. After our Thursday night gig, I typically got home around two-thirty in the morning, and either appeared in court by ten o'clock Friday morning or started taking depositions at nine. I was wiped out, but the payoff was that I came out of my time at the Blue Crystal Club full of confidence and with a solid song list.

Michael Franks also came through, setting me up with Joel DiBartolo (Carmen McRae's regular bass player), Michael himself on rhythm guitar, a steel guitar player whose name I have forgotten (pictured in the center folio), my friend Ken Segall on drums, and me on keyboards. We had time for only one rehearsal, but these were all solid musicians and they picked up the songs immediately.

The Santa Anita concert was a huge success, and William Morris was ready to sign me, but once again, tension and tequila temporarily put my music career on hold. This time it wasn't Leroy and Brandt, but my own manager. Bill Meyer and I had agreed that it was essential to conceal my reputation as a nationally recognized trial lawyer. Bill realized that no record company would take a musical "hobbyist"—a lawyer with a full-time commitment to a firm that bore his name—seriously. But contrary to our agreed-upon strategy, with both of us drunk on tequila at an after-party celebrating the success of the concert, Bill boasted to the William Morris representative that I was also a "famous trial lawyer."

I knew through my boozy haze that William Morris would no longer be interested in me, and worse, might circulate the word around the industry that music was just a hobby for me. In my tequila-crazed anger, I grabbed Bill and was about to throw him out of the Beverly Hills Hotel window (don't worry—we were on the first floor) when cooler heads prevailed. Bill and I were separated before I could do any serious damage to him, but my music career went back on hold.

Eventually, Bill and I buried the hatchet, and perhaps to assuage his guilt, he offered to invest $10,000 of his own money in order for me to record three songs at A&M Records under the guidance of Jimmy Bowen, a big-time producer. Those several days working in a major recording studio were thrilling. The backup orchestra of fifteen double- and triple-scale professional studio musicians was spectacular. Everybody involved judged the session a success, and Bowen indicated there should be no trouble getting me a record contract. Once again, however, Bill screwed things up by setting off a heated argument with Bowen. And once again, it appeared that my music career wasn't meant to be.

— — —

In 1975, Gerald Ford was President and I was forty-four, just beginning to suspect I wasn't getting any younger. If I was going to have a musical career, it was time to take control of it; time to get off my ass and stop relying on others.

After several years of nonstop legal work, I had accrued a four-month paid sabbatical from the firm and decided to take it in Los Angeles, where my friend and favorite former drummer, Ken Segall, currently lived. I told him about my plan to put a band together and play clubs in LA, and he eagerly signed on and even offered me a four-month flop in a spare bedroom of his rental just off Lankershim in North Hollywood, around the corner from the famous Palomino Club, one of America's most prominent country-rock showcases. It was a friendly, musical neighborhood, perfect for auditioning musicians and rehearsing a band. Our hope was to start playing small clubs in LA with the goal of eventually scoring a gig at the Palomino. This would necessitate an extended separation from my teenage children, and I hoped they would understand.

A secret objective I didn't allow myself to even dream about was the possibility of securing a record contract and maybe even a gig at the world-famous Troubadour. For one thing, it was highly doubtful I could attract the attention of record companies in just three or four months of performing. For another thing, I'd agreed to take on a huge trial in Napa, California, scheduled to commence in about six months. Final trial preparations were already underway.

What to do?

I decided to trust Jim Haydel and Bruce MacLeod, two highly competent lawyers I'd worked with in the past, to prepare the case for trial. They were willing, and so was the client, so I went ahead with my sabbatical and moved into Ken Segall's rental on Hart Street.

Putting a band together in LA wasn't difficult. The city was overrun with musical talent, and it was clear we could find a competent bass player, lead guitar player, and piano man (I would front the band on guitar). Before the internet, the way one found available musicians was to visit the local musicians' union. There, you were handed a separate Rolodex (a rotating file of index cards) for each instrument you were interested in. The Rolodex provided a thumbnail sketch of all available musicians, including experience, style of play, level of proficiency, and telephone number. We contacted two musicians for each of the three positions that needed filling, then auditioned each pair. We were blown away by the quality of talent that showed up to compete for a chance to play with a band without a single gig lined up, backing a musician they had never heard of.

We selected a bass player, a lead guitar who could double on steel, and a piano man, then commenced rehearsals with Ken on drums, working with the chord charts I had prepared for every instrument. With a couple of weeks of intense work, the latest version of the Joe Silverhound Band resurfaced and began playing my original tunes at small clubs. A month later, we scored our first gig at the Palomino Club. We were well received, and during the next three months we played the Palomino three times, once opening for one of my favorite musicians, Hoyt Axton ("When the Morning Comes"). We were paid the going rate for new bands, $750 for each night we performed, which was good pay in the midseventies. At the end of the evening, owner-manager Tommy would take me into his closet-sized office, open a cash box, and produce our money in small and medium-sized bills. I followed my usual practice of splitting any income from performances four ways among my band members.

Based on our success at the Palomino Club, I was able to secure an appointment with Doug Weston, owner of the Troubadour. Audition tape in hand, I was met at Mr. Weston's front door by the most beautiful girl I had seen in years, which took me by surprise since I'd heard rumors that Weston was gay. She took my tape and turned the volume up when Joe Silverhound started singing.

My heart sank, however, when I was immediately seated at a table with six or eight luncheon guests who continued chatting while my tape played through speakers in all the rooms. Nobody seem to be listening to the music, but I got the impression from glances that Doug was hearing enough to be favorably impressed.

It was a bad time for me to leave the room, but my bladder insisted and Doug pointed me down a hall. The first thing I saw through the open bedroom door to my right was two naked young men with facemasks attached to a hose connected to the ceiling that I presumed contained nitrous oxide.

"Excuse me," I said and continued down the hall where I found the bathroom and was relieved to see a lock on the door. Back in the dining room, the beautiful girl was silently coming in and out of the room and seemed attentive to Doug but also seemed to be flirting with me. *Reel it in, John. Get a grip.*

"So, what do you think, Doug?" I asked at last, trying to focus on what I was there for. He casually told me to get out my calendar. Holy shit! *I was going to play the Troubadour!*

I acted like I had my calendar in my head because I was going to take any day he offered, no matter what. We agreed on a date and, with a longing look at the beautiful girl, I left, eager to spread the news to the band. Rehearsals immediately intensified.

We played two performances at the Troubadour, alternating with another band. This was a dream come true for me, playing and singing my original songs on the stage where musical idols such as James Taylor, the Eagles, Joni Mitchell, Hoyt Axton, Carole King, Bonnie Raitt, Jackson Browne, Van Morrison, Fleetwood Mac, Bruce Springsteen, and Carly Simon had performed. The room was so acoustically flawless even my gravelly voice sounded respectable, and I could hear every note on every string of my Gibson J-200 acoustic guitar. I was never a great guitar player, but that night, we all sounded good.

On the first night we played, the beautiful girl from Weston's house was enthusiastic in her applause and generous in her flirtatious smiles. I smiled back but resolved to keep my eye on the ball and not get distracted.

The only things missing from one of the greatest nights of my life were my family and close friends. My brother and sister would have loved the Troubadour, but they were school teachers with small children of their own. My father was long deceased, and my mother could not leave her home alone. Some of my best friends made it to the Palomino Club, but not the even-more-important Troubadour performance.

I went next door to a musicians' bar between sets that night to get some air and an Irish coffee and realized I was standing next to one of my musical idols, Robbie Robertson. We chatted for a while and I casually mentioned I was gigging next door at the Troubadour and would love it if he could stop by for my last set. He let me down easy with a courteous excuse, but I didn't mind. We had shared a drink together, and I felt like a professional musician for the first time in my life.

As if there wasn't enough pressure that night, I was told just before our second show that a representative of A&M Records was in the audience to listen to me. I'd been flirting with A&M and Warner Bros. for several weeks and wondered if this might be the clincher.

I didn't sleep well that night. I was starting a major trial in less than two months in Napa; how could I expect famous labels like A&M and Warner Bros. to accept my crazy schedule? *Be careful what you ask for . . .*

Complicating things further was that, after my second set that night at the Troubadour, Doug invited me upstairs to his surprisingly austere office and, without a word, poured Jack Daniel's into two shot glasses and slid one across the desk to me. This was scary. Had he seen me exchanging smiles with the beautiful girl? God knows I'd been careful, not even daring to speak with her or even ask her name. I was concerned Doug might have plans for the hunting knife he always kept strapped around his waist. (If you saw Doug Weston depicted in the movie *Rocketman*, you saw that weapon.) I wasn't quite ready to become a tenor, especially over a girl whose name I didn't even know. I picked up my glass, glad to see my hand didn't tremble, and touched it to his in a silent toast.

He smiled and said, "You did well. Were those all your original songs?"

"That's all my band plays," I said, and took a generous slurp from my glass.

"How would you like to record them," said Doug. "The album would be called *Joe Silverhound Live at the Troubadour!*"

It was while I was recovering from the first shocker that he delivered the next, making a casual reference to the fact that the beautiful girl I had been lusting after (he had noticed) was in fact a very young man.

I don't remember exactly what I said next, but I tried to conceal my excitement about the possibility of an album. I asked for another shot of JD and told Doug I'd have to talk to the band.

Later that night, I began to think it was time for me to get back to San Francisco. I ultimately declined Doug's offer to do the live album, partly on the advice of a trusted and knowledgeable entertainment expert who suggested I hold out for a major studio, but mainly because of the Robert Mondavi case. He had chosen me to take on his second trial knowing that I was on a musical sabbatical and agreed for my partners to start trial preparation—as long as I would be his trial attorney in court. Within two weeks, and with a heavy heart, I was back in San Francisco, mired in final preparation for the trial. Several weeks after that, I stood to make my opening statement in *Mondavi v. Mondavi.* As I considered the competition between an album at the Troubadour and the Mondavi case, it struck me that they involved two kinds of live performances, but with different objectives—entertainment versus justice.

Looking back, I now regret not making the live album at the Troubadour, though I'm not sorry I returned to my responsibilities at the firm. I had my time pretending to be a rock star and wouldn't give it up for anything. Other art forms, like cinema and theater, can alter my thinking and motivate me to action, but nothing instantly affects my emotional state and moves my soul like music.

## Chapter 16

# Back to My Future: The Mondavi Case

> She said you're doing okay
> You're doing just fine
> But it's time to stop gathering grapes
> And start making some wine
> —"Teachers" (1970)

IN 1906, AN ITALIAN immigrant named Cesare Mondavi came to America to work the iron mines in Ely, Minnesota. He returned to Italy only long enough to marry his sweetheart, Rosa Grassi. The newlyweds then settled back in Minnesota where they established a boarding house for fellow Italian émigrés.

When Prohibition was declared in 1920, Cesare and Rosa were selected by their tight-knit community to travel to California to ensure a supply of grapes for their home-fermented "sacramental wine." I was yet to be born, but the Mondavis' trip to California in 1922 would have lasting consequences for me sixty years later.

The Mondavis fell in love with California and settled there permanently. By 1943, Cesare and Rosa had saved enough money to consider—at the urging of their young son Robert—purchasing a decrepit winery, originally established by a Prussian winemaker named Charles Krug. The winery was located in the Napa Valley, already the heart of California viticulture, owing to soil composition and weather. The purchase price was $75,000 and included the Charles Krug name.

Robert (known as Bob) and his younger brother, Peter, worked in the winery until it was time to go to college. Both attended Stanford, bringing different personalities but a common desire to succeed in the wine business. Even in their younger days, Bob manifested the more aggressive personality, while Peter was more introverted. Bob was always pushing Peter to achieve more, and when Peter tried, he usually succeeded. Differences aside, the Mondavi family made their first domestically sold wine in 1944, only a year after purchasing the Charles Krug Winery.

In 1943, Cesare created C. Mondavi and Sons—a family partnership based in Napa—for the purpose of holding all his business operations, including a household table grape shipping business located in Lodi, California. The general partners were Cesare (20 percent), his wife Rosa (20 percent), Robert (20 percent), and Peter (20 percent). The limited partners were their daughters, Mary Mondavi Westbrook (10 percent) and Helen Mondavi Ventura (10 percent). The partnership survived Cesare's death in 1959.

In 1962, a sudden rainstorm in the Central Valley rendered the partnership's Lodi table grapes unfit for shipment. To salvage some value from the grapes before spoilage occurred, they arranged to have them crushed and made into wine. This wine was then purchased by Krug (an intrafamilial transaction) for use in a newly created jug wine called CK Mondavi.

This accidental first sale of Lodi jug wine—from one wholly owned entity (CK Mondavi) to another (Krug)—awakened the partners to the possibility that they could minimize double taxation (once as Krug corporate income, and then again as dividend income to the Krug shareholders) by making inflated-price Lodi wine sales to Krug a regular feature of the family businesses, i.e., Krug would purchase partnership wine paying above market prices, thus diminishing its taxable profits. This was a perfectly legal tax avoidance method that had Bob's full approval, since only the US government was the loser.

But not for long.

— — —

By 1965, the reborn Charles Krug Winery had established itself as one of the finest in California. Bob, being more outgoing, focused on marketing, while Peter became the principal winemaker. They were a team, at least until the differences in their personalities led to friction, eventually resulting in a fistfight in Peter's kitchen during a family gathering. Peter had been accusing Bob of spending too much company money promoting the winery rather than focusing on quality of the wine. Bob, on the other hand, frequently charged Peter with a conservatism that would ruin their hopes of efficiently expanding sales. The night of the family gathering, Peter took it a step further.

"He accused me of taking money that didn't belong to me," Bob later claimed. "I told him to take his accusation back."

Peter's allegation related to Bob's purchase of a fur coat for his wife, Marge, so they could make a good impression at a White House function to which they'd been invited. Bob had presumably expensed the purchase, so Peter's accusation was tantamount to a charge of embezzlement and was more than Bob could take. Bob totally lost it, socked Peter, then grabbed him by the collar and threw him around the kitchen.

Whether justified or not, that did it for Mama Rosa Mondavi, who sided with her younger son. Sisters Helen and Mary also supported Peter, and together they turned to a Mondavi board member, San Francisco Mayor Joseph L. Alioto, who was also the nation's leading antitrust lawyer for plaintiffs. The mayor was very popular and had been spoken of as a possible Democratic candidate for President of the United States.

In 1965, with Alioto's help—and unbeknownst to Bob—a nefarious scenario was unfolding in which a new partnership was formed by Peter, his mother, and his sisters for the primary purpose of freezing out Bob from company profits. The new partnership would continue to charge the Krug Corporation artificially elevated prices for sales of its own Lodi grapes and bulk wine, but Bob's interest in that partnership would be eliminated. The ploy would continue to diminish Krug's own profits and value, but the members of the new partnership—minus Bob—would be well compensated.

When Peter informed Bob about the new limited partnership, Bob was livid. He was still a stockholder of the Krug Corporation, but it now had a policy of not paying dividends to shareholders because they would be taxed. Thus, Bob was now effectively cut off from any cash flow from either Krug or the new partnership. To make matters worse, he could not sell his Krug stock because corporate bylaws required he first offer his shares to the Krug Corporation, which would only be required to pay book value—probably a fifth of the true value, especially now that the new partnership was siphoning off most of Krug's profits. Krug's accountant further blessed the intracompany sales plan with a patina of legality by opining that the scheme would both reduce taxes and minimize the value of Krug so the family wouldn't be hamstrung with estate taxes when Rosa died.

When Bob realized he was shut out from both the partnership and Krug corporate profits, he consulted with his lawyers and then announced, in July, 1966, that he would endeavor to start his own new winery. Soon thereafter, Joe Alioto, using Bob's announcement as an excuse, finally dropped the last shoe. Acting in his capacity as Krug's general counsel, he wrote Robert, advising him that his employment by Krug was immediately terminated. The battle lines were now drawn, and Bob was left with no choice but to consider the possibility of litigation and continue trying to finance his own winery. The fight that had started in the kitchen would now be continued in the courtroom.

Later that same year, the Robert Mondavi Winery was born. Without sufficient capital of his own, however, Bob was forced to rely on Molson Brewery, a Canadian company, as his financial partner, and they—not Bob—would own a majority interest in the new business.

Soon after production commenced, Bob began competing with Krug for wine grapes. As a result, the family filed a lawsuit to remove Bob from the profitable family trust and its growing wine empire. Bob was represented by Cliff Adams, and the hearing on the motion would have made for good comedy, except for the outcome, which—from Bob's standpoint—was pure tragedy. Rosa Mondavi, a key witness at the hearing, was still not fluent in English, necessitating a translator. As (bad) luck would have it, the judge presiding at the trust hearing was fluent in Italian, and the Mondavi family's lawyer, Joe Alioto, was also of Italian descent, and multilingual. The stage was set for disaster and, at one point in the proceedings, the parties—*including the judge*—became impatient with the delay caused by Rosa's translator and began talking over him, rapidly exchanging questions and answers in Italian.

Adams was understandably at a loss—as was Bob's cause.

When the judge ruled against Bob, he tried to fight back. In November, 1972, Bob's law firm, Busterud, Draper & Adams, filed a complaint on his behalf seeking dissolution of the new partnership and an injunction prohibiting further transactions between it and Krug.

## Release the Kraken

This action provoked a quick response. Bob had poked the giant and was about to feel a family's wrath. Peter, after all, had Alioto—one of the best and toughest undefeated trial lawyers in America—who had just been waiting for his cage door to be opened. Responding to Bob's filing, Alioto answered on behalf of Peter and the family, denying all of Bob's allegations—and that was just for starters. He then brought out the big guns, cross-complaining against Bob, the Robert Mondavi Winery, and Molson in a blistering twenty-seven-page pleading that accused Bob of everything but copulating with farm animals. A partial list of charges against Bob included breach of fiduciary duty; unfair competition against his family; various antitrust violations in his acquisition of grapes, vineyards, and distributorships; conspiring to take over the wine industry; paying exorbitant rates for grapes; and theft of family secrets.

Bob felt devastated and outmatched, an opinion probably shared by his lawyers as loss after loss piled up in court proceedings. Something was going to have to be done to rescue Bob from the brink of financial ruin and irreversible failure.

But what could he do? Peter and Alioto's newly contrived CK Mondavi partnership scheme was working to perfection. In the 1970s, jug sales of wine out of the Lodi area, including the new partnership's wines, were skyrocketing. If the limited partner device were challenged, Peter would simply testify that the high prices charged to Krug were fueled by the enhanced reputation of Lodi wines and the exceptional quality of the bulk wine they provided. A trial was inevitable, and Bob saw no hope for victory.

## The Challenge

I could write a book about this trial, but will settle for a few anecdotes instead, since the full history has already been masterfully told by Julia Flynn Siler in her thoroughly researched book *The House of Mondavi: The Rise and Fall of an American Wine Dynasty* (Gotham Books, 2007), in which she meticulously traces Robert Mondavi's desperate journey to make his way back into the wine business.

Bob continued to produce wine but was far from content. He owned just 25 percent of his own winery—Molson owned the rest—and he was being pursued aggressively by his family on the numerous theories listed above, including a disturbing claim for treble damages (multiplying the jury's verdict by three) for alleged antitrust violations:

> Robert had to take it [the claim for antitrust treble
> damages] seriously, since the argument was being
> made by the formidable Joseph Alioto, known
> nationwide as "the King of Antitrust." (Siler 104)

Bob was becoming more terrified every day. Every member of his family—mother Rosa, Peter, and even both sisters, Mary and Helen—was united against him. This was heartbreaking to the eldest son of a close-knit Italian family, and Bob fell into a state of fear and depression. It appeared Peter would finally have his revenge for having suffered years of abuse as the younger, inept brother, culminating in being physically beaten and humiliated in his own home.

Bob's fears were justified, for Alioto had a reputation for never losing an antitrust case. Moreover, Bob wasn't thinking clearly and, in desperation, naïvely sought direct help from the fox guarding the henhouse: Alioto himself. Bob mistakenly assumed that Alioto—a theoretically objective member of the Krug board of directors and a family friend—would give him an objective opinion about what he should do. To Alioto's credit, he told Bob he was in "deep trouble" and that he "had better go out and hire the best damned lawyer [he] could find."

Bob took Alioto's advice to heart and made the hard decision to change trial counsel. Working with Adams, the two men accumulated a list of the best trial lawyers in Northern California, and then—based on their reputations and track records—pared the candidates down to six, then three. The final step would be personal interviews with the short-listed candidates.

I didn't know it at the time, but I was one of the three on the short list, and was invited to be interviewed. I was flattered but had reservations. For one thing, I was busy handling other cases, while trying at night to advance my career as a musician. My life was confusing, to say the least, and—as detailed in Chapter 15—I had planned on spending my imminent four-month sabbatical in Los Angeles, getting away from the law business for a while, putting a band together, and finally getting serious about my nascent singer-songwriter career:

> Because Martel hoped to land a contract with a big record company, he kept his other life as a lawyer under wraps while he was pursuing his music career. He was juggling several complex cases, including defense of a subsidiary of the Bank of America in Washington, D. C., while performing weekends fronting a trio at the Blue Crystal Lounge in San Francisco. He was drinking a lot—regularly tossing down multiple shots of tequila offered by fans between breaks at the clubs—and leading a complicated life as a single man. His marriage to his first wife had ended in 1969, undermined by his long hours at work. His personal life at the time was [described by Martel as] "somewhere between a shambles and a shipwreck." (Siler 102)

## Act One: The Seduction

Reservations aside, I decided to meet with Bob Mondavi and Cliff Adams in early 1975—before I left on my sabbatical—in my penthouse office in the Russ Building at 235 Montgomery Street. I was prepared to engage in the ritual known by trial lawyers as "the beauty contest."

After listening to Bob and Adams for a half hour, briefing me on the facts of the case, I immodestly related my record of nearly one hundred trial victories and only four defeats, and added whatever else I thought they wanted to hear. After fifteen minutes of questions and answers, Bob rose suddenly and headed for the door, signaling the end of the meeting. Once there, he stopped, turned—looking like a man who had forgotten his coat—and said, "I like the cut of your jib, John, but why should I hire you over the other attorneys I've met with?"

"Because I never lose, and I don't intend to start with you."

He smiled, knowing hyperbole when he heard it, but I could tell he was impressed that I had the balls to utter it. The interview ended and Bob and Adams left.

Siler, in preparation for *The House of Mondavi*, engaged in exhaustive interviews with all participants in the trial. She writes:

> They [Mondavi and Adams] quickly agreed that Martel
> was the gunslinger they'd been looking for. (104)

Indeed, Adams called me within two hours and said simply, "He wants you."

I was both elated and apprehensive, unsure who seduced whom. The stakes would be incredibly high, and a loss would be catastrophic to my reputation and my near-perfect trial record. Then there were my music aspirations. I already had my drummer, Ken Segall, lined up, as well as a place to stay for three or four months in Los Angeles. I was thinking that Mae West was wrong when she said, "Too much of a good thing is wonderful." It was the shits.

I sensed that if I didn't go forward with my Los Angeles plans, I never would. Which one of these opportunities should I say no to? How could I decline what would be one of the most significant and highly publicized lawsuits in the country? And how could I abandon my music dreams after so much planning?

You already know that I took Yogi Berra's advice: "When you come to a fork in the road, take it." I would continue planning for the LA music trip and try to assure Bob and Cliff I'd only be gone for three months, would stay in close touch by telephone, would be back well before the start of the trial, and preparation would continue in the capable hands of my experienced colleagues, Jim Haydel (who would later become one of my very best friends) and Bruce MacLeod, a recent top graduate of the University of Chicago law school.

After several suspenseful days, Bob and Cliff rendered their verdict: they hired me.

## Pretrial Preparation

One of the problems Jim and Bruce encountered while preparing the case for trial during my sabbatical was the absence of any organized accounting system at the Charles Krug Winery. Alioto was stonewalling Bruce's informal requests for production of Krug's accounting records, including documents demonstrating bulk sales from the new partnership to Krug. But the judge granted a "motion to produce" brought by Bruce and ordered "full disclosure of all financial documentation."

Our celebration was short-lived, however, for what Bruce found when he arrived for his court-ordered document inspection was a motley collection of shoeboxes overflowing with scattered purchase orders, receipts, and billings, strategically located in a suffocating railroad caboose. This, of course, was intentional and carefully orchestrated. It was summer and hot in the Napa Valley, and the caboose wasn't air-conditioned. Moreover, when we demanded additional documentation—specifically the corporation's traditional accounting records, ledgers, and other standard accounting documentation—Bruce was told that "this is the way Peter always did it." There simply was no organized accounting system.

Ironically, Alioto had probably seen his client's careless bookkeeping muddle as his secret weapon, curtailing our ability to sequester and attack Peter's managerial machinations. They did not, however, reckon with our own secret weapon—Bruce McLeod. When I returned from Los Angeles, my soul refreshed from over three months of music, I was relieved—but not surprised—to see that Bruce, working with our expert forensic accountant in the steaming hot caboose, had performed the miraculous feat of creating a retrospective cost accounting system out of the scattered scraps of paper Peter had supplied under court order. Talk about sweating it out! Indeed, the financial records Bruce organized were sufficiently accurate to serve as the basis for our expert witnesses' opinions to be offered at trial on the issue of Peter's alleged mismanagement and fraud.

One of the significant discoveries Bruce made as he waded through the torrent of documents were notes—apparently unknown or overlooked by Alioto's office—by George Vierra, Krug's winemaker, criticizing certain tanks of bulk wine sold to the Krug Corporation by the new partnership at typically inflated prices. These notes would be important in countering Peter's claim that the quality of the bulk wine justified the high prices charged to Krug. Parenthetically, when I saw what Bruce had accomplished, I silently resolved to never take on a major case without him as my backup.

From the outset, Jim, Bruce, and I had decided to take an aggressive position in our amended pleadings and started by adding claims for breach of fiduciary duties. We also considered filing a demand for dissolution not merely of the new partnership, but for an involuntary dissolution of the Charles Krug Winery, an idea hatched by Jim.

"A corporation as successful as Krug has never been dissolved by a court," Jim warned. "The Busterud firm considered the idea but dismissed it outright when they researched it and found it to be unprecedented, but I think our situation meets the criteria for involuntary dissolution."

"Draft it up, Jim," I said, "and we'll ask for it as an amendment to our pleadings. Sure, it's never been done before, but doing the impossible is where the fun is."

Jim's theory was that Bob was a significant minority shareholder and that Peter Mondavi was guilty not only of gross mismanagement but fraud as well, justifying dissolution of the Krug corporation. We would try to show that Peter's archaic managerial style, plus his minimizing of the corporation's earnings by paying too much for wine purchased from the new partnership, would justify a court ruling that dissolution was the only solution sufficient to guarantee the protection of an innocent minority shareholder. In July 1975, we filed our second amendment to our pleadings.

After our motions were filed, I received a call from Joseph Alioto asking if I would be interested in discussing settlement possibilities. Had Joe blinked? Was he betraying weakness? In any event, this was an encouraging development. I replied that I would be willing to talk and we agreed to meet one-on-one at his mayoral chambers in City Hall. Orthodox trial lawyer tactics would deem it a mistake for me to meet in his office instead of my own, or at a neutral location. I never have put much store in this view, reasoning that this flexibility would instead suggest ultimate confidence in my case—a good thing. If one were truly confident in one's position, why would he or she haggle over the location of a meeting?

The day arrived and I appeared at Mayor Alioto's office on schedule. His secretary was pleasant but formal as she invited me to be seated. I wasn't surprised to then be kept waiting—not so long as to constitute overt rudeness, but long enough to impress upon me that the mayor was the man in charge here. Had I made a mistake?

"You may go in now, Mr. Martel," said the spider to the fly, at last. I opened the door to the mayor's chambers and was shocked at the sheer size of his office and the forbidding distance I would have to travel just to reach his desk. I can still hear the tap-tap-tapping of the heels of my leather shoes echoing against what appeared to be marble flooring as I approached an oak fortress of a desk, behind which Alioto didn't even deign to rise.

Yes, I had made a mistake. Advantage Alioto.

This was our first face-to-face meeting, and I couldn't deny the power of his renowned presence, even while seated. While standing, Alioto was just over six feet tall, probably weighed 180 pounds, and was possessed of a large and commanding head that radiated authority.

When I had finally reached my destination in front of his desk, he did take my extended hand, but his manner was somewhat curt as he unnecessarily pointed with his other hand to the single chair in front of his desk. As expected, I disappeared into the chair like Amelia Earhart, so that Joe—only an inch taller when we were standing—was now at least a head taller. This was the oldest trick in the book, and I tried not to let it bother me.

"You suggested this meeting, Joe," I ventured, trying to achieve a modicum of control, "so tell me what you have in mind."

He was glad to oblige and flashed me a disingenuous smile. "The solution is obvious, John. Your client goes his way and my clients go theirs."

I saw where he was heading and realized I had embarked on a fool's errand; worse, I had been suckered in like the kid from Modesto he probably took me for.

"I agree, Joe," I said, "but only after your clients make substantial financial reparations for their fraudulent and capricious exclusion of Bob from the family business." I was relieved and not a little surprised to hear that my voice betrayed neither anxiety nor anger.

Joe smiled, but there was no sincerity. "It'll work the opposite way, John. Bob will have to stop competing with his family for grapes and pay several million dollars for the damage he's done to Krug so far. I'll let him and Molson keep his winery, and my clients are willing to be patient and accept a long-term payout."

I knew I was wasting my time and, in an effort to salvage a tiny bit of the control that every trial lawyer seeks to achieve in an adversarial meeting, I rose to my feet.

"We're obviously far apart, Joe. I'm sure that being mayor of this great city is very demanding on your energy and time, so I'll leave you to it."

This time, I didn't offer my hand, but quickly turned and tap-tap-tapped my way out of the cavernous room. I walked quickly enough so he wouldn't think I was bluffing, but I was slightly disappointed he didn't stop me from leaving.

## Final Trial Preparation

On the defensive side of our engagement, it soon became clear that one of my most difficult tasks would be preparing Bob for his testimony at deposition. Bob wasn't a man tortured by self-doubt—he knew everything about the wine business. Since I, on the other hand, knew little about it, I was concerned that client control—an essential element to victory in any lawsuit—would be challenging. I've found that the difficulty achieving this control is often directly proportional to the success the client has achieved in his chosen vocation. Bob, among his peers, was on the verge of revolutionizing the wine business in the United States, and unfortunately, this could be trouble if the deposition got rough and I couldn't control him.

As I feared, it quickly became apparent that controlling Bob at his deposition was next to impossible. During our first preparation meeting, Bruce and I discovered that Bob had an odd quirk. Before we could even finish asking a question (in the manner we anticipated Alioto would do at Bob's deposition), he would either answer too quickly before the query was even finished or provide an answer that was so defensive as to be unbelievable. Moreover, his hasty answer was almost always prefaced by the phrase "For the simple reason that . . ."—after which he would proceed to give a hopelessly damaging or irrelevant response. After an hour of this, I called a recess and sent out for an old-fashioned shopkeeper's bell.

When we resumed, the instant he interrupted Bruce or me with "For the simple reason that . . ." I would hit the bell. After a few minutes of this, lawyers and staff members began emerging from all over the top three floors of the office, concerned a fire alarm was going off. This Pavlovian training was ultimately successful in slowing Bob down long enough to consider the meaning of a question before he tried to answer it.

## Playing Doctor

Still, the defensive response problem remained. Instead of gilding the lily as most clients do, Bob consistently undermined himself with almost every answer. I once facetiously told Bruce that when Alioto asked Bob to state his name for the record, Bob would probably deny having had anything to do with it, blame it on his parents, and then apologize for it anyway. I realized that if I couldn't reverse this tendency, Bob would be his own worst enemy at trial, particularly given Alioto's reputation as one of the best cross-examiners in the nation.

After an unsuccessful week of this preparation, I told Bob I wanted to do something I could only do with his permission—something I admittedly had never tried before. I wanted to consult a psychiatrist I had used as an expert witness in another trial about why Bob was responding in such a compulsive and defensive manner. Bob readily agreed, so I went up to my office and called the doctor.

After telling him what I knew about the background of the case and Bob's family life, he reluctantly rendered an opinion, with the disclaimer that he had never done this sort of thing before and wouldn't take responsibility for its accuracy. After hearing his diagnosis, it was with considerable reservation and trepidation that I returned to the conference room where Bob had been patiently waiting.

"The psychiatrist is of the opinion," I told Bob, "that you're suffering from guilt over your separation from the family, despite the fact that they—not you—are at fault. The first step to fix this is to internalize that you're an innocent victim of fraud perpetrated by your family, particularly by Peter, and their personal legal counsel, Joe Alioto."

I paused and let what I had said sink in. Bob looked down at his hands and then slowly and silently nodded his head in agreement. I was encouraged to go on.

"The psychiatrist also said that it sounds to him as if you're feeling guilt about seeking to dismantle your deceased father's life's work, the Krug Winery. In addition, you may also be suffering unconscious guilt about having succeeded in making a better wine than your father did."

I had his attention and was encouraged to continue. "I want to suggest to you, Bob, that your father would have expected nothing less of you, and that you should share in his pride, not feel shame. Can you do that?"

I held my breath, not knowing how Bob would react to my brazen and presumptuous invasion of his privacy. To my amazement, he totally accepted the analysis of the psychiatrist.

"Oh my God," he said, and we could see the heavy load of pain and shame seem to lift from his shoulders. He sat upright, resuming his normally excellent posture, and his defensiveness and verbal quirks all but disappeared. Gone was "For the simple reason that . . ." and now he was answering questions honestly in a way that made sense for our theory of the case.

The following week, all pretrial motions had been argued and ruled upon by the judge, discovery and trial prep was finished, and both sides were prepared for trial.

Showtime!

# Chapter 17

## Mondavi, Act Two: The Trial

> Down and out in Modesto, feelin' forsaken
> A bottle of grape in my hand
> When I heard about you and him, from a guy sittin' in
> With my rockin' and rollin' hillbilly band.
> —"I Should Have Taken My Time" (1975)

THE TRIAL COMMENCED IN May of 1976. Siler captured the stress of the moment:

In anticipation of a long trial and large crowds, the case took place in a double-wide trailer that had been converted into a large temporary courtroom. Joseph Alioto represented Rosa, Peter, Mary, and the Krug directors. On the other side, John Martel, his longish curls hinting at his other life as a rock musician, represented Robert. The opening statements were, respectively, described as bombastic and intense by a reporter who covered the trial. . . The courtroom was packed as friends, rivals, reporters, and the simply curious waited for the story of the Mondavi family's feud to unfurl fully in public for the first time. As one lawyer observing the scene recalled, the opening round histrionics "made the Scopes trial look like a cotillion intermission." (115)

Additional drama and pathos—not that more was needed—was provided by Rosa Mondavi's tragic death soon after the start of the trial, setting the stage for a most uncomfortable funeral. Peter and Bob, deadly combatants in the opening days of a trial from which only one could survive, stood awkwardly close to one another, solemn mourners, staring at each other across the casket that contained the remains of their beloved mother. Each might have been thinking, *what have we done*? Once again, Siler—quoting at length from Anthony Cook's article in *New West* magazine—captures the drama:

> The first awkward moment came after the Lord's Prayer. Monsignor William Serado . . . offered a blessing for the dearly departed, Rosa Mondavi: Let us offer each other the sign of peace. Almost in unison, the mourners shifted their eyes to catch a glimpse of Rosa's two sons and two daughters standing in the first three pews with their families. What would they do? Time stopped, as the morning sunlight filtered through the stained-glass figure of St. Helena, the mother of Constantine. Then reluctantly, Rosa's children exchange tentative, embarrassed handclasps. The moment passed and they turned away from one another to stare straight ahead at the altar . . .
>
> Father Sixtus Cavagnaro, a close friend of Rosa's during her last years, stood up to speak. . . . Signora Mondavi is gone, he said. So what good does this greed do? Let your mother rest in peace. Stop this family war before you are all six feet under!" (116)

## The Battle Resumes

The requisite handshakes and apparent residual goodwill between the members of the family lasted only until they reached the door leading out of the church. Then, as if nothing had changed in their lives, the parties resumed the process of girding themselves for battle.

Recognizing that the trial would last several weeks or possibly months, Bruce and I had moved into the Silverado Resort condominium rented for us by Bob. Fortunately, Bruce was a compatible roommate. His constant smile and calm blue eyes gave him the innocent look of a schoolboy, but those of us who had worked with him knew that— to any overreaching opponent—this gentle appearance barely concealed a savage beast. He was eager to join the Mondavi fight, even though he would have to leave his young wife in San Francisco for the duration of the trial.

Computers were still in their functional infancy in 1976, so four-drawer file cabinets ringed the walls of the living room. I intuited that Judge Robert Carter, having shown himself to be a hard-working, no-nonsense adjudicator, would push us with a killer, long-day schedule once trial began. Organization, planning, and teamwork would be essential.

Most of my more difficult cross-examinations of defense witnesses would be focused on the complex bulk wine transactions, specifically the quality and cost of each one. These examinations would require a precise sequence of questions together with the introduction of as many as one hundred documents into evidence. It would be impossible for one person to cross-examine witnesses seven hours a day in court and then prepare that night for seven hours the next day. The facts were simply too complex. If we were to survive, Bruce and I would have to develop a workable division of labor.

We decided on a plan in which I'd work with our own witnesses to prepare them for their direct examination while Bruce outlined anticipated cross-examination of adverse witnesses, with annotated references to documents and previous deposition testimony I'd need to offer into evidence during their testimony. Unfortunately, this would make it impossible for Bruce to attend court sessions, but he handled the disappointment with his typical positive attitude.

We also adopted a routine where I would return to the condominium after a day in court and, if not too exhausted, jog with Bruce around the golf course. While jogging, I would tell him between gasps what had transpired during the day in court and he would tell me what he had achieved at the condo. When we returned to our rooms, it would be dinner time—which usually consisted of microwaved frozen meals accompanied by a bottle of white wine from the cases that Robert's children regularly dropped off at our condo.

After dinner, I studied what Bruce had prepared for me so far during his day. He'd resume work around seven and continue working all night. I'd turn in early, around nine-thirty or ten, and then wake up around five in the morning and integrate the additional work Bruce had produced during the night for my use that day. We'd both be only half awake, and our only morning communication was usually a dull-eyed handoff by Bruce of a yellow legal pad with handwritten proposed questions and citations to impeaching evidence. Bruce would then fall into bed and sleep until eleven, then shower and have breakfast by noon before resuming work until I returned from court around five-thirty in the afternoon, at which point we would start the whole process all over again. Amazingly, we survived this endless relay race for over two months without a single argument or harsh word between us.

Although we pushed ourselves to the limit, I was convinced that if neither one of us broke down from exhaustion during the anticipated two months of trial, we had a good chance of prevailing.

## The Trial

My first witness after lengthy opening statements by both sides was Bob's son, Michael Mondavi, whose function was to explain the background and history of the family and the Krug Winery. I selected Michael for this task rather than Bob because it was important to get off to a good start. I still had lingering doubts about Bob's ability as a witness, and Michael was a natural. Although Alioto was ready for him, he inflicted no damage I was unable to repair on redirect examination.

Fortunately, my concern about Bob's testimony was unjustified. Later, Bob would survive two full weeks of rigorous interrogation by a master cross-examiner without serious injury. When Alioto finally gave up his effort to break Bob and court was recessed that day, we had another surprise. While relaxing later outside our condominium at Silverado, Bob's sons, Michael and Tim showed up celebrating and bearing a magnum of their finest reserve cabernet sauvignon as an expression of their gratitude.

— — —

Several witnesses (and four weeks) later, Bruce and I were exhausted but encouraged. Trial work is a demanding mistress, and those who win her favor must be fully committed to the point of obsessiveness. Sad to say, the best trial lawyers are neurotic as hell, using each confrontation as a means of proving themselves worthy. What follows is an excerpt from an interview I later gave to Douglas Martin of the *New York Times*:

> Some lawyers, of course, so thrive on their contentious work that for them burnout is unimaginable. "They have a blood lust for this kind atavistic violence," Mr. Martel said.
>
> But most, he and others say, use their insecurities as a powerful motivator. "Show me a lawyer who has little to prove, and I'll show you a lawyer who will prove very little," Mr. Martel said. ("From Courtroom Wars, Battle Fatigue," November 20, 1987, B6)

I was first referring here to naturally combative lawyers like Joe Alioto. Unlike me, he possessed the type of personality that thrives on contentiousness. He was created for battle, a natural killer with an inborn instinct for the jugular. I, too, am capable of rigorously fighting for my client, but I'm not a naturally combative person. This quirk in my personality didn't hinder my work as a trial lawyer any more than it hindered Steve Young's success as a Super Bowl quarterback or Andre Agassi's as a tennis champion. Always role-playing the part of omnipotent killer did, however, take a toll on me over the years—as it did on them.

*Image 1. My parents, Alice and Henry, and Baby John Martel. Modesto, California, 1931.*

*Image 2. Trial lawyer Baby John, inspecting his first briefcase. Modesto, 1931.*

*Image 3. Playing on the Modesto High School basketball team, 1947.*

*Image 4. Home on my first military leave with Dad, Mom, sister Mary, and brother Lloyd. Modesto, 1951.*

*Image 5. Pilot training cadet at Spence Air Base. Moultrie, Georgia, 1952.*

*Image 6. Wedding day with Ann Moore. Honolulu, Hawaii, 1957.*

*Image 7. The Joe Silverhound Band and friends at the Santa Anita Park summer weekend concert series. Arcadia, California, 1974. Left to right: Drummer Ken Segall, singer-songwriter Michael Franks, Joe Silverhound (me), steel guitar player (name long forgotten), and bass player Joel DiBartolo.*

*Image 8. A promotional photo of Joe Silverhound. San Francisco, California, 1978. Jay animated this portrait in his closing credits for Key & Peele. (Photo by Robert Altman.)*

*Image 9. At my wedding to Susan Spalding, with her brother. Hearst Castle, San Simeon, California, 1980.*

*Image 10. Celebrating a major legal victory with Robert Mondavi. Mondavi Winery, Oakville, California, 1982.*

*Image 11. At my Sausalito, California, home in 1984.*

*Image 12. With Melissa and Jay. Maui, Hawaii, 1990.*

*Image 13. Hosting a theme party at River House. Ben Lomond, California, 1990. Left to right: Suzy Katz, me, Bonnie, Carol Gordon, Jack Gordon (behind the wheel), Ron Cowan, and Bennett Katz.*

*Image 14. My law FB&M partners (left to right: me, Jerry Braun, Thomas Elke, and Frank Farella) at Farella Braun + Martel's in my San Francisco office, 1991.*

*Image 15. Bonnie and me in Maui, 1991.*

*Image 16. Wedding day with Bonnie Laird. Sausalito, 1994.*

*Image 17. Winning the 100 meter hurdles at the USA Track & Field National Masters Championships. San Jose, California, 1997.*

*Image 18. Family photo from son Jay Martel's wedding to Sarah Hemphill. White Sulphur Springs, California, 2002. Front row, left to right: Melissa Martel (daughter), Jay Martel (son), Sarah Hemphill (new daughter-in-law), me, Bonnie Martel, Amy Eggleston (niece), with daughter Angelina in her lap. Back row, left to right: Jenny Martel Johnston (niece) holding son Lucas, Josh Johnston, Tom Phillips (son-in-law) holding granddaughter Riley, Todd Hillstrom, Lisa Martel Hillstrom (niece), Jill Martel (sister-in-law), Lloyd Martel (brother), Mary Martel Eggleston (sister), Don Eggleston (brother-in-law), Nicole Eggleston (niece).*

*Image 19. Christmas at the Martels. River House, Ben Lomond, California, 2006.
Front row, left to right: me, granddaughter Riley Martel Phillips, Bonnie. Middle row,
left to right: Jeff's friend Melissa, Bonnie's granddaughter Sarah Lantis,
daughter Melissa Martel, daughter-in-law Sarah Hemphill, holding granddaughter
Cleo Martel. Back row, left to right: Bonnie's son Jeff Lantis, son-in-law Tom Phillips,
son Jay Martel.*

*Image 20. Meditating at the Caruso hotel. Ravello, Italy, 2008.*

*Image 21. With Bonnie at Deer Valley, our favorite ski spot. Park City, Utah, 2010.*

*Image 22. My eightieth birthday party at the Fairmont, 2011.*

*Image 23. Book jacket photo for The American Lawyer, 2012.*
*(Photo by Bonnie Martel.)*

*Image 24. The birthday boy at ninety-three. River House, Ben Lomond, California, 2024.*

True, I had a huge trial victory in Richmond under my belt, yet I often felt like a schoolboy in Alioto's mature presence, and not just because of his age (more than fifteen years my senior), but because of a confidence derived from his vast courtroom and life experiences. When, for example, during a pretrial motion before Judge Carter, I proudly cited an antitrust case involving Metro-Goldwyn-Mayer, Alioto casually rose to his feet.

"Interesting that Mr. Martel brought up that case," he said. "I remember driving to court *the day I argued it.* I was riding in the back of Sam Goldwyn's limousine and remember telling Sam then, as I will tell the court now, that . . ."

Sure, he was name-dropping, but here I was, arguing my position secondhand out of a law book case Alioto had actually tried! I wondered how many more humbling experiences I would have before this trial was behind me.

Physically, Joe was a rock—which I learned the hard way one day during my cross-examination of one of his witnesses. Alioto had a nasty habit of coming up behind me and looking over my shoulder at my documents as I cross-examined his witnesses. Whenever I requested it, the judge would dutifully admonish him to step back and Joe would retreat . . . temporarily. Incorrigible, he would just come back, looking over my shoulder a few minutes later.

One day, I decided I'd had enough. If the judge couldn't control him, I would do it myself. I could always tell when Joe was coming up behind me, particularly if it was after lunch, during which he usually consumed a significant amount of garlic. On this day, I acted as if I didn't realize he was hovering again and spun around like I'd forgotten something on my desk. As I turned, I drove my elbow as hard as I could into his solar plexus. (Have I mentioned that trial work can be a rough game, a buttoned-down alley fight?)

I was prepared to profusely apologize and help him to his feet, but that wasn't to be the case. Joe didn't budge. He just stood there smiling at me as if to say, "Is that all you got?" The only minor injury suffered was to my elbow.

In fairness, Joe didn't have a monopoly on dirty tricks. Big case litigation can be a vicious game. For example, I read in the *Chronicle* one morning that his wife, Angelina, was on a tour of missions in California, the implication being that they were having domestic troubles. To confirm this, the first page of the *Chronicle* announced that Alioto had been seeing a woman from Boston named Kathleen Sullivan, an attractive East Coast political figure. Kathleen's wealthy and aristocratic father apparently became aware of the illicit relationship and was quoted as having told her to stay away from "that damn sheriff from San Francisco." My own spies in Napa told me Alioto was seen visiting a florist nearly every day during the lunch recess.

The temptation was too much to resist. I held off until I could get maximum impact, and that moment came during my cross-examination of Peter Mondavi. I approached Joe during a recess.

"Sorry about your marital difficulties, Joe. Damn nasty of the *Chronicle* to put it on the front page."

Joe's head snapped around and his face reddened. "Those bastards!"

Time for the kill. "Yes, stories like that," I said, my forehead pinched in sympathy, "must make it hard for both your wife *and* Kathleen."

His face seemed to swell with anger, but still more at the *Chronicle* than at me. "When I get through with those bastards," he said, "I'll own the goddamn paper and fire every fucking one of them!"

When court resumed, I continued my cross-examination of Peter. I could be wrong, but Joe seemed both angry and distracted. Incidentally, those "bastards" were accurate in their reporting. Joe and the former Kathleen Sullivan were married in 1978—the year after the judge's ruling in the Mondavi case—and enjoyed twenty years of apparent marital bliss until Joe's death in January, 1998.

It's well known that trial lawyers will fight like badgers in court, then play golf or have a drink together afterward and think nothing of it. Joe taught me that adversarial tactics should not be taken personally. When our courtroom battle ended, we shook hands and said goodbye without rancor, and later became friends. Two months after the trial, I was hosting my aged mother for breakfast on Nob Hill in San Francisco and saw Joe, eating alone. He saw me, too, and came over to our table, graciously met my mother, told her how proud she must be of me, and then told her why in his own words. Rivalling our visit to the Pope in the Vatican, Mom later said meeting the mayor of San Francisco and hearing him rave about her son was one of the highlights of her life.

## Act Three: Peter's Cross-Examination

Peter's cross-examination was, as they say in boxing, the main event— what the people who filled the courtroom every day had been waiting for. Bob had held up under Alioto's withering cross surprisingly well, and now it was Peter's turn.

And mine.

Tension was high because it all came down to this: I would have to expose Peter as a fraud to ensure victory. I would have to destroy his reputation. He knew it, and I knew it.

I first mounted Exhibit No. 500 on an easel, a huge poster board on which was listed a summary of all fifty-one bulk wine sales to Krug by the new partnership. I had previously laid the foundation for my interrogation by putting this document into evidence through the testimony of our expert accountant.

My strategy was to take Peter step-by-step through each bulk wine transaction and ask him for his justification in allowing the new partnership to charge such a high markup to Krug. As anticipated, Peter had to claim that the price was justified by the high quality of the wine being sold. Once he made that claim about each transaction, I confronted him with Krug's winemaker George Vierra's handwritten notes criticizing the quality of some of the wine.

Despite this, Peter was surprisingly fast on his feet in making up rationalizations to justify the high price charged to Krug, but after two weeks of cross-examination, I had forced him to admit to several gross errors in managing the winery, revealed his lifelong antipathy toward his brother, and ultimately extracted an admission that the reasons for Bob's expulsion from the partnership were a combination of Peter's own greed . . . and having lost a fistfight.

Upon completion of my cross-examination of Peter, the judge announced an afternoon recess, and I felt certain we had made our case. I was ready for my closing argument, so I walked outside into the fresh air, only to despoil it by lighting a cigarette (I quit one year later, after thirty years of smoking). I inhaled deeply and began to relax for the first time in several weeks, reasonably certain we had done a good job and had a good chance of winning.

But it wasn't over, because just then, Bruce drove up, slammed on his brakes, and came running over to me from his car holding a notebook and several sheets of paper.

"We can get him!" shouted Bruce.

"No, Bruce," I said, "We already got him. I just finished his cross-examination."

"No," said Bruce. "You're not finished with him. You can prove that Krug sold wine that wasn't legal! Look what I just found—"

"Bruce! You're not listening. I killed him on cross. We are going to win. We're finished. It's over."

Bruce raised his voice and I was concerned that people were watching us. "Look at these figures, John!" he said, holding out enough documents to paper the walls of the courtroom. "I just found these documents that show Krug sold cases of chenin blanc that contained insufficient alcohol to qualify as wine."

Among Bruce's many attributes was a healthy and prodigious stubbornness, but at that moment in my life, it was seriously unwelcome. I can vividly recall standing outside the courtroom while Bruce thrust page after page in front of my face, some of which had words and numbers scrawled across them and others that appeared to me to be a cross between random chicken scratches and the Lord's Prayer engraved on the head of the pin. Bruce's sheets of paper were filled with figures, interspersed with arrows and references to courtroom exhibits that were meant to prove each of his points seriatim before moving on to the next exhibit. When I got to the last page, I saw a percentage that was indeed less than the legal minimum limit of alcohol. My memory is a little dim now, forty-two years later, but I think it was something below 8 percent.

I realized what I was holding in my hand was a wine detective's journal. Bruce had somehow traced specific grapes from the day of their harvest into the crush, then into fermentation tanks, later into oak barrels and, finally, into bottles. It was an overwhelming achievement.

"I don't doubt you for a moment Bruce, and I'm sure if I had an hour or two, you could guide me through your work and I could turn it into a viable cross-examination." But we didn't have an hour. We had fewer than ten minutes before court resumed.

"You've got to do it, John!" Bruce urged, with an insistence in his voice bordering on desperation. Although he would probably deny it, what it sounded like to me was, "You've got to do it *for me*." While I'd had the glory of being out in front of the bright lights and excitement of the courtroom for the past two months, Bruce had mainly been stoically and brilliantly laboring back in the dull confines of our condominium. As I ground out my cigarette, my state of relaxation vanished, replaced by my usual courtroom anxiety. I knew if I could pull it off, this revelation would not only be a shocker, but a clincher. We would win and win big for Bob. Krug would be dissolved! In any case, this was Bruce's masterpiece and I owed it to him. I just hoped I wouldn't fuck it up.

I took a deep breath. What I had going for me was confidence in Bruce's intellect and a solid familiarity with the hundreds of exhibits I had placed into evidence. I would have to try it, for better or for worse.

When court resumed, I approached the witness, exhibiting a confidence I didn't feel. I was either about to shock the wine world and win the case or establish beyond doubt that I was a barking mad lunatic.

Girded with MacLeod's discovery, Martel challenged the witness directly.

"So that there's no mistake about it, sir, I am about to show the Court that some of your wine wasn't really wine at all," Martel said.

The courtroom exploded. After a half day of systematic questioning, during which Martel filled up a huge chalkboard with scribbled dates, vineyard locations, vat numbers, and chemical data, Peter was confronted with evidence that some of his juice could not be classified as wine under the state of California's rules. (Siler, 121–122)

Bruce had explained at the recess that certain chenin blanc grapes were identified in Vierra's records as having a relatively low sugar content. Bruce's theory was that Peter had negligently halted the fermentation process before residual sugar had been converted to alcohol. This would mean that not enough sugar had fermented to reach the minimum required alcohol level.

I took a last look back at Bruce's eager face and began to take Peter methodically, point by point, through each step on Bruce's pages, feeling like I was walking on marbles and could fall on my ass at any moment. Striving for a smooth delivery, I followed his crazy arrows and directions from one exhibit to the next, each time extracting a reluctant concession of the point from Peter. When Peter eventually saw that I was nearing success, his usual recalcitrance turned to obstinate anger and, finally, outright refusal to continue, requiring the judge's frequent admonitions to answer my questions. What Peter had foreseen—before the gallery or even his own lawyers—was that the next question or two could represent the end of the venerable Krug Winery.

Finally, inexorably, I had indeed reached Bruce's last page and was ready for the ultimate question, the coup de grâce.

"Mr. Mondavi, is it not a fact that Krug sold to the public bottles purporting to be chenin blanc wine *that in reality contained nothing more than grape juice?*"

The gallery exploded and Alioto jumped to his feet, objecting furiously. But the judge overruled the objection, and Peter stared at me with eyes that bulged like a pair of golf balls. He opened his mouth to speak but nothing came out. He looked so stricken I almost felt sorry for him.

Almost.

"Answer the question Mr. Mondavi," I insisted.

He looked up at the judge and saw no sympathy there.

"I suppose it's possible," he said at last.

"Do we have to go through the exhibits again, Mr. Mondavi? I'll ask you once more: is it not a fact, Mr. Mondavi, not just a possibility, that Charles Krug sold chenin blanc that was below the legal minimum limit for alcohol and was technically not even wine?"

The courtroom was totally silent. Finally, he nodded and, in a barely audible voice said, "I guess so."

Another muffled rumble went up from the gallery and the judge gaveled for order.

If I thought we'd won the case before the recess, I was sure of it now, and I noticed that Alioto, for perhaps the first time in his professional life, recognized that he'd been beaten.

— — —

One of the key issues in the case was whether Krug had suffered damage and lost sales caused by Bob's unlawfully claimed competition. We had countered that any damage suffered by Krug was caused by its own mismanagement—mainly Peter's. And we had decisively proven it. Moreover, I dared to hope the court would agree that we had proven Peter's mismanagement was bad enough that the only way Bob's interests as a minority shareholder could be protected would be to dissolve the Charles Krug Winery completely. I pressed the point home in my closing argument.

## Postscript

The final judgment, entered February 9, 1977, not only ruled in Bob's favor on the antitrust and other claims brought by Mr. Alioto, but found the directors guilty of fraud and ordered the dissolution of the Krug Winery—the first dissolution of a corporation as profitable as Krug in the history of American law. The national press exploded:

> In a stunning decision arising from a long feud between two Mondavi brothers, a judge has ordered that Krug, which earned $3.5 million on sales of $17 million in fiscal 1976, be sold to the highest bidder by next February. The judge placed Krug, which has been valued at up to $47 million, in the hands of a three-member board of receivers who will oversee it until it is sold. (David Deitz, "In California—A Battle for a Winery," *New York Times*, May 15, 1977, 107.)

As other national newspapers and periodicals like *Time Magazine* blared the news of Bob's victory after a three-month trial, Peter had no choice but to quietly pay Bob approximately $17 million to prevent the sale of Krug. The judge had also found the board members, including Bank of America senior executive Fred Ferroggiaro and John Alioto (who had taken his father Joe's seat on the board when the latter became mayor of San Francisco), guilty of fraud, with punitive damages. He also awarded Bob himself half a million dollars in the way of punitive damages, and another half million for attorney fees.

Bob made good use of his new wealth. He bought out Molson's interest in the Robert Mondavi Winery, a company that in 2004 would be purchased by Constellation Brands for the sum of $1.3 *billion*! He gradually got used to the idea that he was finally the owner of his own winery and, despite the tortured path he took to get there, regarded the result as having been worth the pain. Sadly, the family was irreversibly torn apart and Peter never fully recovered from the litigation, as summarized in the *New York Times*:

> Robert's lawyer, John Martel of San Francisco, who described the trial as the "final unraveling of a gifted and emotional family," said Krug would become "the largest and most successful U.S. corporation ever to be involuntarily sold." (Deitz, 107)

It was an intense and exhausting trial, and I had not gone easy on Peter during my marathon cross-examination, a verbal assault that eventually required a special orthopedic chair to ease Peter's physical and mental discomfort on the stand during the final week of my questioning. I make no apologies for this, any more than Joe Alioto felt guilt over his architecture of the scheme that expelled Bob from Krug. Trial lawyers are often called hired guns, and for good reason. Our obligation is to do anything we can, legally and ethically, to achieve success for our client. I have found over the years that many people criticize lawyers for being too coldly vicious—until they get in legal jeopardy themselves. Then they, too, want a lawyer who is coldly vicious, a gunslinger.

I've also observed that most clients want to forget about their lawyers as soon as their litigation is complete. If they won their case, they rationalize that it was because they had been totally in the right, and the victory simply vindicated their claims. If they lost their case, it was solely because of poor lawyering.

This flawed logic is only human, I suppose, but Bob was an exception to the rule and never ceased to publicly credit me with saving his winery and bringing justice to him and his wife and children. A typical example of this occurred about fifteen years later. My beautiful wife Bonnie mentioned she would like to celebrate her birthday at the famous French Laundry restaurant in Yountville. Reservations there are next to impossible, so I reluctantly called Bob to ask if I could use his name to obtain one. He immediately said he would take care of everything. We were expected at his home, where Bonnie's birthday celebration would begin, at six in the evening. Upon our arrival at the Mondavis' palatial hilltop mansion, we found Bob in the act of lighting the last of over one hundred candles that surrounded his and Margrit's massive living room. Additional light was provided by a blazing fire in a hearth that could have comfortably accommodated an Oldsmobile. There wasn't a single servant or assistant of any kind anywhere in evidence.

After hors d'oeuvres and champagne in the Mondavi kitchen, we went on to The French Laundry, where the chef—obviously honored by Bob's appearance—regaled us with a thirty-course sampler of everything on the menu. In between courses, we enjoyed vast quantities of Bob's finest cabernet sauvignon and taste tested it against fine French wines, like a perfectly aged Château Margaux. Removing my wallet wasn't permitted. It was a night to remember, topped off by Bob's insistence that we do it again the following year—which we did with great pleasure.

Bob was also generous with frequent invitations to meet privately at the winery with such musical luminaries as Dave Brubeck, Paul Desmond, Herbie Hancock, and others. He even insisted that a huge reception following my second marriage be held at the winery. I'm told it was previously unheard of to allow a wedding reception to take place there.

The good news for our firm didn't end with the highly publicized victory. Bob invited me to walk with him around the block after judgment had been rendered, and asked if we'd like to represent the Robert Mondavi Winery as general counsel. Clifford Adams would relinquish his role as outside counsel to become an officer of the winery.

It wasn't long before our burgeoning clientele of wineries required Farella, Braun + Martel to establish its first branch office, in St. Helena, deep in the wine country. Today, FB&M probably represents more wineries than any other law firm in the United States.

As for my own reputation, the Mondavi trial undoubtedly contributed to my being listed among the "Top 10 Trial Lawyers in America" by the *National Law Journal*, and years later—perhaps the biggest shocker of all—having my photograph (pictured alone) on the front page of the November 20, 1987, issue of the *New York Times*.

Do I ever wonder what might have happened if I'd said no to the Mondavi case, stayed in Los Angeles with my band, and possibly garnered a recording contract? Do I wonder how my life would have been changed? Of course I do. Doesn't everybody fantasize about being a rockstar, and hearing your songs played on the radio? Although that unforgettable night at the Troubadour produced music that will play in my heart forever, I knew the courtroom wasn't finished with me yet.

## Chapter 18

# The San Francisco Newspaper Case: *Pacific Sun v. The Chronicle, The Examiner* and The Hearst Corporation

> You ask me to unmask you
> Know you really want me to
> But I guess I just ain't strong enough
> To save both me and you.
> —"Unwanted Child" (1975)

IN 1849, GOLD WAS discovered in California, and hopeful miners flocked to the West. One of these fortune seekers, a man named George Hearst, had carved out a meager living for ten years digging small veins of gold before finally striking it rich during the silver rush of 1859. His success didn't come easy, and indeed would require a demonstration of spectacular courage, persistence, and strength.

George and his partner, together with eight pack mules bearing several tons of specimen ore they judged to be promising in appearance, risked their lives traveling by foot over the treacherous Sierra Nevada, hoping the fruits of their years of labor would be assayed as silver ore.

Exhausted from his journey, George waited as the ore was smelted in San Francisco, then held his breath at the assayer's office. Everything was at stake. Drained both physically and mentally, his money was also totally depleted. Finally, the assay was delivered and to his relief and amazement, the ore was valued at $2.5 million dollars. George Hearst was suddenly one of the richest men in California and, over a hundred years later, his courage, persistence, and ultimate good fortune would have a tremendous impact on my own life.

The new millionaire and his young wife, Phoebe Apperson Hearst, would have but one child, a son they named William Randolph. The young man, doted upon by his parents (especially his mother), would have his formal education supplemented at some of the finest museums and cathedrals in Europe. When he came of age, he quickly found his passion in journalism and persuaded his father to give him control and management of a newspaper called the *San Francisco Examiner*. The rest is history. At one point, the William Randolph Hearst publishing empire would total thirty newspapers across America, with the *San Francisco Examiner* remaining its flagship property.

But by the mid-twentieth century—long before the advent of computers and cell phones—the public's interest in reading newspapers began to wane. Sensing a coming economic and cultural calamity, Congress decided to carve out an exception to the antitrust laws for the benefit of certain daily newspapers. It was called the Newspaper Preservation Act of 1970 and permitted the formation of a "Joint Operating Agreement" (JOA) between two competing major daily newspapers in a single city if it could be shown one of the newspapers was failing. Two competing papers who qualified for a JOA under the Act were permitted, among other things, to discount prices for customers who subscribed to both papers and to allow reduced rates to advertisers who purchased ads in both. These were activities that would have been clearly unlawful under the antitrust laws but for the exception carved out for JOAs in the Newspaper Preservation Act.

When the afternoon *San Francisco Examiner* began facing declining circulation and revenue, it eventually joined the increasingly more successful morning *Chronicle* in forming a JOA. The losers in this scenario were smaller, satellite newspapers who couldn't begin to compete with the coordinated discounted subscription and joint advertising prices suddenly being offered with impunity by the bigger publications. This was particularly anathema to the *Pacific Sun*, located in Marin County, and the *Berkeley Barb* of Alameda County, since neither believed the *Examiner* or the *Chronicle* was a truly "failing newspaper," and hence not legitimately qualified for protection under the Act. Armed with legal opinions that confirmed these beliefs, they brought an antitrust action against the two major dailies in San Francisco federal court.

The *Chronicle* was owned by the de Young family, and in the ensuing first jury trial, they joined forces with the Hearst Corporation to present a united front at trial. Both papers were represented by Richard Archer, one of the top antitrust lawyers in Northern California. The plaintiffs also joined forces and were ably represented by Arthur Shartsis for the *Pacific Sun* and Richard Harrington for the *Berkeley Barb*, both experienced and highly competent trial lawyers—as Richard Archer was soon to find out.

After a lengthy trial in 1980, the six-person federal jury was irrevocably hung, five to one, in favor of the plaintiffs *Pacific Sun* and *Berkeley Barb*, and a mistrial was declared by the court. Once the defendants recovered from their communal shock and relief at having so narrowly escaped disaster, they, along with hundreds of other JOA-protected newspapers, breathed a collective sigh of relief that could be heard across the entire nation. The *Chronicle* and the *Examiner* were particularly thankful for that single juror who'd stubbornly held out and saved them, at least for the present, from catastrophe.

The loudest sigh of relief was heard all the way from Hearst's New York City headquarters, where a plaintiff's verdict would have been particularly disastrous. Without the JOA permitted by the Newspaper Preservation

Act, not just the *Examiner* but many of the other daily newspapers in the Hearst Empire would most likely have failed. For Hearst, the JOA wasn't a business tactic to pump up profits; it was a lifeline.

But there was little time to relax, for a new trial date was promptly scheduled and the defendant newspapers, aware of how close they had come to losing, fired defense counsel Richard Archer and immediately set about retaining, as one newspaper lawyer put it, "The best lawyer money could buy." Word went out across California that the defendants would soon be inviting a limited number of top trial lawyers to compete in another high-stakes "beauty contest."

Fresh off my nationally prominent victory in *Mondavi v. Mondavi* against the previously undefeated Joe Alioto, I—though hardly a logical candidate for the engagement—was invited to appear for an interview. Similar to my initial naïveté about wine, all I knew about newspapers, to paraphrase Will Rogers in 1879, was "just what I read in the papers." I had never heard of the Newspaper Preservation Act, nor did I consider myself an antitrust specialist. I was also still exhausted from Mondavi and trying to schedule a wedding with a new woman in my life named Susan Spalding. Yet the challenge was impossible to reject. Although a part of me hoped I'd fail, I couldn't help but try. What was wrong with me? I needed another major case like I needed water in my shoes. For once, was my father right?

Sitting outside the conference room on the appointed interview day, trying to relax before my turn on the stage, the door opened and out came Jim Brosnahan, a friend and one of the nation's best-known trial lawyers. My hopes, already dim, flickered even lower as I wondered why they hadn't hired Brosnahan in the first place instead of Richard Archer. Jim was perfect for this kind of case. He and I exchanged a knowing smile. This wasn't the first rodeo for either of us.

"Mr. Martel?" a three-piece suit inquired from behind Jim.

"Yes," I replied. *What the hell, I'm here. I might as well do my song and dance for these guys.*

As I entered a large conference room, I was surprised to see no fewer than ten serious-looking men sitting around a long oak conference table, all of them wearing dark suits, white shirts, and striped silk neck ties. I'd never been interviewed for a job by such a large group. I later learned they were New York lawyers representing the Hearst Corporation, local lawyers representing the *San Francisco Chronicle* and the *Examiner*, plus various experts and consultants. As I was shown to my seat at the head of the table. I drew a deep breath.

"Tell us first, Mr. Martel, about your experience in newspaper litigation."

My answer was candid, if uninspired, and had only the virtue of brevity: "That's easy. I have none. I'm afraid you've been misinformed about my trial experience."

"Okay," said another lawyer, "how about litigation in the publishing industry generally."

"Same answer," I said, noticing some of the suits exchanging troubled looks.

"Okay," said the man closest to me, "how about antitrust litigation?"

"I'm afraid I'm not an antitrust specialist either."

To my surprise, a lawyer I'd never met at the end of the table spoke up.

"Were there not antitrust issues in the Mondavi case you recently won against Joe Alioto?"

Encouraged, I agreed that although the Mondavi matter was essentially a fraud and mismanagement case, Alioto had asserted an attempt to monopolize, along with several other antitrust theories. My memory refreshed, I also mentioned having won the jury verdict several years before in Richmond, Virginia—an antitrust case. For the first time, some of the stone faces around the table softened with mild interest, while some even smiled, probably misconstruing my oversight as modesty. I didn't wait for another question. It was time to quit dancing around the subject.

"Gentlemen," I said, "let me save us all some time. If you're looking for a newspaper or publishing specialist, I'm not your guy. But I do know a little bit about your case, having followed it in the daily press, and I suggest to you that you do not need an antitrust lawyer or a publishing specialist. What you need is the best *trial* lawyer you can find. I may or may not be that lawyer, but I do know how to talk to a jury and make complex things seem simple. I also think I know what jurors want to hear, and how they want to hear them. Moreover, I don't like losing, and I don't have much experience at it either."

There followed an awkward silence throughout the room. Had I come on too strong?

Finally, I was asked a few general and insignificant questions about previous cases I'd tried and was then excused from the room. As I left, I saw the next candidate waiting his turn.

I didn't have long to wait for the verdict. I was called later that day by one of the Hearst lawyers from New York and was shocked to learn they wished to retain me.

They must have liked "the cut of my jib."

As in the Mondavi case, I greeted my good fortune with mixed emotions, given the fact that I was scheduled to be married in a little over a month and had a honeymoon booked on Maui. I knew I'd be facing a period of intense preparation. The marriage—which would last only slightly longer than the trial itself (and with a less successful result)—got off to a rocky start as I spent most of my honeymoon not on the beach but in our hotel room reading daily transcripts from the first trial.

I made it a condition of my retention that I be given the freedom to surround myself with my own chosen expert witnesses. All experts from the first unsuccessful trial were to be excused (i.e., fired)—the same fate suffered by the previous attorney, Richard Archer. I would launch the retrial with a clean slate.

The second thing I did was to be sure Bruce MacLeod was available to work backup with me, and I was relieved to find he was willing and able.

## Preparation

Trial lawyers know that preparation is at least 50 percent of the ball game, and a retrial of a lawsuit presents both advantages and disadvantages to a lawyer new to the conflict. Because the plaintiffs had nearly prevailed in the first trial, I knew they would stick pretty much to the same game plan. This was an advantage for me, because I could study the transcripts of the experts' testimony and prepare my cross-examination knowing they had little room to alter it.

The bad news was that my opponents, Shartsis and Harrington, knew the case intimately and I didn't. I would have only a few weeks to prepare for an incredibly complex case that they were fully conversant with, both in terms of the facts and the applicable law. Moreover, they had their witnesses already prepared and ready to testify, and their legal briefs already drafted. I had nothing but my predecessor's failed strategy and, thankfully, once again, the assistance of young Bruce MacLeod.

I quickly got to work researching and recruiting my own stable of expert witnesses, including Marvin Stone of Denver, Colorado, as my forensic accountant; Irwin Stelzer—head of National Economic Research Associates (NERA) in White Plains, New York—as my general economist; and John Morton, a publishing expert, as my newspaper economist. All three of these professionals were at the top of their respective fields.

It was clear that the alleged anticompetitive conduct by the two major dailies was in fact illegal unless protected by the Newspaper Preservation Act. The key to a successful defense, therefore, would be proving that the *Examiner* was a failing newspaper, thus qualifying both newspapers for immunity under the Act. My client representatives, Randy Hearst and Phelps Dewey, needed no persuasion on the point. The difficulty would be getting the publisher of the allegedly failing *Examiner*, Charles Gould, to fall on his sword.

I immediately asked Phelps to set up an interview with Mr. Gould, but only after first scheduling one with iconic journalist Herb Caen.

My preliminary research indicated that his 1958 departure from the *Examiner* to work for the *Chronicle* had resulted in an immediate impact on the circulation of both papers, reducing the *Examiner*'s and increasing the *Chronicle*'s. This, compared to cold statistics, would be something jurors could easily grasp. Because of his fame and popularity among subscribers, Caen would be a potent witness for the defense. He could say, for example, that it was apparent the *Examiner* was going down and he wanted to take to the lifeboats before the ship sunk.

I was aware that Caen's popularity with subscribers wasn't shared by local restaurateurs, who viewed him as a blowhard and a freeloader. He was known to order a meal and simply walk out without paying, knowing that no restaurateur would dare criticize him. One word in his daily column, Baghdad-by-the-Bay, could make or break a restaurant. He was also unpopular with some of his fellow journalists at the *Chronicle*, one of whom told me that "Herb thinks the paper works for him, not the other way around."

— — —

"Come in," Caen said, beckoning me with a scowl that said he wasn't happy about taking the meeting. Phelps had warned me to expect rude behavior, and, true to form, Caen's manner was curt from the beginning.

"What-can-I-do-for-you," he spat out in an irritated barrage of words that implied he had no intention of doing anything at all for me.

"It's not what you can do for me," I said, returning his tone. "It's what you can do for your newspaper."

Perhaps I should have sucked up to him like everybody else did, but I was under pressure of my own. Our instant and mutual dislike was evident. He looked up at me, his expression suggesting he was surprised to see me still there.

"You got five minutes," he said, returning his gaze to the papers in front of him, "but I know nothing about the case, nothing that can *help* you." The implication was that if I pushed him, he knew things about the case that could hurt me. "So, let's cut this short, *okay?*" he added.

"You can keep your precious five minutes, Mr. Caen," I said, "but you'd better hope we win the case, or you might have to find a new newspaper to work for you."

Herbert Caen never testified.

— — —

The other thing Bruce and I had to do in a hurry was get up to speed on the internal workings of a newspaper—and the newspaper industry in general. While this may appear to be a formidable task, the hallmark of any good trial lawyer is the ability to quickly assimilate a great deal of intricate information about the case at hand, then simplify it so a lay jury will easily understand it. In preparing for the trial, I'd have to fully understand the technical and economic complexities involved in publishing a newspaper, as well as the meaning of the Newspaper Preservation Act and its application to our case. This meant countless hours of research and staff interviews.

There was much to do, and the clock was ticking.

## The Patty Hearst Matter

In the spring of 1980, the trial commenced with jury selection in *Pacific Sun v. Hearst Corporation*, Judge Robert Aguilar presiding. Judge Aguilar was a new appointee, and this would be his first trial. It turned out to be a baptism by fire, a high-stakes trial that shook the walls of the federal district courthouse for over three months.

It didn't take long for conflict to arise among the lawyers. The first six potential jurors were seated in the box, awaiting the presence of the judge and the commencement of voir dire, when I noticed a book sitting on the plaintiffs' counsel table in front of Shartsis. It was perched on the corner in clear view of the front row of jurors. I casually strode behind Shartsis and saw that the book was *Every Secret Thing* by Patty Hearst.

Patty had been convicted on March 20, 1976, of willingly participating in a bank robbery with members of the Symbionese Liberation Army, a California revolutionary gang. She'd also been described by her own lawyer, F. Lee Bailey, as being "more unpopular than the Boston Strangler." The plaintiffs' tactic was clear: Guilt by association. Since Patty's father, Randolph Hearst, would be sitting beside me during the trial, this was an obvious effort not only to rattle Randy, but to further discredit the family. I seized the book and walked directly to the court clerk, demanding an immediate conference in chambers with the judge. The clerk looked surprised, but my tone of voice must have left little question about the earnestness of my request, because she quickly rose and disappeared into chambers. A minute later, my two adversaries also looked surprised at being summoned to chambers. When I explained to Judge Aguilar what they had done and showed him the book, he angrily admonished them "not to try a stunt like that again." Chastised, the plaintiffs' lawyers returned to their table and a scowling Judge Aguilar took the bench.

Round one for the defense. The book was no longer in sight, and plaintiff's counsel had succeeded in inspiring the antagonism of the judge before the trial had even begun.

## The Trial

As usual, the plaintiffs and defendants sought different kinds of people to sit on the jury. For the defense, I sought college-educated people who could grasp the complexity of our proof and would adhere to the letter of the law, while the plaintiffs sought blue-collar workers who'd tend to favor the little guy and react to the inherent unfairness of big newspapers apparently trying to drive smaller newspapers out of business. We were not blessed with a heavily educated panel from which to draw, demonstrated by the eventual foreman of the jury, James Lopez, who worked in a Burger King in the South Bay. I would have to find a way to keep the case simple and clear.

Few people understand the work that goes into a pretrial study of prospective jurors. Up through the late 1970s, only a very basic jury study was available to trial lawyers. From this weekly subscription service, we were provided basic data on the prospective jury panel, including political affiliations, employment details, neighborhoods, and a summary of the results of the previous week.

In early 1980, I heard about a new and growing field of professionals called "jury consultants." In the early stages of this vocation, the consultant merely observed jurors as they were seated in the box and surreptitiously communicated with the trial lawyer the consultant's opinion on whether to accept the juror. I decided to try it. A week before the trial started, I contacted a jury consultant who agreed that we needed intelligent, politically conservative jurors.

On the first day of trial, she sat herself in the third row of the gallery. As I began questioning prospective jurors, she unobtrusively rendered her opinion for or against, based on the juror's answers on voir dire, of course, but also on their appearance, clothing, jewelry, and body language. She was reading the books by their covers.

Our system was rudimentary in the extreme. Upon completion of my questioning of the prospective juror, I'd casually glance back at the consultant who would either tug her ear, meaning she would dismiss the juror, or touch her shoulder, meaning the juror looked like a winner for our side. I found her assessment of jurors almost always agreed with my own, and that fact alone gave me added confidence.[1]

With voir dire completed, it was time for opening statements. I knew that in this case, as in all trials, it was important to gain the jurors'

---

[1] I was asked to address the American College of Trial Lawyers the following year at their annual spring meeting in Maui, Hawaii, on the use of jury consultants, "a new and burgeoning industry." It seemed that, off a single case, I had somehow become an expert in the field.

trust as early as possible. By this I mean not just that I'd tell them the truth, but that I'd show them I had a better grasp of the facts than my opponent and would therefore be more likely to *know* the truth. Because diminished newspaper readership was critical to making my case, I decided I'd try to accomplish this from the jump in an unorthodox way. I would memorize long columns of six-figure circulation and revenue numbers and recite them in my opening statement without referring to a single document or note.

Sounds boring, right? And risky, too. What if I got one of the numbers wrong? Plus, the three to four minutes it would take to recite these columns of numbers could indeed bore the jury to tears. So why do it?

First, the numbers were key to winning the case. Second, as mentioned, I have rarely used notes in my opening statements or closing arguments because they interfere with the all-important eye contact with the jurors. Third, I believed the recitation of numerous and lengthy figures by memory would demonstrate to the jury that I was the lawyer in possession of superior knowledge of the facts of the case—the person they could trust for an accurate presentation of the evidence they would be hearing in the next several weeks. The main benefit, however, was the first one: without a single witness being called, jurors who were still awake at the end of my recitation would have learned about the *San Francisco Examiner*'s diminishing circulation and revenue numbers.

## The Plaintiffs' Star Witness

Of the many witnesses over the course of the three-month trial, five of them are worth noting for what they reveal about our justice system.

The key witness for the plaintiffs in the first trial was a newspaper economist whose testimony had clearly carried the day. I knew he'd be a formidable witness and that I'd have to destroy his credibility on cross-examination.

When he appeared to testify in the retrial, however, I saw that the man was not only intelligent and well-qualified, but also instantly likable and almost pixie-like in appearance—the ideal expert witness. I began to see what poor Richard Archer was up against in the first trial. As he testified on direct examination, it was obvious the jury not only believed him—they liked him. I would have to be careful.

Bruce and I had devised what we hoped was a winning cross-examination, but it would have to be handled with surgical delicacy. Golf professionals say you should hold the club in your hand no tighter than you would a bird. That's the way I would have to cross-examine this congenial witness. Going too easy on him would be suicidal, but being too rough could attract sympathy for him and antipathy toward me. I might win the battle but lose the war. Thus, my strategy required taking it slowly, hoping he'd eventually kill himself so I wouldn't have to.

Though Randy Hearst understood this, my approach wasn't satisfactory to the small army of lawyers representing both newspapers who sat in the back of the courtroom every day, kibitzing, assessing, and second-guessing my progress. This group of trial amateurs simply wanted bloodshed, and they wanted it fast. I began to dread court recesses.

"You've got to hit him harder!" said one who cornered me in the hallway.

"You're not getting anywhere," said another. "The jury still loves him."

"He's lying, but the jury doesn't know it," said a third lawyer. "You need to smash him, crush him! You've got the goods on him. Use them!"

This was no way to relax during a recess. I was exhausted from a month of trial, fighting two able opponents in court and then having to defend myself to my client representatives during the recesses.

"Be patient, gentlemen," I urged. "You can't crush a lovable pixie, and if I do, the jury will turn on me. Remember, we come into this litigation as bullies, using our wealth and power to destroy the little guys."

I knew what I was doing, and I had to take my time doing it. I told them, "Let's remember the old saying: 'Give a man enough rope and he'll hang himself.'" I was allowing the expert witness plenty of rope, while secretly building the scaffolding that would eventually bring about his demise.

Bruce and I had discovered in our pretrial research that the righteous-appearing expert had taken the opposite position on economic issues in a former lawsuit and charged a substantial fee for his testimony. When it was finally time to open the hatch under his feet, I acted almost surprised and disappointed in him while he tried in vain to lie his way out of the conflict in his testimony. As he fell through the figurative opening and hung himself, I could almost sense the jurors' disappointment when they realized the man was a charlatan. I believe most of my back-of-the-room critics finally saw the wisdom in exercising patience and caution. Their deferential body language told me I wouldn't be pressured by them again.

## The Defense Experts

By contrast, our own expert witnesses were superb. Marvin Stone, for instance, my expert accountant, opined that the failure of the *Examiner* was inevitable based on the diminishing circulation and paid ads (the "downward spiral" in which one deficit feeds the other, into ultimate bankruptcy). Simply stated, diminishing paid ads impact the ability of the newspaper to hire good reporters and staff, leading to lower product quality, which in turn reduces circulation, which in turn reduces the willingness of advertisers to place ads in the paper, and so on.

Mr. Stone wasn't only brilliant, but human and humorous as well. On his cross-examination, for example, an opposing lawyer sneered, "Mr. Stone, I noticed that you seem to be taking a long time before you answer. Are you having trouble coming up with believable answers to my questions?"

"Not at all," replied Marvin, after a pregnant pause, "it's just that I'm being paid by the hour."

The jury broke into laughter, and after that Marvin could do no wrong, having achieved a sense of wit and humanity in their eyes.

Our star expert economist, Irwin Stelzer, a leader in his field, gained the jury's approval in a different way. I noticed that his fiancée was in the back of the courtroom as he took the stand.

"I will try to make this brief, as I know you have a date to get married in Hawaii in two days."

"That's correct, Mr. Martel," said Irwin, smiling.

"Is that your fiancée sitting in the back of the courtroom?" I asked.

The jurors turned as one to look at the blushing fiancée, then suddenly broke into a communal smile. Irwin was no longer a robotic economist; he was a human being to whom they could relate. Mr. Stelzer was also one of the finest forensic experts I've ever had.

Many trial lawyers fail to understand that to be truly effective, the expert witness must be not only authoritative, trustworthy, and competent, but personable and likable as well. A perceptive reader might wonder whether I was taking a dangerous liberty pointing out Irwin's fiancée. It *was* risky, but like so many other risks I took, it worked, and, in the process, not only humanized a big-time New York economist in the eyes of six ordinary San Francisco citizens but allowed me to begin to take control of the courtroom, the ultimate objective of any trial lawyer.

## Charles Gould

One of the more challenging issues facing the defense would be the fact that Charles Gould, the publisher of the *Examiner*, was going to be placed in the humiliating position, once again, of having to testify that his newspaper, the Hearst flagship property, was failing with him at the helm. Mr. Gould was a man of great prestige and pride, well into his seventies, and undoubtedly not as quick as he once had been. His admission of failure would amount to a public shaming, and it took several long meetings to persuade him to take a bullet for the team.

I finally convinced him he wasn't alone. Newspaper expert witness John Morton would testify to three key points: failure of major dailies like the *Examiner* was almost inevitable now with the popularity of television news; failures were so common that Congress had to act; and Herb Caen had stabbed him in the back.

That seemed to comfort Gould, and he ultimately came around to accepting his fate, performing as admirably as possible at trial. The hardest part was weaving his way through his sworn testimony from the first trial, during which he *hadn't* been willing to accept the reality of the *Examiner*'s imminent failure. This time, he somehow came through relatively unscathed and even appeared to gain the jurors' sympathy.

As he left the witness stand, he knew he had done well and went directly to where I sat. The old man seized one of my hands in both of his and raised it in the air as if to declare "the champions!" It was one of the most amusing and embarrassing episodes in my nearly fifty years of trial work. The jurors were smiling. Fortunately, they had developed such sympathy for the old guy by then that I suspect they found it charming.

## Hearst Castle

Meanwhile, compounding my anxiety level was the matter of my second wedding to a woman who seemed perfect. She was smart, independent, and pretty. She was employed as a marketing executive with Henredon Furniture, had previously worked in New York City as a Ford face model, and had helped raise her younger siblings after their father died young and their mother became an alcoholic. I would have been content with a quick trip to Las Vegas, but this was Susan Spalding's first wedding, and she wanted it to be spectacular. Aware that one of my clients was the Hearst Corporation, she saw no reason why we couldn't be married beside the beautiful Neptune Pool at Hearst Castle. But this would require overcoming two problems. First, with the sole exception of Marian Davies' daughter, nobody had ever been allowed to be married at Hearst Castle. Second, the Hearst family no longer controlled Hearst

Castle, having turned it over to the California Department of Parks and Recreation. Susan, however, was adamant, and reminded me that the future of the Hearst newspaper empire was resting on my shoulders.

"Don't they understand the importance of keeping you happy?" Susan asked me over a costly dinner at the restaurant Stars, one of many such dinners during our intense courtship.

She was right, of course. The Hearst Corporation wanted to keep their lawyer happy at all costs on the eve of a bet-the-company trial. But the problem—ownership of the Castle having passed to the state— remained, and even Susan realized this seemed insurmountable, until fate intervened in a most amazing manner.

One of the features of the Hearst Castle experience had always been the famous wild animal menagerie. African and domestic beasts of all kinds roamed the property: antelope, zebras, camels, llamas, kangaroos, ostriches, emus, bighorn sheep, oxen, giraffes, yaks, and various species of deer from India, Europe, and Asia. There was even an iced enclosure for polar bears. Fortuitously, a herd of zebra had recently crossed from Hearst Castle over to the adjoining Hearst Ranch and showed no interest in returning. When State Parks sought permission from Randy Hearst to cross onto his property in order to bring the zebra back to Hearst Castle, he saw an opening.

"We'll be happy to return the zebra," Randy told the Parks representative, "but we have a small favor to ask."

The marriage, for better or for worse, was celebrated on July 26, 1980, at the spectacular Neptune Pool, accompanied by a string quartet, and guests all garbed, as requested, in Gatsby-era attire. It was a sensational affair and, sad to say, the high point of the short-lived marriage.

## Postscript

As it turned out, the Hearst trial fared much better than the marriage, as noted in this Associated Press article:

SAN FRANCISCO (UPI)—Two daily newspapers, the Examiner and Chronicle, have been cleared by a jury of violating antitrust regulations by combining non-editorial operations. ("Papers Cleared of Violation," *Napa Valley Register*, June 16, 1981)

The upset, turn-around verdict was an example of how hard work by a burned-out trial lawyer, combined with a drive to win and occasional flashes of competence, could shock the experts and flip a one-five jury vote in the first trial into a six-zero victory in the second. When the verdict came in, I was stunned, ecstatic, and ready to give in to my complete exhaustion.

## Chapter 19

# The Menendez Brothers and O. J. Simpson: Murder, Inc.

> I went through that door, they were watching TV
> Sure surprised to see me standing there.
> Well I turned off that set with the first shot you bet
> Then I burned off that stranger in my favorite chair.
> —"I Should Have Taken My Time" (1976)

ON AUGUST 20, 1989, José Menendez and his wife, Kitty, were watching television in the den of their Beverly Hills mansion. Suddenly and without warning, the peaceful night was shattered as sons Lyle and Erik burst into the room and brutally slaughtered their parents with multiple blasts from 12-gauge shotguns. Following a highly publicized trial, two juries—one for each defendant—were unable to find them guilty, and a mistrial was declared.

The nation was shocked. How could this have happened? Had our justice system become hopelessly inept? I shared the angst.

How did a San Francisco trial lawyer specializing in commercial law get involved in two Los Angeles criminal murder cases? *Or, what's a nice business lawyer like you doing in a trial like this?*

It started with a phone call. I was attending a family anniversary celebration in Santa Rosa, staying at a forties-style hotel called The Flamingo
(pink flamingos everywhere—I'm not kidding). I don't remember telling
anybody I would be there for the weekend and was therefore puzzled
when I was paged and called to a telephone near the pool. On the line
was the district attorney for Los Angeles County, Gil Garcetti. I've always
been curious how he knew I'd be at The Flamingo on a Sunday, but I never
asked him. I guess when you're the district attorney of Los Angeles County, you have your sources and can make things happen.

Mr. Garcetti recounted that he'd been talking with Arlo Smith, the
district attorney of San Francisco, with whom I'd recently lamented
about cases in which public prosecutors were being overwhelmed by
expensive high-profile defense attorneys with large budgets. As a result,
I feared the public was losing trust in the justice system. Arlo shared my
concern with Gil, who was calling to ask if I'd be willing to come down
to Los Angeles and consult with his staff on the Menendez brothers'
retrial. Here, being handed to me, was an opportunity to take action on
the issue Arlo and I had been discussing. I told Gil I'd take it up with my
partners, and with my firm's approval, I flew down to Los Angeles the
following week.

When I arrived at Mr. Garcetti's office, his secretary apologized and
told me he was running late. It turned out he was meeting in the adjoining conference room with a dozen leaders of the Black community,
apparently in regard to the two-part documentary, *Leaving Neverland*,
which told the story of two men who had accused Michael Jackson of
sexually abusing them when they were young. I would later learn that
Gil often negotiated with these Black ministers, granting them a receptive ear in return for their agreement to help keep the peace in the predominantly Black population of South Los Angeles. (This arrangement,
probably originating after the Watts riots and frequently useful to both
parties, would prove the undoing of the prosecution in *People v. O. J.
Simpson*, as will be seen.)

The conference room door eventually opened and a dozen solemn and distinguished-looking Black men, many wearing the white collar of the clergy, strode out and headed toward the elevator. Gil greeted me and apologized for being late. He led me back into the same conference room and tried to explain how his team had been unable to achieve a conviction in a case where the defendants admitted blasting their parents to death with shotguns. He asked me if I'd be willing to work with a senior prosecutor named David Conn, who would first-chair the prosecution of the retrial.

I told him I'd be willing to serve as a consultant and expected no fee; my firm regarded this engagement as a public service. This was partly true, but it was no secret the publicity would be good for the firm, and for me individually. I was then introduced to Mr. Conn, a likable and experienced prosecutor. After a half hour, it was clear we would work well together.

My next step was to enlist the services of the finest jury consultant in America, Reiko Hasuike. Reiko, with the approval of her company, also agreed to work pro bono.

I had worked successfully with Reiko in Hawaii on a case involving the Bank of Hawaii and was certain we'd collaborate effectively in this one. I would partner with Conn in conceptualizing a new strategy, then conduct mock trials with Reiko to refine what kind of jurors would be most likely to convict, how we might identify them, and how best to present our case to them in a way that would mesh with their psychological predilections. Mock trials were growing increasingly important in major cases. Reiko's firm, Decision Quest, and my law firm were among those instrumental in the growth of the technique's popularity. Our firms absorbed most of the mock trial cost in the Simpson case.

Reiko and I put together a mock jury demographically comparable to the actual jurors we'd expect to draw at the retrial. We then presented a simulated trial to this jury, complete with a "judge" and advocates on both sides of the case. I played the part of defense counsel, Leslie Abramson.

Watching the mock jury deliberate through one-way glass allowed us to focus on what had worked and what hadn't in the way we'd presented our case.

It's widely accepted now among trial lawyers that many jurors make up their minds early in the trial, even during opening statements by counsel, so it's obviously important that the case be presented from the very outset in a clear manner that doesn't create cognitive dissonance in the minds of the jury. Reiko explained that jurors come into court with a set of basic beliefs and ideologies that are unlikely to change during a trial. The use of mock trials would allow Conn to select jurors whose personal beliefs and values were most likely to fit with our view of the issues, and to present those issues to the jury in a manner most consistent with their own beliefs and values, avoiding theories that might conflict with them and risk causing cognitive dissonance.

As luck would have it, I intercepted a notice of a presentation to be given to a criminal defense lawyers' organization in San Francisco by none other than Leslie Abramson, Erik Menendez's lawyer in the first trial. Posing as a defense lawyer, I gained access to the meeting and was able to watch, undetected from the rear of the room, as Ms. Abramson pontificated about her "victory." It was obvious she'd successfully manipulated Judge Stanley Weisberg in the first trial, and I now knew that my first job was going to be to change Judge Weisberg's view of the law applicable to the case. The second trial of the brothers was consolidated into one jury trial with Leslie Abramson as lead counsel.

After studying the testimony given in that trial, I proposed a radically new approach, both legal and factual, to prosecutor Conn. First, we'd persuade the judge that he'd erroneously admitted numerous character witnesses to testify for the brothers, and that he must totally abandon the instructions given to the jury in the first trials that allowed the brothers to claim self-defense, even though they were wrong in thinking they were in peril. Second, Conn should present the facts of the case to the new jury in a fresh, focused, and dramatic fashion that would leave them no choice but to render a verdict for the prosecution.

In January 1994, two separate juries had been unable to choose between murder and manslaughter verdicts, largely because the brothers each claimed they'd acted in *"imperfect* self-defense" (as the theory was labeled), acting in the *mistaken* belief that their sexually and physically abusive parents would kill them if they didn't act first.

With the competent assistance of my associate, Kelly Woodruff, we prepared legal memoranda that argued as follows:

a.  That the defense had shown insufficient evidence the brothers had been sexually and psychologically abused by their father, and, therefore,

b.  That there was therefore no legitimate justification for them claiming they had killed in the mistaken belief that they were in danger of being killed themselves.

This deprived Abramson of her "imperfect self-defense" theory, the centerpiece of her defense in the first trial, and successfully persuaded Judge Weisberg to completely change his approach in the newly consolidated trial. Abramson appealed, but our approach was eventually upheld by the state Supreme Court. This was a major step forward.

Finally, the trial judge was persuaded to refuse to allow television cameras to be present in the second trial, based—in part I hope, but cannot prove—on a comment I wrote in 1959, during my senior year, for the *California Law Review*, called "Fair Trial v. Free Press in Criminal Trials," in which I argued that:

> Flames of public sentiment can be quickly fanned white hot, especially now with the ubiquitous television set bringing all the court room emotion into the family living room . . . Not even experienced counsel can be depended upon not to under or overplay their roles under the pressure of mass audiences [guaranteed by television]. (Vol. 47, no. 2, 372)

On March 20, 1996, after a lengthy trial, the defendants were convicted of first-degree murder and conspiracy to commit murder. On July 2, 1996, Judge Stanley Weisberg sentenced Lyle and Erik to life without the possibility of parole, accepting the jury's recommendation that they not be put to death. They remain incarcerated to this day.

I have always been opposed to capital punishment, even when I helped send Ray Hamilton and Thomas Purvis to death row in San Quentin as a prosecutor in Alameda County. Accordingly, I was pleased with the Menendez verdicts and the recommendation of life without possibility of parole, and Garcetti was both complimentary and grateful. I accepted his thanks and concluded our firm had served the cause of justice well, and that I was finished working with the City and County of Los Angeles.

But then O. J. started killing people.

## The Case of *People v. O. J. Simpson*

> Murder is like potato chips: you can't stop with just one.
> —Stephen King, *Under the Dome*

Once again, Gil Garcetti came back to me for help. How could I say no? It would literally be "The Trial of the Century" and I wanted to try again to be useful in obtaining justice, anticipating that Simpson would have a blue-ribbon team of lawyers at his disposal.

And, once again, I was quoted in the *Los Angeles Times*:

> The [Menendez] arrangement, [Martel] said, has worked well, increasing his belief that lawyers in private practice should aid prosecutors who face high-powered defense teams.
>
> That belief, Martel said, grew from what he perceived as the public's loss of faith in the criminal justice system after the Menendez juries deadlocked.

"I was hearing people say, 'You can get away with murder if you have enough money,'" he said. (Andrea Ford, "JOHN MARTEL: County's Answer to the Dream Team," July 29, 1995, A24)

Four months after the Menendez verdict, I was back in Los Angeles, this time scheduled to work with Bill Hodgeman, the senior counsel on the case. His associate would be an experienced but little-known attorney named Marcia Clark.

I immediately liked Hodgeman and saw him as an able and secure trial lawyer, much like Conn had been in the second Menendez trial. Like Conn, Hodgeman seemed self-assured enough to accept suggestions from an outsider.

We did, in fact, work well together for months, and a modest degree of optimism began to evolve during pretrial preparation. DNA and other blood evidence against Simpson began to accumulate, and Simpson's "Dream Team" was beginning to look vulnerable. My involvement in the case—never intended to be a secret—was trumpeted in the article quoted above by *Los Angeles Times* staff writer Andrea Ford. It led with the following headline, blared in bold print across the top of page A24:

## JOHN MARTEL: COUNTY'S ANSWER TO THE DREAM TEAM

The first sentence of the column read as follows: "O. J. Simpson has his team of celebrity lawyers, and the prosecution has its own stars. But until recently, no one knew that John Martel was among the latter."

Under my photograph, the caption read: "District Attorney Gil Garcetti persuaded prominent San Francisco lawyer and novelist John Martel to help the prosecution counter Simpson's dream team defense." Garcetti must, at this point, be considered an additional, albeit unwitting, suspect in my personal investigation about why I've had an insatiable desire for success. Garcetti, after all, supported my quest.

Ms. Ford went on to describe me as "the highly regarded Bay Area civil defense lawyer and writer of legal fiction—called one of the top 10 trial lawyers by the National Law Journal."

This was all very exciting and flattering, especially when I became the informal spokesperson for the prosecution, appearing three times on the *Today Show* with Katie Couric and Bryant Gumbel and an equal number of times on *Larry King Live*. While I was on the talking-heads-limousine-ego-trip circuit, I felt I was contributing something worthwhile and being recognized for it. Videos of these appearances show me to be confident and optimistic, but this posture became more and more difficult as I began to see that, despite the state's overwhelming evidence, the current prosecution team—with the exception of Hodgeman— seemed unequal to the task at hand.

You already know how the case turned out, so I might as well give you my reasons why we failed to win "The Trial of the Century." There were several.

First, in order to keep peace with the Black clergy from South Los Angeles, Garcetti agreed to allow a transfer of venue from the Santa Monica Courthouse, where the trial would normally have been held— and where a predominantly white jury would have been a certainty— to the Stanley Mosk Courthouse in downtown Los Angeles, where a predominantly Black jury would surely be impaneled.

I'm not second-guessing Garcetti's decision. I wasn't in his shoes nor did I face the incredible political pressure this incendiary murder investigation created in the Black community, not to mention the ever-present possibility of rioting. Garcetti was going to be wrong no matter what he did, but turning the fate of a Black icon—even one who publicly denied his Blackness—over to a Black jury in Los Angeles County was obviously risky business. In fairness to the prosecutors, they went into the trial with two strikes against them, and a curve ball on the way.

Bring in . . . the lame, and the blind.
—Luke 14:21

The second major reason for the prosecution's ultimate failure was the stress-related collapse (and feared heart attack) suffered by Hodgeman as the trial was commencing, an event that elevated Clark to the position of lead counsel and brought Christopher Darden in as second chair. As Jeff Toobin, in his best-selling book on the trial writes, "His [Hodgeman's] absence deprived the prosecution of a day-to-day center of gravity, a voice of calm and maturity."

I could not agree more. The prosecution had lost its compass. In Biblical terms, the lame were now leading the blind and, with Johnny Cochran and the Dream Team on the other side, it was no longer a fair fight. As for my role, where Hodgeman and I had been a compatible team and developed a solid strategy, Clark seemed to resent both my presence and my suggestions, perhaps sensing my growing concerns about her ability to handle a case of such magnitude.

Although she had successfully tried many murder cases, it seems to me Clark never quite understood that this trial—with its cultural, historical, and sociological overlay—was going to be different, *sui generis.* This would become obvious to me in the two mock trials Hodgeman and I organized, again working with Reiko Hasuike and her boss, Donald Vinson, the same jury consultants I had brought into the Menendez case. Don was the CEO of Decision Quest (Reiko Hasuike's employer), and he controlled the purse strings. To Don's credit, his company contributed over a million dollars in creative courtroom exhibits and visual aids that would have convinced any fair-minded person of Simpson's guilt.

Why, Clark probably wondered, did an experienced prosecutor such as herself need help from a San Francisco commercial litigator like me? Not an illogical question, to which the *Los Angeles Times* sought an answer. One response came from a prominent attorney, David Alexander, who had worked with me on a victorious case against the City of San Francisco and was quoted as follows:

> Martel's instincts with juries are "uncanny" . . . [and he] also has extraordinary strategic skills.
> "This is a major league guy, and if you've got a major league contest, this is the guy you want." (Ford, A24)

In my opinion—and all my remarks in this chapter are nothing more than my opinion—Clark lacked both good "instincts" and "extraordinary strategic skills." These shortcomings became painfully obvious to me, especially once Hodgeman was functionally out of the picture. Nor did Clark seem to grasp the extent to which this trial was going to be "a major league contest," the highest of high-profile cases—one that would require an abundance of creativity with focused considerations of history, culture, and public relations. What we got instead was Christopher Darden, a young, relatively inexperienced prosecutor.

Clark's shortcomings were dramatically displayed to some of us in the second mock trial we held in Arizona at a secret location, selected in order to avoid the ubiquitous and hungry press. Incidentally, a good example of her arrogance was on display in her late arrival in Arizona. The district attorney representatives, the jury consultants, and I had convened on schedule at a hotel in the early evening hours, ready for a planning conference about what we hoped to accomplish the following day with our demographically selected mock jury panel.

As ten o'clock neared, Marcia still had not arrived, and a few phone calls eventually revealed what may have happened. The rumor was that she had been apprehended packing a sidearm as she went through the metal detector at Los Angeles International Airport, and then caused a furor when airport security officers didn't recognize her. We were told she was detained by unimpressed authorities, and that's why she was late.

I had played the role of Clark in the first mock trial in Los Angeles, but she played herself in the second one in Arizona, and her strident manner and presentation were viewed with open disdain by the mock jurors we "impaneled" the next day. Almost as unpopular with the Black mock jurors was Nicole Brown Simpson, mainly because she was a white woman who had dared to marry their Black icon. Female Black jurors unabashedly called her a "blonde bitch." As for Ron Goldman, he was just another white man, a friend of Nicole's who'd been in the wrong place at the wrong time.

The Arizona mock jury's verdict was decided overwhelmingly for the defense, and there was a whiff of failure in the air. Everybody but Clark seemed to sense trouble and recognize the disaster that lay ahead. Although the DNA, timeline, and overwhelming circumstantial evidence were laid out clearly, the jury wasn't persuaded. Moreover, the few white jurors on the panel were the only ones who favored the prosecution. A new approach was called for, but Clark displayed complete confidence she'd prevail at trial and apparently took nothing away from the Arizona experience, not even the harsh criticism of her own manner and performance by the mock jurors. I had no choice but to join in that criticism, which effectively ended my productive involvement in the case.

It was clear the verdict would be racially drawn. Ironically, Simpson, a man who had rejected his Black roots, was about to become a symbol of downtrodden Black America. In a 1994 interview with the *Huffington Post* Robert Lipsyte recalled an evening he had spent with Simpson twenty-five years earlier, during which O. J. told him he had overheard a white woman saying, "Look, there's O. J. sitting with those ni..ers" to refer to some Black friends he had been with at a wedding, though she exempted Simpson himself from the categorical insult. When asked if that was terrible for him, O. J. replied, "No, it was great. Don't you understand? She knew that I wasn't Black. She saw me as O. J." But now that he was in trouble, with the likely jury being predominantly Black, Simpson cleverly took his lawyer's advice and embraced his race.

— — —

As the trial began on September 24, 1994, it became clear the available jurors would indeed be mainly African American. The stage was set for "jury nullification," in which a jury renders a verdict as a function of what they view as a higher moral imperative, exercising its power to ignore the facts and the law, even if the verdict happens to be in conflict with both. In a 1995 article on the subject in the *Los Angeles Times*, Robert Weisberg, a law professor at Stanford, explains that ". . . jury nullification has been part of the American tradition since the days when the colonials were the defendants and the [English] were the prosecutors and judges."

The predominantly Black jury (eight out of twelve) saw the Simpson case in the context of a history of racial intolerance and abuse toward African Americans, ironically, in my opinion, having little to do with a defendant who, before he was charged, seemed determined to be treated as white. One juror admitted that the jury was primarily responding to the Rodney King beating by Los Angeles cops. Another juror later asserted that the verdict was in response to police detective Mark Fuhrman's repeated use of the N-word and his lying about it.

Given the overwhelming evidence in support of Simpson's guilt, together with the subsequent, racially balanced civil jury's verdict in favor of Ron Goldman's family, *concluding that Simpson in fact killed Ron and Nicole,* there is really no logical way to look at the Simpson verdict other than jury nullification. When viewed in that light, it can therefore be concluded that there was nothing the prosecution could have done to win the case once Garcetti allowed the venue to be moved from Santa Monica, guaranteeing a predominantly white jury, to Downtown Los Angeles, guaranteeing a predominantly African American jury.

Compounding the dominant race issue was Clark's seeming denial of its cultural importance. Add to that Judge Lance Ito, who in my opinion was inept, and you had a recipe for disaster. The most glaring example of the poor prosecutorial judgment that was rampant throughout the trial—even exceeding the decision to put the bigoted Fuhrman on the stand—was the infamous glove experiment. By the time Simpson spread his fingers in order to make it impossible to pull the glove on, I had retired from the case of my own volition, essentially unnoticed, and returned to San Francisco, where I watched the drama unfold on television like everyone else. Seeing what Darden was trying to do with the glove, my heart raced and my mouth went dry. When the inevitable occurred, and Cochran pronounced, "If it doesn't fit, you must acquit," my anxiety turned to rage. I picked up the phone and called Bill Hodgeman, who had returned to work after his emergency, but not as a trial participant.

Me: "What the fuck just happened with the glove, Bill?"

Bill: "Yeah, it was a mistake."

Me: "Were you involved? Couldn't you stop it?"

Bill: "The issue was put to a vote last night. Marcia and Chris voted to go forward with it. I was obviously in the minority."

Me: "All he had to do was spread his fingers. It was an insane gamble."

Bill: "I understand."

Bill sounded so downhearted I could no longer vent my frustration to him and said goodbye. Left unspoken was our mutual recognition that the trial was heading off a cliff and no one could stop it.

Following the trial, I was sometimes asked to speak on the subject. At a regional meeting of the American College of Trial Lawyers in Washington state, for example, I opened my speech by silently removing a glove from my pocket and making a show of trying hard, for at least fifteen or twenty seconds—and in vain—to pull it onto my upright hand. When I had everyone's attention and it was obvious the glove appeared to be far too small, I simply closed my fingers, slipped the glove easily onto my hand, and said, "If it doesn't fit, you must acquit." This stunt always got a laugh.

But what happened in the Simpson case wasn't funny. Any time an obviously guilty defendant "beats the rap," people lose faith in our justice system. Was Simpson "obviously guilty" or was this just sour grapes on my part, having been connected with the prosecution?

The evidence of Simpson's guilt should have been conclusive, but the verdict was no surprise to me, and I felt no sense of personal responsibility. Given the confluence of circumstances, there was nothing I could have done. Some of the predominantly Black jurors I have quoted above admit they acted on racial grounds. Moreover, jury nullification is the only possible explanation for rejecting the overwhelmingly persuasive blood evidence in the case. Further probative of Simpson's guilt is the verdict in the civil trial of *Goldman v. Simpson*, a case filed by Ron Goldman's father sixteen months after the criminal case concluded. Following a lengthy trial, the jury unanimously found that Simpson was guilty of the murders of both Ron and Nicole and awarded damages to the Goldmans in the amount of $33 million.

Undaunted, I have continued to advocate for the involvement of private firms to aid financially handicapped counties in the prosecution of complex murder trials, especially where big money or complex social issues are on the side of a wealthy defendant, requiring a leveling of the playing field. At least, we were able to do that successfully in the Menendez case.

# Chapter 20

## Other Trials and Tribulations

> So walk across the stormy sea
> Once more Jesus for me if you care
> 'Cause I wouldn't know I was home
> If I was there.
> —"Shipwrecked Sailor" (1971)

### Part One

**AND THEN THERE ARE** the other hundred or so cases I have tried. Most of them were of no national interest and only a few even made it into the newspapers. But they were all important to me. Each brought a new learning experience, and there was always something—besides winning—at stake. In addition, I nearly always identified with and befriended the clients I represented and sympathized with the problem that forced them to put their fate into the hands of the justice system. It was important to me that they not be disappointed by the treatment received.

## Milani v. Alberto-Culver

Some cases are memorable in part simply because of the way they came to me. I was approached by phone one day to participate in a "beauty contest" of lawyers vying to represent Milani Foods, famous for their 1890 French Dressing, in potential litigation against corporate giant Alberto-Culver, makers of Alberto-Culver VO5 hair products. I was scheduled to meet with two members of the family who had owned Milani Foods, Larry and Joseph Hoffman, at noon on the same day I was scheduled to see hand specialist Dr. William Green at eleven o'clock in the morning. I had injured the little finger of my left hand the previous weekend when I tackled my son (who was bigger than me) while playing football on a Santa Cruz beach. Days passed, the pain persisted, and I knew I had to do something about it. Dr. Green was one of the top hand surgeons in San Francisco, and I was lucky to get an appointment with him, though I knew I'd have to hurry back to the office in order not to be late for my meeting with the Hoffmans.

Green took one look at the distorted finger and said, "I'm going to have to rebreak that finger and reset it properly."

"I was afraid of that," I said, "How soon can you get me in?"

"You don't understand, John. You've already waited too long. I should do it immediately."

"Well, okay," I said, "but please hurry. I have to get back to my office." When he told me he'd have to inject my finger with a local anesthetic and that it would take at least fifteen minutes before he could proceed, I told him to go ahead and break the finger without the local.

He shook his head. "Again, you don't understand. There are a ton of nerve endings in that little finger and the pain will be intense."

I told him I couldn't be late for my meeting, and to go ahead and skip the anesthetic. He was reluctant but agreed. I remember him staring directly into my eyes, taking my little finger in his two large hands, and . . . *snap*! I heard a sound like the crack of a pistol, then a red flare went off in my head and the next thing I was knew I was prostrate on a gurney, slowly returning to consciousness. A small bandage covered a needle mark in my arm, probably from a shot of adrenaline. I managed to make it to the meeting, my finger in a cast, only a minute late, got the case, and, eventually, with Jim Haydel's help, won it.

## Manila, the Philippines

On February 12, 1985, I was skiing with a friend at Lake Tahoe, about to start my run from the top of the slope when a member of the ski patrol flagged me down.

"I'm looking for a Mr. Martel," he said, "are you by any chance him?"

Was I that bad a skier? "Guilty. What's up?"

"All I know is that you're supposed to call a Mr. Farella in San Francisco immediately. Are you acquainted with him?"

This was before cell phones, so once I overcame my shock at my law partner having found me, I quickly skied down to the restaurant and placed a long distance call to Frank using my credit card. He sounded relieved to hear from me.

"Thank God. You have reservations on a flight to the Philippines tonight. The Manila Regent Hotel is on fire and people are jumping off their balconies and dying." Frank didn't need to remind me that the Regent Hotel chain was one of our major clients.

"So, I told Bob Burns," he continued, "that you'd get there first thing in the morning. Can you get to San Francisco in time to catch the night flight to Manila?"

When I arrived in Manila early the next morning, I was met at the airport by a client representative and taken to a hotel separated from the Regent only by a vacant lot. I was shocked to see that the Regent was still smoking. Looking at the hotel across the lot was like watching a scene from *Apocalypse Now.*

After a hurried breakfast, I met the representative and we entered the smoke-filled hotel, assured that the last burning areas had been

229

extinguished. The death toll now exceeded sixteen people, mainly jumpers. That had always been one of my worst nightmares, and I felt heartsick, imagining people just a few hours ago faced with a choice of death by fire or by leaping into the night through a five-story window. When we had total privacy, he told me the real story—a defense lawyer's worst nightmare.

"Why," I asked him, "didn't the ceiling sprinklers I see in all the rooms control the fire?"

After some initial reluctance, he eventually came out with it. "We suspect the former management here found out they could save the cost of connecting the overhead fire sprinklers to the water source by simply bribing the safety official in charge of compliance."

"You've got to be shitting me!"

"No, Mr. Martel, you've got to understand the way things are done here under Marcos."

To make matters worse, although the fire was promptly reported, all essential emergency services failed to respond. The Marcos government officials didn't seem to care about problems with an American-owned hotel. When someone finally called the American Embassy, two fire trucks were dispatched to the scene, only to crash into each other as they came from opposite directions in a tragicomic scene that could have been inspired by the Keystone Cops. The trucks hit each other head on, locking front bumpers that could not be separated, thereby blocking the main entrance into the property.

The scene was set for a full-on tragedy. While people had been literally leaping to their deaths to avoid being burned alive, the "firefighters," according to one observer, finally entered the hotel and allegedly went straight to the bar in the downstairs area and helped themselves to cocktails. Then, when they became drunk and bored, I was told they apparently began looting vacated rooms. If a room wasn't occupied and not yet on fire, they smashed the door open so the breeze from Manila Bay carried the flames into the room, justifying their presence inside so they could then loot that room, as well.

On hearing reports of the looting, the US State Department finally pressured the police to enter the hotel, but the manager told me they simply joined the firefighters in the drinking and looting. I'd heard of the corruption at all levels of the Marcos government, but this was overwhelming.

As I began the search for local counsel, I was soon joined by FB&M partners John Cooper and Randy Wulff, who flew in from the states. It was obvious to all of us that this was an indefensible case, one that would have to be settled. Ultimately it was—by local counsel and the client's insurance carrier.

The first UPI news report tells the beginning of the tragic story:

> Fire raced through the luxurious Regent of Manila hotel early Wednesday killing 16 people, including at least two Americans, and forcing some guests to leap from windows in the fourth hotel blaze in the country in as many months. At least 20 others, including an American and a Taiwanese, were reported injured in the pre-dawn fire, authorities said. Firefighters battled for more than eight hours before putting the blaze out.
>
> It was the fourth major hotel fire in the Philippines since October.
>
> Authorities blamed the previous fires on opponents of President Ferdinand Marcos seeking to destabilize the 20-year-old regime. (Fernando del Mundo, February 12, 1985)

While I was traveling in a cab to meet with a prospective local counsel, the driver pointed out a building where he claimed at least one hundred of Imelda Marcos' political opponents had been buried in the foundation during construction.

I was eager to leave Manila, but the memory of those poor deceased souls traveled home with me and haunts me still.

## Melvin Belli, King of Torts

On July 10, 1996, newspapers across the country announced the death of Melvin Belli, the most famous lawyer of his era. Typical was this headline in the *New York Times*:

### Melvin Belli Dies at 88
Flamboyant Lawyer Relished His Role as King of Torts
By Richard Severo, July 10, 1996

Melvin Belli, an impresario of a lawyer who pioneered new techniques and huge settlements in personal injury cases and who defended Jack Ruby, the man who shot and killed Lee Harvey Oswald, died yesterday at his home in San Francisco. He was 88.

Other celebrity clients of the "King of Torts" included Errol Flynn, Chuck Berry, Mohammed Ali, the Rolling Stones, Lana Turner, Tony Curtis, and Mae West. He had won over $600 million in judgments during his legal career and was clearly the most famous lawyer of my generation.

"His name on a court pleading is worth a billion dollars!" former Belli associate David Sabih claimed. "He brings in fifty new cases a day."

But no party lasts forever, and Belli's took a hit when he became the defendant in a case instead of the lawyer bringing one. The plaintiff was a former Belli partner named Vasilios Choulos who'd been enjoying the partnership until the day he showed up for work and found that his key would no longer open the main exterior door. According to Mr. Choulos, Mr. Belli had changed the locks on all the doors and on November 23,

1981, "announced nobody was working around here and he would do better by shutting the place down."

Litigation ensued when Belli not only changed the locks on Choulos's private office but also intercepted his confidential mail. In one case, Belli called the father of one of Choulos's clients and said he had "fired Choulos" for incompetence, then took on the case himself.

Word on the street was that the litigation between the two partners promised to be the most vicious courtroom battle in history. After the initial complaint had been filed by Mr. Choulos, I received a call from Sabih, who had remained in Belli's favor and been made a partner. Sabih said Belli wanted to retain me to represent him in the litigation against Choulos. He asked me to come to the famous Belli Building at 722 Montgomery Street for a meeting with Mr. Belli.

I agreed to a meeting but withheld my commitment to take the case. For one thing, Belli was known to be incredibly erratic as well as derelict in the payment of bills. The story around town was that Belli had to retain a different caterer for his annual Christmas party each year because of his failure to pay the previous year's bill.

I confess to being mildly anxious upon entering Mr. Belli's office later that day. Mr. Sabih greeted me with a smile and showed me around the iconic brick building Belli had famously restored, joining two structures into one and making it a must-see on any tour of San Francisco.

I took in the crystal chandeliers and red velvet drapes, masks from Kathmandu, and apothecary jars from Belli's grandmother's drugstore. In a corner stood a statue of a Swiss Madonna wearing an ostrich plume from South Africa. Belli's personal vintage rolltop desk sat behind a front window where people on parked Gray Line tour buses could steal a glimpse of the famous man at work. I did not ask Sabih to show me upstairs, where Mr. Belli kept a cannon to be fired whenever he won a huge verdict, accompanied by the raising of a Jolly Roger flag.

Regarding the lawsuit, Mr. Sabih explained that once the partnership between Mr. Choulos and Mr. Belli was dissolved, Mr. Choulos opened his own firm, developing a successful practice with a specialty in product liability law. Sabih showed me the complaint that had been filed by Choulos and provided me with a copy. I told him I would need an advance of $10,000 (serious money in 1980, at least to us!) and would also have to discuss the case with my partners before I could commit to undertaking Mr. Belli's representation. Sabih seemed to understand my concern and took me in to meet the Great Man.

We got right down to it—or I should say, Mr. Belli did. His rage at his former partner was shocking. I grew up in a rugged agricultural community, played collegiate sports with some fairly tough characters, and spent five years in the military, but never had I heard such profanity from the lips of a single individual. At times during his peroration, I wasn't sure whether Belli was angry at Mr. Choulos or at me, such was the violence in his expression as he described what Mr. Choulos had done to him and his reputation. At one point in the meeting, following a string of violent invectives, he reached into a drawer under his desk and withdrew a pistol.

"John, if you don't kill the motherfucking cocksucker in court," he said, wildly waving the pistol above his head, "I'll shoot the rotten son of a bitch myself, I swear to God."

I was relieved when Sabih came forward and managed to calm his boss down. I indicated I would study the pleadings and get back to him the next day. I still hadn't committed to undertaking Mr. Belli's representation, but they didn't seem to notice. Suddenly everybody was all smiles as I was escorted out with Sabih's promise to deliver a $10,000 retainer later that afternoon.

I convened the partners in an emergency session and wasn't surprised to have them almost uniformly opposed to undertaking Belli's representation. They acknowledged the public relations and practice development value of being able to boast that when the most famous lawyer in the world needed a lawyer, he turned to Farella, Braun + Martel. They feared, however, that we'd get sucked into nasty and never-ending litigation for which we would never be paid.

I finally persuaded them to agree we would take the first step: analyzing the pleading and proposing a response to Choulos' complaint.

"I already have an idea for a cross-complaint," I told them, "One that could bring the litigation to a quick end."

I agreed with the partners, however, that under no circumstances would we file my proposed cross-complaint until after receiving the promised advance of $10,000.

I called Sabih and told him I would draft a pleading in response to the complaint upon receipt of the $10,000 retainer. Sabih pointed out that the pleading was due in the next day or two. I told him I'd be ready and that I had some ideas for a cross-complaint that might succeed in ending the matter in a hurry. He was enthusiastic about taking the offensive and assured me he'd bring the check and pick up the draft pleading the following day.

He arrived on schedule the next day and seemed impressed with the cross-complaint we'd drafted. He apologized for not having the check and assured me it was prepared back at the office and that upon obtaining Belli's signature, he would deliver it to me personally.

He did return to his office, where—I later learned—he retyped my draft pleading showing Belli and himself as propria persona counsel for defendant and cross-complainant Melvin Belli. I never saw the check. Having the benefit of our creative cross-complaint, Belli apparently saw no further need for our services and, since we were never formally retained with an engagement letter, he saw no need to pay us either. I had screwed myself. My embarrassment as I gathered the partners was exceeded only by my anger and determination to sue Belli for our fee. Once again, the partners were reluctant to go forward.

"If you fight with a pig in the mud," one said, "you just get dirty, and the pig likes it."

"But we can't let the bastard get away with this!" I said, both furious and humiliated. Furious because Belli had stolen my work product; humiliated because I had been trying to use Belli's fame to bolster my own, and my partners knew it.

Somebody, I don't recall who, summarized the dilemma this way: "Suppose we end up in litigation over the fee and you each call a press conference to make your case to the public. Which one of you do you think will attract the most attention from the press, Melvin Belli or John Martel?"

There it was. *Belli's more famous than you, John, and always will be.* I nodded and we reluctantly walked away from it. A lesson learned: get the money up front, especially when dealing with a world-class celebrity deadbeat. A more constructive lesson I learned was that although partnerships can be troublesome at times, whether in business or relationships, they're essential to success. My ego had set a trap for me, and my desire for retribution could have made it far worse if cooler heads hadn't prevailed.

## Construction Litigation (Frank Lloyd Wright)

The defense of architects and engineers was a significant part of my life as a lawyer, most notably during my association with the Frank Lloyd Wright Foundation, for which I was honored to serve as West Coast lead trial counsel.

It started with the case of *Chrisofi v. Green* in 1962. Before his death, Mr. Wright had two principle protégés: William Wesley Peters, based at Taliesin West in Scottsdale, Arizona, and Aaron Green, located in San Francisco. I came to know and become friends with both men. My introduction to the Wright Foundation was a lawsuit arising out of a palatial residence in San Mateo County designed by Aaron Green for the Chrisofi family. The Chrisofis had wanted a home in the Frank Lloyd Wright style and sought out Mr. Green.

Practicality and function were never the hallmarks of a Frank Lloyd Wright design. Instead, artistic beauty and coalescence with the surrounding environment were considered preeminent. The Chrisofi home, when completed, met these creative standards, but soon developed massive amounts of water pooling in the ceiling, apparently resulting from either a leaky roof or upward evaporation of moisture into the roof from an indoor swimming pool.

Sorting out responsibility for the problem resulted in a nearly three-month battle of scientific expert witnesses, leading to the then-longest trial in the history of San Mateo County. The primary defendants at trial were the design architects, Aaron Green for the Frank Lloyd Wright Foundation, and the construction contractor, Sam Crawford, and—as is often the case— there was finger-pointing all around, a regular circular firing squad that unfortunately almost always benefits the plaintiff. Judgment was ultimately rendered against the contractor for alleged building defects while unexpectedly (and happily) absolving the architect from any design liability.

The trial had an important and immediate impact on my professional life. I had just left Bronson, Bronson & McKinnon, and *Chrisofi v. Green* was my first major case for the CNA Insurance Company, the Wright Foundation's malpractice insurer, working with my new partners at Elke, Farella, and Braun. The trial achieved national prominence in the design community, in part because it was the first major malpractice lawsuit against an architect who had been successfully defended, and also because of the sheer length of the record-setting trial.

The surprising victory resulted in invitations for me to teach lawyers across the country on the subject of professional malpractice under the auspices of the Practicing Law Institute. I also once addressed the National Society of Professional Engineers at their annual meeting in Las Vegas, Nevada.

Much to my surprise, I had become the leading national expert on professional malpractice defense, a specialty that became a major building block for our young firm. I was tasting fame, at least within the legal community, and I liked it.

## The Marin County Civic Center

In 1958, a short, elderly man sat alone and unnoticed on a hillside in Marin County, looking down on a sylvan landscape. He had nothing in his hands but a sketchpad and pencil. He was an architect, designing in his head and sketching on paper what many observers would later call the most beautiful government building in the world. The man was Frank Lloyd Wright, the most famous architect of his generation, and the building—his last—would become known as the Marin County Civic Center.

Ground was broken for construction of the project in 1962, but Mr. Wright didn't live to see it. The Civic Center was completed in several stages, again under the supervision of Wright's protégé, Aaron Green. The Veterans' Memorial Auditorium phase of construction wasn't completed until 1971. (Incidentally, I performed on the Auditorium's stage in the midnineties, singing one of my original compositions, "It Kills Me."). The Civic Center was designated a National Historic Landmark in 1991.

I was again retained to defend the Frank Lloyd Wright Foundation in a suit brought by the owner of the Civic Center, the County of Marin. The case involved another leaky roof, but this time on a grand scale. I was pleased that the matter was ultimately and amicably settled without the necessity of a trial. By now my reputation as a trial lawyer was becoming known, which gave me powerful leverage in settlement negotiations. Litigants are more willing to settle a case when they know the opposition is represented by a lawyer who isn't bluffing and has the courage and competence to take the case to trial—and win. My intense drive to achieve victory at all costs and against all odds was apparently serving me well.

I was proud the case settled without the necessity of a trial and gratified to represent the Foundation for more than thirty years. If you're ever driving anywhere near Highway 101 and San Rafael, a tour of the Civic Center is worth your time.

## The San Jose Center for the Performing Arts

The Center, located in downtown San Jose, California, is a state-of-the-art theater designed in 1972 by the Frank Lloyd Wright Foundation and Taliesin, its West Coast headquarters. Taliesin retained a Yale University consulting engineer to design a movable ceiling for the Center in order to offer perfect acoustics, whether lowered for a string quartet or raised to accommodate a full concert symphony. It was a promising concept—on paper. The problem was that the ceiling proved to be too flexible for its own good, and during the final week of construction, it fell into the newly-installed orchestra seats below, leaving two workers dangling on ropes high in the air. The workers were rescued with only minor injuries, but the ceiling was badly damaged and the orchestra seats were demolished.

I was called in immediately by the Wright Foundation. Working with the owner of the building, the City of San Jose, and several potential defendants, it was clear that the first priority was to lift the massive ceiling high enough off the orchestra seats to permit an analysis of what had caused the failure. This was certain to become another lengthy courtroom battle of expert witnesses unless responsibility for the failure could be agreed upon.

A meeting was called to order by the San Jose Board of Supervisors, attended by the Board and other city officials, as well as potential litigants and lawyers representing the design and construction teams who were about to become defendants in a costly and inevitable litigation. The purpose of the meeting was to entertain verbal bids for the project of raising the ceiling, with timing as well as cost being important.

The bid presentations were held in a giant conference room with at least twenty-five San Jose officials and potential litigants present. Each bidder took their turn, and it became clear after a few hours that safely lifting the giant ceiling ten or fifteen feet in the air would be an expensive and time-consuming undertaking.

When the final bidder was called, he stood out, not attired in coat and tie like the others, but in jeans and a T-shirt. The scruffy contractor looked to be in his sixties and badly in need of a shave (and probably a bath, as well). He was obviously impatient with what he'd heard from the other bidders and said the following to the shocked onlookers:

"You all are makin' way too big a fuckin' deal out of this project. Gimmie a broomstick, some baling wire, and two Blacks, and I'll have the fuckin' thing up in a week and a half!"

The room was stunned into shocked silence, although I could hear muffled tittering. The bidder was asked to leave by the politically sensitive Board of Supervisors and the contract was awarded to a Los Angeles company, Stagecraft, Inc. After the expert opinions were delivered, and numerous meetings among counsel took place, the case was settled without a trial.

— — —

As a result of my professional association with the Frank Lloyd Wright Foundation and my friendship with Aaron Green, I became an admirer of their work. I've been in several of their structures over the years, and even managed to spend two nights in the iconic Frank Lloyd Wright-designed Tokyo Imperial Hotel the week before it was demolished to make room for a more economically efficient building. The Imperial, famous not only for its design but for its durability, had survived—albeit with serious damage—the devastating Tokyo earthquake in 1923.

Although my friends Wes Peters and Aaron Green are long deceased, Taliesin partner John Rattenbury was an amiable host to my wife, Bonnie, and me at Taliesin West's Scottsdale headquarters before he passed away in 2021.

## Patrick Declert v. Freeman Paving

This was a heartbreaking case and full of irony. I'd only recently left Bronson, Bronson & McKinnon and was on my own with my new firm.

I was retained to defend an engineering firm that had designed a road-way with a sharp curve that allegedly caused the plaintiff, young Patrick Declert, to lose control of his car while trying to negotiate the curve, admittedly traveling at high speed. He collided with a heavy-duty light pole, destroying the automobile and dooming the plaintiff to a life of quadriplegia.

Patrick was a handsome young man, and the jury, as expected, was obviously sympathetic. Despite the solid evidence of contributory negli-gence—his admittedly high speed was established by expert testimony and skid marks—we all knew cases like this could result in runaway "sympathy verdicts" well into the millions. I had learned as a young prosecuting attorney that jurors will twist facts to justify their decision in favor of a more desirable litigant.

Co-defending the case with me was my old firm, Bronson, Bronson & McKinnon, representing the pavers of the roadway. The irony was that Bronson was represented by Vernon Goodin, the very same attorney who had hired me out of the district attorney's office in 1962 and then become my mentor at the firm. As described earlier, there had been some bitterness at my sudden departure from BB&M, but my friendship with Vernon had survived it.

Co-counsel relationships in major trials are often difficult and always awkward. While both defendants may realize the desirability of main-taining a united front against the plaintiff, there is almost always conflict on the issue of tactics and, of course, primary liability. In this case, the paving contractor, Vernon's client, blamed the designer, my client, for not taking into account the possibility that someone would exceed the speed limit, while the designer, my client, assigned fault to the paver for his application of the surface. One thing that usually unites codefen-dants, however, is the desire to minimize the seriousness of the injury and the amount of financial damages awarded the plaintiff.

Even here, though, there is sometimes tension among codefendants. Trial lawyers can be egomaniacs who think they're the best and smartest lawyers in the courtroom, and therefore seek to control the proceedings, sometimes to their detriment. There have been times when I've fallen into this category. When you're as driven as I was, it's possible to conflate the healthy confidence that you will win with the dangerous belief that you cannot lose. In this case, for example, I vividly remember doing a very credible job of cross-examining the plaintiff's chief medical witness, the treating physician. When I had completed my examination and was walking back to counsel table, Vernon gave me a subtle nod of approval and I breathed a sigh of relief, confident now that any verdict would not exceed low seven figures.

A recess was called and Vern and I met outside the courtroom. He congratulated me on an excellent cross-examination. I hoped he would add that there would be no need for him to give the doctor a chance to slip off the hook I'd so expertly, if precariously, inserted. Instead, he shocked me by announcing his intention to ask the doctor *if Patrick retained the capability of achieving an erection!*

I clearly recall my response.

"With all respect, Vern," I said, trying to control my astonishment, "if you ask that question, the answer will most assuredly be in the negative, whereupon the jurors will come out of the jury box and beat the shit out of both of us and then deliver a verdict in the amount of several millions of dollars."

"I think there's a chance he's not impotent," Vern said.

"You're wrong, Vern, and even if you are right, he's still a quadriplegic."

I couldn't dissuade him, however, and wondered if he was pulling rank, taking this opportunity to remind me that he had once been my boss. That made no sense, though, because Vernon Goodin wasn't a petty individual. We returned to court.

"Do you wish to cross-examine, Mr. Goodin?"

"Just one question, Your Honor."

I moved my chair as far as I could from Vernon's, trying to somehow disassociate myself and my client from what was about to happen.

"Dr. Millsap," Vern said, "can Patrick achieve an erection?"

I stared down at the table in front of me, glad at least that he had not asked the doctor if Patrick could still get a hard-on, a woody, a boner, a tentpole, or a pocket-rocket.

To my amazement, the otherwise stoic physician broke into an enthusiastic smile and said, "Oh, yes. It's highly unusual, but Patrick has full sexual capacity and fertility."

"Thank you, Doctor," said Vern, as I dared to glance at the jury. They were smiling along with the doctor, seemingly relieved at hearing this new information.

The result of Vernon ignoring my arrogance and his violation of the rule that all beginning trial lawyers are taught—never ask a question on cross-examination to which you don't already know the answer—was that we settled the case for well under a million and our clients were delighted.

## Vincent Coppola

Vincent Coppola and his wife, Barbara, were model citizens of Mount Kisco, New York, where they lived with their four children. It was 1976, and Vinni was employed as the vice-president of a sales organization, while Barbara was a registered nurse. Both were active in the local PTA. They were a happy, typical American family.

This was all about to change.

Vinni received a call one day from a man who told him he "had the money" and was ready to "acquire the goods." Vinni had first tried to explain that he "didn't know what this was about," but the voice at the other end of the phone was not to be dissuaded.

"You don't have to play cute with me, Mr. Coppola. I know who you are and we need those guns now and have the money. So, where do we meet?"

Vinni, a conscientious citizen, figured out the confusion, for it wasn't the first time he had been mistaken for a notorious local Mafia Don known as "Trigger Mike Coppola." Perspiration was breaking out across his forehead as he frantically tried to think of what to do.

"Call me back tomorrow," Vinni said, and hung up the phone. He then called the police who at first took him for a crank, but then eventually referred him to the Bureau of Alcohol, Tobacco and Firearms (the ATF), who had heard rumors and took him quite seriously. They suggested he set up a meeting with the stranger, who later turned out to be the contact man for Colonel Manuel Alfonso Rodriguez, El Salvador's Army Chief of Staff since 1972.

Vinni wondered what he was getting himself into, but over the objection of his wife he cooperated and set up a meeting as directed by an ATF agent. The time and place proposed by the agent was May 15, 1976, at the Mount Kisco Holiday Inn. The ATF would wire the room with hidden cameras and agents, posing as Mafia underlings for "Trigger Mike," and would be armed and ready to step in to make arrests.

The day of the meeting arrived, and Vinni was a nervous wreck, a kitten up a tree. *What if one of the buyers knew what the real Trigger Mike looked like? What if he was shot before the agents could intercede?*

The meeting took place and the plan came off without a hitch. The thwarted transaction, which consisted of the unlawful sale of ten thousand Bushmaster automatic machine guns, was recorded on videotape before ATF guns were drawn and six men were arrested. The colonel was carried off from the meeting place shouting curses and death threats at Vinni.

It soon became apparent that Vinni was indeed living under a threat, possibly from the colonel's associates, but also perhaps from the real Mafia gang members who had been standing by for a call from a "Jim Grey" and were not amused by Vinni's interference with their business.

To make matters worse, Vinni's wife did not regard her husband as a hero, but rather, a fool. Things deteriorated between them even more when an ATF agent explained that Vinni's testimony would be essential to convicting the Colonel and his associates and would only be effective if Vinni were still alive at the time of the trial. To ensure his safety, Vinni and his family would have to go into the US Witness Protection Program. They were stunned.

On May 20, 1976, at six in the morning, the entire Coppola family of six was loaded into a station wagon with only a few personal belongings. They were not told where they were going and were instructed not to tell anyone they were leaving. The Coppolas' lives were about to be completely uprooted. They had to quit their jobs, take their children out of school, and move away without a forwarding address, not even telling their closest family members where they were going. Indeed, they were instructed, once settled, never to tell *anybody* where they were. After several weeks of temporary stays at low-rent motels, they were finally deposited like so many packages into a small home in Pleasant Hill, California.

Barbara Coppola would later write a letter to a friend, which said in part:

> I was unable to contact anyone for fear we would be traced. It was never my intention to pick up and leave like a thief in the night. I don't know and probably never will know what you all thought of us. I can only hope that you read the papers or watch TV and learn the truth. Vinni was only doing what he felt in his heart was right for our country. Please remember us and if and when it is ever possible, I hope to see you all again.

Their disruption was worsened by the US Marshals' inability or unwillingness to provide them with new Social Security numbers, as promised, so they could resume something resembling a normal life. They had no credit cards, drivers' licenses, or even a relationship with a bank. They were provided a house and a monthly stipend of $1,068 per month, an amount that soon proved insufficient for a family of six. They lived for a while in Pleasant Hill, before being moved again, this time into a Walnut Creek, California, condominium.

Barbara couldn't work as a registered nurse because she had no documentation and no way to get any. Vinni, who had been making $4,000 a month in New York, eventually landed a job as a commissioned used car salesman, using their adopted name, "Carson." Just when things couldn't get any worse, he began to suffer heart problems.

Their nightmare seemed to be over on September 21, 1976, when Vinni was returned to New York for his testimony against the defendants. The result of the trial was that all six defendants were convicted and sentenced to prison for five years, except for the Colonel, who was given ten for his predominant role. Once reestablished in Mount Kisco, Vinni was presented with the city's highest civilian award, the Civilian Service Award. Walter Cronkite did a feature on him.

Sadly, however, the misadventure had taken its toll on the Coppolas' marriage. Divorce followed, but they reunited around the notion of seeking compensation from the government for their suffering. Although everybody they consulted told them the government flatly refused to settle Witness Protection Program cases, and that taking it on would be futile, they eventually contacted my secretary and made an appointment.

I was, of course, touched by their story and what they'd been through. I could give them little consolation, however, because of the things they had already heard about suing the government, particularly in the context of the ironclad waivers they admittedly had signed. After a brief discussion, they pleaded with me to try anyway. Based upon the credibility of the couple, and the story they told, I couldn't say no and told them I would file a complaint in federal court—probably doomed to failure, but they left my office smiling.

Upon receiving the complaint, a US attorney called and explained that there would never be a settlement and that I would have to go to the Supreme Court if I ever expected to get the case to trial. I told the federal attorney that's exactly what I was prepared to do, if necessary, and that I wanted to start with the deposition of the head of the US Marshals Service and the US attorney in charge of the Witness Protection Program as soon as possible. I told him a gross injustice had been perpetrated on my people, and that I was prepared, if necessary, to rip away the veil of secrecy that surrounded the program. That got his attention.

There followed several weeks of argument and delay before the US attorney in charge of the litigation finally blinked. He called and asked me "what the Coppolas wanted in order to go away." He suggested the possibility of a highly confidential nuisance settlement, perhaps something in the vicinity of $5,000. My clients were prepared to take anything they could get at this point, but I told him I wouldn't insult them with an offer less than ten times that amount. I had found their weakness and intended to exploit it.

He chuckled and was about to hang up when I told him I would immediately be filing a request with the federal court seeking the depositions of everyone with knowledge of the Coppolas' case. He laughed at me again and hung up. Now it was getting personal.

After I filed moving papers to the federal court seeking an order requiring production of key personnel for deposition, he called back and told me that perhaps a bit more was possible, "despite the signed waivers." I assumed he may have been talking about $10,000 but wasn't sure.

"If you continue to talk nuisance settlement," I told him, "I just want to assure you that I'm going to be the biggest nuisance you have ever dared to imagine." Although I knew the clients would take whatever he offered, I told him to come back to me with a more reasonable number and hung up on him.

We finally settled at a strictly confidential figure several times the earlier number, an amount that pleased the Coppolas. Getting the money into their hands, however, was when things got really strange.

I was told to be in front of the Watergate Hotel in Washington, DC at ten in the morning on a given day, and that I would be escorted to a location where I would receive the entire settlement in cash. This was highly unusual, but I agreed, after insisting on receiving round-trip airfare and a paid hotel booking at the Watergate in advance of the payment meeting. On the morning following my arrival, an unmarked car pulled up to the curb in front of me at the Watergate.

"Are you Mr. Martel?" asked the driver.

"Yes," I said, "and who are you?"

"Agent Smith, sir," he said, flashing his ID too quickly for me to read his name. "Please get in the car."

He was a pleasant-enough looking fellow and the ID looked authentic, so I got in and asked, "Okay, where are we going?"

"I am not at liberty to reveal that, sir, but I am told you will receive your settlement fund upon arrival."

Agent "Smith" was a man of few words—no words actually—during our trip to a small community on the outskirts of Virginia, where we parked in front of an obscure-looking post office.

"Please follow me, sir," he said, and we entered the building. They seemed to be expecting Agent "Smith," and he swiftly entered a door to the back of the post office, beckoning me to follow.

When I was a small boy, one of the few outings my father took me along for were trips to the post office to pick up his mail. It was the first US government building I had been in, and I remember looking upon the back room of the post office as a mysterious place, the seat of great power. I smiled to myself, thinking that—at last—I was now inside one, seeing not very powerful-looking people, some with eyeshades, some with rubber gloves, sorting through scattered boxes. Not one person looked up as we walked swiftly by. I followed Agent Smith down a dark hallway and into a small office where I was introduced to a "Mr. Brown."

I gave him my name and said, "Brown, huh? I guess the name Smith was already taken?"

Neither of them smiled, and Brown asked to see my photo ID.

I presented it, and without hesitation, he produced a small travel bag containing multiple stacks of hundred-dollar bills wrapped in rubber bands. He asked me to take my time counting the money to be sure the right amount was there. I did so, signed a simple receipt that was pocketed by Agent Brown, and was then driven by Smith directly to the airport from which my return flight home was soon to depart.

I kept my travel bag between my legs throughout the flight and didn't close my eyes.

When I later handed the cash to Vinni, not taking any fee, he smiled and thanked me, but without much enthusiasm. He probably wished it were more, and who could blame him?

## Part 2: Pro Bono Litigation (Free Legal Services for Those with Limited Means)

### The Rivera Asylum Case

Responding to a request from the local Lawyers' Committee for Civil Rights Under Law, I undertook the representation of a Guatemalan refugee named Diego Rivera, in connection with his application for asylum—a topic much in the news as I write these words in 2022.

Back in 1978, Rivera, then only seventeen and on his way home late one night, became an unintentional witness to one of Guatemala's notorious civilian death squads as they dumped dead bodies into a Guatemala City construction site. He ran home, sure he hadn't been observed, but to his everlasting regret, he'd underestimated the National Civil Police Death Squad.

Reality set in a few nights later as he was arrested and questioned for hours. He continued to deny he'd seen anything. Over the next eleven years, however, he was repeatedly arrested and imprisoned under false charges, subjected to brutal beatings and other forms of torture administered by prison authorities and the renegade National Civil Police. He understood that this harassment and torture was to remind him he "saw nothing" that night.

Rivera eventually could take it no longer, and after being grazed in the head by a sniper's bullet during a parade, he knew it was only a matter of time until he'd be assassinated. In his twenties, he was married with two young children when the four of them escaped to the United States. They managed to avoid the attention of immigration authorities for several years, all the way until their two kids were in high school, with a younger brother recently born in the United States. But their luck ran out. As Rivera and his family were about to be deported, he heard about the asylum program and applied, claiming he and his family would be killed to ensure his silence if they were forced to return to Guatemala.

When I heard about the case, I immediately agreed to take it on. I'd recently traveled to Guatemala researching my fifth novel, *The American Lawyer*, and had some familiarity with the repressive nature of the country. Analyzing the case, I saw two critical problems. The main one was whether the hearing officer—who had the power of a judge—would believe Rivera's unsubstantiated story about events that allegedly happened twenty-five years in the past. A related question was whether we could convince the hearing officer that the current democratically elected government was still a danger to Rivera and his family.

We prepared sworn declarations, detailing the history of Rivera's torture and abuse before escaping Guatemala. Once again, I sought out an expert, this time hiring a prominent psychiatrist to interview Rivera and to opine whether, in his clinical judgment, Rivera was telling the truth about both his past and current fears. I told the doctor to pressure Rivera in his responses and to be willing to testify at the asylum hearing himself if Rivera's answer was in the affirmative to both questions.

After several sessions with Rivera, the doctor indicated a willingness to testify favorably. This, coupled with Rivera's own sympathetic presence, gave me cautious optimism that we would prevail on the first question regarding his traumatic past. The second question, however, continued to raise doubt. Was Guatemala City still a particularly dangerous place for

Rivera, twenty-five years after his departure? I was coincidentally qualified to deal with this question, having recently—and narrowly—escaped
being kidnapped at gunpoint in Guatemala myself.

Asylum cases were being looked at by the US government with
a jaundiced eye, but the hearing officer assigned to the case was a
retired judge who seemed both experienced and reasonable. She paid
close attention to the testimony of the psychiatrist, to Rivera and his
family members, and to my cross-examination of the immigration
officer assigned to the matter. It soon became apparent that I had more
knowledge of current Guatemalan political and cultural life than the
locally based Immigration and Customs Enforcement (ICE) officer.

In 2006, the Rivera application was recommended for approval
by the hearing officer, and Rivera's final application for asylum and
eventual citizenship was accepted. This meant safety for his family
members, as well.

The family wept upon hearing the good news, and my eyes clouded
up, too. We parted, and I did not expect to hear more from Diego Rivera,
but on the one-year anniversary of the asylum approval ruling, he called
and asked if he and his family could come to the firm and express their
appreciation for what we had accomplished for them. They came with
cookies, and it was an emotional reunion. I will long remember his
daughter's tearful goodbye at the end of our time together: "You not
only saved our father's life; you kept our family together."

Of the many spine-tingling occasions during my fifty years as a trial
lawyer, that was one of the strongest.

## One That Got Away

In June of 1980, I received a call from my entertainment lawyer (who was
also my former law school classmate and friend) Bob Gordon, inviting
me to join him in front row seats at a concert featuring his clients, the
Doobie Brothers, and including one of my favorite vocalists, Michael

McDonald. Bob said that after the performance, we'd go backstage so he could introduce me to McDonald, who Bob believed was a victim of copyright infringement of his number one hit song, "What a Fool Believes," which features a highly unique and catchy rhythmic structure.

The infringing song was called "Steal Away," written and performed by a one-hit wonder named Robbie Dupree. Bob Gordon sent me a comparative analysis prepared by a reputable musicologist clearly establishing that "Steal Away" involved a near-identical rhythmic structure to McDonald's song.

I eagerly accepted the invitation. As a McDonald fan, "What a Fool Believes" was one of my all-time favorite songs. The show—rumored to be one of the final Doobie Brothers performances as a group—was sensational. Afterward, Bob and I went backstage to meet Michael. Following an exchange of greetings, the singer and I went off together for privacy.

"From what I've seen, Michael," I began, after some small talk, "you have a very strong case. The rhythmic structure in "Fool Believes"—and the appropriately entitled "Steal Away"—are obviously identical. More importantly, the structure is highly unique. I'm willing to take it on."

Clients are usually quite encouraged and cheered by my optimism, but Michael seemed reserved. I asked what was bothering him.

"I'm having second thoughts," he said, "I'm not sure I should bring a case against Dupree."

"Why not? The evidence is clear and convincing that "Steal Away" has infringed your original rhythmic structure."

With a somewhat sheepish look, Michael said, "Well, you see, that's just it. The rhythmic structure isn't exactly original to me. I sort of piggybacked on a rhythm I dug up from a Black blues song written before I was born."

They say there is "nothing new under the sun" (Ecclesiastes 1:9), and I'm beginning to think they're right.

We didn't sue.

## Mamie

In 1993, at the age of sixty-two, I was slowly slipping into retirement and still volunteering my pro bono services to the local Santa Cruz Senior Legal Services Committee (SCSLSC). Specifically, I'd offered to handle any litigation matters that required a level of experience and expertise beyond the local staff's capability.

My most satisfying experience for the SCSLSC was on behalf of an eighty-nine-year-old widow named Mamie Teixeira. After the death of her husband in 1989, Mamie sold her home and its surrounding acreage in Fresno, California, to a local businessman named Dwayne Cardoza. As partial payment, she took back a note secured by a deed of trust dated July 7, 1989.

In February 2001, there remained a total amount of $78,000 owed to Mamie on the note, which Cardoza wanted to pay off in order to retire the debt. He wanted to free the property of the mortgage so he could use it to collateralize another real estate purchase he intended to make. Mamie was advised, however, that the tax consequences of taking a lump sum payment would be disadvantageous for her, and she declined the offer.

Cardoza persisted, and on February 21, 2001, the parties finally entered into a modification agreement in which she surrendered the mortgage and reduced the amount owed from $78,000 to $67,000, in return for which Mamie understood she was going to receive a lifetime annuity from Cardoza of $675 a month. She lived in a trailer that was fully paid for, and she believed she could live out her life on a monthly payment in that amount.

After making payments on the annuity for nine years, however, Cardoza claimed he had completed his obligations under the modification agreement and simply stopped paying. When he was $4,000 in arrears on his monthly payments, Mamie was running out of money, and her daughter urged her to seek legal counsel, forgetting that neither of them could afford a lawyer. Eventually, Mamie found her way to the SCSLSC, and the case, because of its complexity and seriousness, found its way to me.

Unfortunately, the written agreement was somewhat ambiguous, giving Cardoza the opening to claim he had only agreed to pay monthly payments of $675 until he reached the amount of $67,000 owed under the modification agreement. It was clear to me that Cardoza's real problem was that at the time he made the agreement nearly ten years before, he didn't anticipate Mamie would keep on living. Worse, at age eighty-nine, she showed no signs of slowing down. He'd made a bad deal and was trying to slither out of it.

When I first met with Mamie at her trailer park, she was living barely above the poverty line. I was furious that a successful Fresno businessman would take advantage of an impoverished old lady, and on November 17, 2010, with metaphorical guns blazing (forgetting that I was, by now, an old man myself), filed a complaint for declaratory relief and charged Cardoza with breach of contract, specific performance, fraud, negligent misrepresentation, intentional infliction of emotional distress, and financial elder abuse. The temporary restraining order was granted, forcing Cardoza to immediately resume payments, including back payments.

Cardoza was represented by Wild, Carter & Tipton—Fresno's oldest law firm. The trial lawyer assigned to the case was Ms. Monrae English, a very attractive woman in her early forties. I mention this only because once she took over the defense, every male judge we appeared before seemed to fall in love (or lust) with her, and I had very little success with pretrial motions other than the initial temporary restraining order, obtained before English's involvement.

Her looks, coupled with a good mind and a highly aggressive attitude, made her a formidable adversary. Indeed, she was one of the most contentious opponents I'd ever taken on. I began to suspect that she ate raw meat and #10 roofing nails for breakfast. Her hostility was most obvious during depositions, which became a cross between *High Noon, Apocalypse Now,* and WWE matches. During one of our several depositions, I thought she was going to come over the table and attack me—and not in a good way. After the fourth adversarial deposition, I realized I was getting too old for this.

Meanwhile, during the course of litigation, Mamie's case suffered two negatives: her health began to fade, and so did Cardoza's net worth. I filed a motion to accelerate Mamie's trial schedule based on her health and age, and the court eventually granted us an expedited trial date. I wanted Mamie's last years to be as comfortable as possible, and free from financial anxiety. I was confident I could win her case. I did my best to conceal from English that Mamie was becoming far too frail to appear at trial, not wishing to weaken my settlement leverage.

As it turned out, English and I settled the case on the courthouse steps on the first day of trial. She'd been claiming that a negative verdict would force Cardoza into bankruptcy and Mamie would get nothing. I was skeptical, but on the morning of trial, English revealed certified financial records establishing that Cardoza could pay not one dollar more than $30,000 without being forced into bankruptcy.

After corroborating the accuracy of the documents and discussing the matter with Mamie and her daughter, we accepted the settlement offer. Mamie was tearfully grateful and, alas, $30,000 turned out to be more money than she would need. She died two years later on August 12, 2012. I remained in touch with her through visits and telephone conversations and took comfort from the knowledge that she had at least felt financially secure during her final days.

Mamie Teixeira was a lovely lady who enhanced my belief that the greatest satisfaction a trial lawyer can have is not dependent upon the size of the case or the fee earned, but rather the opportunity to help a good person achieve justice.

The case also helped me see that it was time to hang up my guns and retire. *Teixeira v. Cardoza* was not only one of my most satisfying cases as a trial lawyer, but also my last. I should probably be grateful to the antagonistic Monrae English for showing me that it was time to pass the baton to younger people. I still occasionally ruminate with awe and wonder at how my Texas friend, Joe Jamail, winner of the largest verdict in history of $10.5 billion in the *Penzoil v. Texaco* lawsuit, tried cases almost into his mid-nineties before his death.

He must have been, well, driven.

## Chapter 21

# Closing Argument—My Life as a Trial Lawyer

> I see now just how truth comes true
> From behind your secret mind
> It keeps on slipping through
> Tripping you
> —"Take Your Time" (1975)

IF I HAVE NOT yet convinced you that my need to succeed was neurotically driven, then consider the fact that one of my role models was the great marathoner, Alberto Salazar. In 1982, Salazar won his first Boston Marathon after the famous "Duel in the Sun" with Dick Beardsley. Salazar won the race in an exciting sprint finish. He collapsed at the end and was rushed to an emergency room where he was given six liters of saline solution intravenously because he had refused to consume water during the race. This was vintage Salazar.

"This might sound extreme," he told a reporter after the race, "perhaps even a little deranged, but I don't think you can make it to the very top rank in any sport if you don't have an aversion to losing—a visceral, physical loathing."

Unfortunately, I felt the same way about the cases I tried. I despised losing as much, if not more, than I loved winning. Losing was simply not an option for me, and, like Salazar, this mindset exacted a price. Salazar's technique for victory in a marathon race, for example, was to run with the lead pack until around twenty-four miles, and then suddenly sprint away in a suicidal manner intended to crush the spirit of his competitors, who assumed he must be insane. With over two miles to go and everyone's muscles screaming with pain, Salazar wanted his adversaries to conclude, "If that crazy bastard wants it that bad, he can have it."

Similarly, a major trial running two or three months inevitably creates fatigue in the trial lawyer's body and spirit. I have witnessed either physical or emotional breakdowns—eye infections, stomach disorders, succumbing to cold or flu viruses—in at least one of the lawyers in every trial lasting more than two months. Eight weeks is a long time to go without much sleep at night, especially when the big-case trial lawyer's every move during the pressure-packed daylight hours is under intense scrutiny by a judge, a jury, and sometimes the press. In the Mondavi trial, I even saw this physical breakdown occur in a warhorse like Joe Alioto. The pace becomes unsustainable.

I often suffered, too, but concealed any pain and fatigue at all costs, and I believe I was usually successful in convincing my opponent that I was loving the struggle, just like that "crazy bastard" Alberto Salazar.

Salazar and I had something else in common. The pressure to win that we both put on ourselves finally took its toll, and we eventually both burned out. In April 1994, Salazar told John Brant, "For most of the last 10 years, I hated running. I hated it with a passion. I used to wish for a cataclysmic injury in which I would lose one of my legs. I know that sounds terrible, but if I had lost a leg, then I wouldn't have to torture myself anymore."[2]

I didn't hate trial work nearly as much as Salazar hated running, but I can relate to his dark conjecture. Much of the anxiety associated with the work derives from the fact that the lawyer never knows what is going to go wrong in a jury trial; he or she only knows that something

---

[2] John Brant, "Duel in the Sun," *Runner's World*, April 2004.

*will* go wrong, and that there will never be enough time to anticipate and prepare for it. The psychologist James Bugental characterized this anxiety as "the existential fear of contingency" and relates a parable about a shipwrecked man on a desert island who knows a tidal wave will come but does not know how high it will be—or from which direction. Thus, his life is spent stacking and moving his limited supply of rocks from place to place, waiting for disaster to strike.

The trial lawyer's shortage is not rocks, but time. There is never enough time and energy to deal with everything that might go wrong in a jury trial, but I never stopped trying, and that meant working late nights and every weekend, staring at documents and depositions through red-rimmed eyes, trying to catch smoke in a bottle. The knowledge that I couldn't anticipate every peril and pitfall that lay ahead, combined with the obsessive need to win the case, began to take its toll in psychic pain. The anxiety was greatest just before the start of the trial, but anxiety also permeated my weekends when both body and soul cried out in desperation for a relaxed hour or two to enjoy my family or the society of friends. Bad as it was, it never occurred to me that I had it in my power to walk away.

## How Did I Win Nearly One Hundred Trials?

Trial work has been difficult at times, but though demanding, the profession has been very good to me, and I hope in some small way I have contributed to the improvement of our justice system and, in the process, served my clients well. When I'm asked how I managed to lose only four cases in nearly one hundred trials, I never know how to answer the question. I will try here.

1. The most important attributes, albeit no secret, are just plain hard work, thorough preparation, and refusing to be outworked by your opponent.
2. Dumb luck.

Here's an example: My second trial for the district attorney's office, a forgery case, matched me against Clinton W. White, a veteran trial lawyer whom Federal Judge Lowell Jensen would later describe as, "a legal giant, a complete guru of the bar." It was a mismatch, but I had a good case with good facts. My handwriting expert had confidently matched the handwriting on several forged checks to the handwriting of the defendant based on exemplars taken from his cell. But then the tidal wave struck. Let me explain.

Regrettably, my handwriting expert witness fell apart on the stand when it became clear that a cellmate of the defendant—not the defendant himself—had provided the exemplars the expert relied on. I knew I was in trouble when the cellmate was called by Clint White as a witness for the defense. The young prisoner shuffled into the courtroom wearing ankle manacles, but looking vaguely amused, and seemed to enjoy testifying that he had provided the sample handwriting as a favor to the defendant.

The result was that my expert witness had implicated the innocent cellmate, not the defendant, as the person who had forged the checks. I remember feeling heat coursing throughout my body and knew my face must be glowing a bright red in front of the jury. I was both angry and humiliated. Here I was, just beginning my career as a trial lawyer, and I was already about to lose a case that should have been a slam dunk.

The next morning, however, I was visited by a miracle. The judge announced in chambers that a juror's wife had called to report that her husband was in bed with a severe case of flu. Both White and the judge assumed I would agree to continuing the trial with eleven jurors, and I was about to do so when I luckily decided to put in a call to my mentor, Jensen.

"Just say no," he said, "and gracefully get out of chambers." The judge unhappily had no choice but to declare a mistrial. White, who went on to gain fame as lead counsel in the famous "Zebra" murder trial, was furious. I had the good fortune never to appear before him when he later became a judge, because he never forgave me—especially when I won the retrial with a new expert witness. Dumb luck.

3. Smart luck.

By this, I mean making chancy, high-risk choices that pay off—something I've done all my life. An example of this was taking on the challenge of making Peter Mondavi admit he sold wine that was actually grape juice. Some lawyers would consider this a foolish risk, but it worked.

4. Perhaps most important, an intuitive sense of how to frame arguments and cross-examine witnesses in a way that does not offend jurors' sensibilities.

Part of this God-given ability is knowing how to ingratiate oneself with members of a jury. This is done by always being honest and building trust during the course of the trial. I learned quickly that if the jury likes and trusts the lawyer, this positive feeling can be transferred to the client and to the client's cause. Trial lawyers lacking this gift can be good, but never great.

5. An understanding of the importance of controlling the courtroom.

This requires the freedom, when necessary, to break free of protocol restraints and wrest control not only from your opponent or an adverse witness, but even from the trial judge. An example of this trait was seizing control of my opening statement from the trial judge in the Richmond, Virginia case. Another example was humanizing my economist in the newspaper case by introducing his fiancée sitting in the back of the courtroom. Again, not for rookies.

6. The good fortune of being able to occasionally "get into the zone."

By this, I refer to the rare but dramatic courtroom occurrence of Maslow's peak experience during a trial—an out-of-body episode in which I can actually see and hear myself as an objective observer and listen in wonder at the words flowing from my mouth. It's extremely rare and unpredictable, of course, but I suspect the peak experience occurred for me when I was 100 percent prepared, and therefore free to do the dance without worrying about either the ultimate outcome or what should come next.

7. Finally, I wasn't allowed to fail as a child and never kicked the habit in adulthood.

Want approval as a child? Please your parents. Want the respect of your peers as an adult? Never lose. I know I'm not unique in this, but I can think of only one time when I came close to receiving approval from my father. As a new USAF pilot, I persuaded Dave Amis to let me borrow his father's Cessna 190 so I could fly from Oklahoma to Modesto and take my father up for a ride. (My mother, was afraid to go up, but that was okay.) When we landed, my father smiled and for once didn't demean the event or tell me I "needed to be a pilot like I needed water in my shoes." Neither, to be honest, did he say anything complimentary. I've continued to chase his approval, often sprinting in a state of exhaustion like a madman to the finish line in order to avoid defeat in law—and in life. Could this be a major clue to the mystery of who or what caused me to be so driven?

## Paying It Forward

I've tried to repay a profession and justice system that has, for better or for worse, provided me with opportunities. I've done this by passing on to other trial lawyers things I have been fortunate to learn in my years of practice. To this end, I've been a teacher in various forums.

I've also tried to shine a light on the dangerous distortion of our justice system frequently perpetrated by movies and television. I've done this mainly in four speeches, presented between 1989 and 1999, to plenary sessions of the America College of Trial Lawyers. One of these is included in the Appendix.

I feel that doing pro bono work for the community is also something every attorney should contribute as a way of paying back.

In summary, I'm grateful for the opportunities the trial court has provided me, and to the advisor at Cal Berkeley who suggested law as a pursuit.

## Chapter 22

# After Law and Music, a Third Calling: My Life as a Writer

Gossip burns hotter than a funeral pyre
It'll be the death of a suspicious mind
But where there's all that smoke there's gotta be a little fire
I guess that love ain't really so blind
—"Gossip" (1975)

MY FIRST LITERARY DISCOVERY, when I was eight, was Howard Pease, a little-known writer of adventure stories who coincidentally was also born in Stockton. Most of his stories featured a young protagonist named Joseph Todhunter Moran, who frequently shipped out on tramp steamers. In my imagination, I shipped out with him.

Among the questions authors are commonly asked during book readings are "Where do you get your ideas?"; "What is your work schedule?"; "Where do you do your best work?"; and, of course, "How did you become a writer?"

I've always felt a little guilty answering the last question, because my path to becoming an author was absurdly easy. Though I studied creative writing as an elective in college and occasionally taught legal writing to the associates at my firm, I had no formal training in fiction writing. I awoke one day at my Sausalito home in 1981, however, and decided to quit fantasizing about being a writer and try to become one. It happened during my brief and tumultuous marriage to Susan Spalding and, to be fair, I must credit her for kick-starting my writing career. I had awakened with an idea for a novel about three sleazy senior partners in a venerable, but financially troubled, San Francisco law firm. The partners had put all their hopes for economic survival on a rarely-handled plaintiffs' personal injury case that could save the firm from bankruptcy and dissolution. They were so desperate to succeed that they poisoned their own clients with toxins to enhance their damages.

Susan liked the idea and told me she knew a highly regarded agent, a friend of a previous boyfriend. The agent's name was Kathy Covey, of Covey & Covey Literary Agency, with offices in New York and Los Angeles. Kathy (whose last name is now Robbins) remains a giant in her field. Susan put me in touch with her. She took my call and, after hearing my idea, suggested a lunch meeting at the trendy restaurant Jimmy's in Los Angeles.

I flew down a week later. She listened, then told me she liked my plot and asked me to submit an outline, which I quickly did. She liked that too, and asked me to submit three chapters, which I also did. She praised the work, and within months I had submitted a draft of the completed novel, which she offered to Simon & Schuster and Bantam Books. Both publishers immediately made similar offers, including a generous advance, but Kathy recommended I choose Bantam because it was run by the grande dame of publishers, Linda Grey. It proved to be an excellent choice, since Kathy and Linda were friends and I knew they'd work well together while dealing with an amateur like me.

As for the question, "What is your work schedule?," during the mid-1980s, the answer would be, "Anytime." In other words, running the trial department of the leading litigation firm in San Francisco, handling my own caseload, and trying to write a novel left little time for sleep.

As for "Where do you do your best work?," my answer is again influenced by the vicissitudes of my "day job." I was traveling a great deal on litigation matters during this early period, and I often found 35,000 feet a good altitude for contact with my muse. No telephone interruptions, nowhere else I had to be. There are many theories about this. It is said that a good writer should be able to write in a boiler room or bus station. At the other extreme, Billy Wilder only wrote in one place, his office, and famously said, "The muse has to know where to find you." My muse apparently had wings and speed skates and was never far away, because I was able to write wherever and whenever I had the luxury of free time. Between 1988 and 2012, I completed five books.

## Partners

Like most first novels, my debut novel, *Partners*, was overwritten, though it spent fifteen weeks on the *San Francisco Chronicle* best-seller list in 1988, climbing as high as number two and earning some modestly favorable reviews. The story featured Rachel Cannon, an attractive young lawyer trying to break through the glass ceiling and become the first female partner in a San Francisco law firm called Stafford, Parrish, and MacAllister. Her troubled career turned out to be good for mine, especially when a Japanese publishing house put frosting on the cake with a surprise purchase of rights to the novel. I drove my Datsun directly to British Motors on Van Ness in San Francisco, signed the check over to the sales department, and drove away in a brand-new 1988 Jaguar Cabriolet sports coupe.

For a first novel, the reviews weren't bad:

> The courtroom shenanigans are a pleasure to read, and Martel excels at building motivation. (*Publishers Weekly*)

> First novelist Martel, fifty-seven, himself a famed, very big-time trial lawyer based in San Francisco, has a sharp eye for character and a quickly paced plot that is unclichéd and absorbing at every turn. (*Kirkus Reviews*)
>
> This book is well-written; the characters are three-dimensional. I enjoyed it more than I did the Turow book. (*The Practical Lawyer*)

I didn't realize it at the time, but Scott Turow and I were launching a new genre of literature in the late eighties that would become known as the "modern legal thriller." He published *Presumed Innocent* in 1987; *Partners* followed a year later. Another thing Turow and I had in common was that we were both full-time trial lawyers—unlike John Grisham, a former Mississippi legislator who came along in 1989 with a little book called *The Firm* that turned the world of popular legal fiction upside down, reaching number one on all best-seller lists.

Foolishly, some might argue, neither Turow nor I gave up our day jobs; indeed, we rigorously pursued them. I came to know Scott but never thought to ask him how he felt about relinquishing the head start he and I carved out in the publishing industry.

I began working on another novel while agent Kathy Covey went through a divorce—two of them actually: a personal one from her husband, Richard, and a professional one from me. I think Kathy saw that publishers were trending toward nonfiction, plus she didn't seem enthusiastic about my second novel, *Conflicts of Interest*. We separated as good friends and remain so to the present day. I was content to look for an agent closer to home, so I called my friend, the novelist and former trial lawyer Richard North Patterson, to see if he had any ideas about how to find a reputable agent on the West Coast.

"Sure," he said, flashing his typically generous smile, "use mine. His name is Fred Hill, and he's sometimes a pain in the ass but gets results."

## Conflicts of Interest

Thus began my sometimes tumultuous, always rewarding relationship with the Frederick Hill Literary Agency, based in San Francisco and Los Angeles. Fred was said to be one of the premier agents in the United States and he proved it by getting me an advance for *Conflicts* in the high six figures, plus foreign rights. I recall getting the news at a pay phone somewhere in Europe.

*Conflicts* was published in 1994 by Simon & Schuster and was more favorably reviewed than *Partners*. The critics loved the antics of hillbilly lawyer Seth Cameron and his clairvoyant girlfriend, Rosie Wheeler.

> A mix of legal action, government secrets, high-stakes dealings, and streetwise romance makes this [an] exciting thriller. (*Booklist*)
>
> Like Grisham and Turow, John Martel is an accomplished spinner of legal thrillers. (*Marin Independent Journal*)
>
> An exciting and authentic tale. (*The Sunday Times*, London)
>
> John Martel is one of the best. (*Rocky Mountain News*)

The traditional advice to beginning writers is: "Write about what you know." *Conflicts* embodied my roots in the Central Valley of California, my experience as a lawyer, and my nearly five years as a USAF pilot. Maybe that's why it worked. My writing career was gathering momentum, but in 1997, at the age of sixty-six, I found myself at another fork in the road. Was I a writer, or a trial lawyer? Both professions were jealous mistresses, demanding my full-time commitment.

I've already related how I declined an offer of a recording contract at the Troubadour to try the Mondavi case. Would I once again turn my back on art in favor of law and the Montgomery Street lifestyle? That would have been the logical and practical choice. My name was on the masthead of the best law firm in San Francisco and arguably the West Coast, a firm I'd helped create. Moreover, I knew there were better singer-songwriters and novelists than I could ever be, though I refused to take second place to anyone as a jury trial lawyer, and yet...

It wasn't that simple. While I thoroughly enjoyed trying—and winning—cases, I was *in love* with the process of writing. Litigation, as rewarding as it had been, had taken its toll, whereas writing novels, like music, fed my hungry soul. Besides, I'd been matched with—and defeated—the best lawyers in the courtroom, but challenges remained in literature. Although my first two novels were regional bestsellers, I had yet to achieve the win of national recognition. Always hungry for fresh approbation, I craved the satisfaction of writing a national bestseller. I was only in my early sixties but felt compelled to make a decision. What to do?

Once again, I rationalized my way out of the emotional cul-de-sac I'd driven my aspirations into and again adopted Baseball Hall of Famer Yogi Berra's advice. Confronted by another fork in the road, I took it, and while racing headlong into another challenging trial, I contemporaneously went to work on my next novel—I'd call it *The Alternate*, vowing to make it a national bestseller.

## Easier Said Than Done

Yet another major problem for me qua novelist was that, while Grisham could grind out a book a year, it took me, working only at night or while traveling by air, writing in whatever free time I had, about five years on average. I began to understand that this made it impossible to maintain a loyal readership, not to mention keeping my name up front in the minds of publishers and retailers. I did have a loyal following of fans who continually pestered me for my next book, but my law practice was keeping me from the kind of commitment demanded by both disciplines. Could it be that I wasn't working hard enough? Wasting too much time in bed at night?

## The Alternate

Unfortunately, my editor at Simon & Schuster, Bill Grose, retired to Florida, so Fred placed me with a new publisher, Dutton, for the publication of my third novel, *The Alternate*. The book would be my biggest all-time seller, making the charts of both the *New York Times* and *USA Today* in 2000. The book also spent several months on the *San Francisco Chronicle* hardcover best-seller list.

*The Alternate* tells the story of Amanda Keller, a frustrated daytime television actress who saw her role as the alternate juror in a high-profile murder case as an opportunity to resuscitate her fading acting career. Thematically, it was a study of a troubled mother-daughter relationship, unrequited love, insanity, and—inevitably—murder. My fans loved it, and so did the critics.

> The twists and turns . . . are page turners, but the reader will not get lost in the maze. Lawyer-written court novels may be a dime a dozen, but this one is a standout from start to finish . . . a masterly story of murder, madness and the law. (*Library Journal*)
>
> [A] fast moving thriller . . . The Alternate is, without a reasonable doubt, an exciting and enjoyable novel. (*San Jose Mercury News*)
>
> [It] proves that some lawyers do have a talent for writing fiction . . . a thriller that moves like a highspeed train. (*The Orlando Sentinel*)
>
> [The Alternate] confirms—like Grisham and Turow —that John Martel is an accomplished spinner of legal thrillers. (*Gannett's Marin Independent*)
>
> Publication of *The Alternate* gave me my national bestseller.

## Billy Strobe

A writer's books are like his children. We conceive and nurture them, and when it's time, we have to let them go. Because of this relationship, it usually does no good to ask any author to pick a favorite, because the answer will generally be, "My latest."

This isn't the case with me. My fourth novel, *Billy Strobe*, holds a special place in my heart. The critics, who can sometimes be harsh, especially with legal thrillers and especially when they're written by a lawyer, loved *Billy*, heaping lavish praise on the novel:

> This is the fourth novel by the high-profile attorney (more than a hundred trials, only four defeats) and it may be his best. It is certainly better than most of the output of John Grisham and equal to the best of Philip Margolin . . . **This is a legal thriller in the manner that Dickens might have written it.** (*Booklist*, starred review)
>
> Full of twists and turns, wit and well-drawn characters, Martel's fourth novel (after 1999's *The Alternate*) . . . [presents] a realistic portrait of a young man coming to grips with the truth about his father and himself. . . Powerful prison sequences have the ring of authenticity, as do the courtroom and office scenes, attesting to Martel's professional expertise (he is one of the nation's top ten trial lawyers, according to the *National Law Journal*). This satisfying summer legal thriller should assure Martel the growing readership he deserves. (*Publishers Weekly*)
>
> San Francisco author and lawyer John Martel hits the ground running in *Billy Strobe* . . . A refreshingly gritty approach to a decidedly button-down genre . . . Martel pulls no punches. (*San Francisco Chronicle*)

> Compelling reading . . . The story, and the writing,
> hold one fascinated. (*The Boston Globe*)

*Billy Strobe* was released by Dutton in early September 2001, and was supposed to be my big breakout novel. Excellent reviews and a national book tour that featured full houses in Oklahoma City and Houston bookstores (after kicking off with packed appearances in California) set the stage for a runaway novel.

What could possibly go wrong?

My wife Bonnie and I had spent the night after my Oklahoma City book reading in the home of our dear friends Dave and Susan Amis. I vividly recall emerging from the guest bedroom on the morning of September 11, 2001, and seeing the sorrow on Dave and Susan's usually smiling faces. I then saw the horrific pictures on television, played over and over again, planes intentionally crashing into downtown New York City buildings. Was this really happening?

The death and suffering being depicted was soon too much to take, although the courage of the first responders was awe-inspiring.

All flights were canceled, of course, and I assumed my appearance scheduled that day at Murder By The Book, in Houston, had been canceled as well. I called one of our sponsors to tell him I was sorry I couldn't be there, forgetting what I had learned about Texans, having been stationed at four Air Force bases in the state during the Korean War. That lesson, simply stated, is that Texas considers itself independent from the rest of the country. "Cancel? Hell no," cohost Joe Jamail said, "Get your ass down here. We've got over a hundred people coming, eager to hear you speak, and the bar will be open."

A bar? In a bookstore? Only in Texas. I reminded him that all flights were canceled, but Bonnie, my ever-resourceful wife, interceded.

"We could rent a car and drive to Houston," she said, and was able to reserve the last available car in Oklahoma City. There were few other cars on the road and of course no planes in the air. The drive was surreal, like being in a sci-fi movie after an apocalyptic disaster. I didn't want to violate my commitment to Murder By The Book but couldn't imagine people showing up for a book reading on this horrific day.

We made it to Houston in plenty of time, and I was shocked at the turnout. I also noticed that during my introduction by the great trial lawyer, Joe Jamail, there was no mention of the tragedy that had just befallen America. When it was my turn to speak, I felt compelled to acknowledge it.

More than 165 hard copies of the book were sold that day alone, placing the novel in the top ten bestsellers for the entire year, as monitored by the *Houston Chronicle*. Alas, the tour ended there, and my scheduled New York appearance was canceled. We sat stranded for a full week in Houston at the home of dear friends, and my cohosts, Harry and Macey Reasoner, who were coincidentally stranded in New York. In the comfort of their home, we waited for the airport to reopen so we could return to our own.

In my sorrow over the disastrous suffering in New York City, it never crossed my mind to consider how my writing career would be irreversibly altered by the events of 9/11. All novels released around the time of the attack suffered the same sales paralysis. People didn't want to buy thriller fiction; they were living it.

I was also belatedly learning a hard lesson about how publishing works. It can best be understood by picturing a book on an imaginary conveyor belt that slowly chugs along—through line editing, advance publicity, promotion, and pitches to retailers—until the book is finally released, warehoused, and distributed to retailers. The book will then either sell or die very quickly. *Billy*, of course, died at birth. Fred Hill explained to me that the conveyor belt had continued to inexorably chug along, bearing new books scheduled for distribution. There was no second act for a novel, no stopping the conveyor belt or climbing back on it.

I suspected that exceptions were somehow made for franchise novelists such as Patterson and Grisham, and I couldn't forgive Brian

Tart, my representative at Dutton, for not supporting a reissue. It was clear that *Billy* had become collateral damage in a much more serious tragedy, and *Billy*'s bad luck would turn out to be mine as well. There was the mass-market paperback edition, of course, but that sold only 130,000 copies, far below Dutton's expectations. Another hard lesson learned: A book's paperback (mass-market) edition tends to piggyback on hardcover results in the marketplace.

## Billy Strobe, the Movie

Six months after *Billy*'s release, Fred Hill finally delivered some good news. Our book-to-movie agent for *Billy Strobe*, Angela Cheng Caplan, had called Fred to report that producers Larry Mark (now deceased but a major producer with his own film company) and Jonathan King (now Chief Creative Officer for Narrative at Concordia Studio) had fallen in love with the novel and wanted to option it for filming by Sony Pictures. A movie based on *Billy* would mean not only a boost to my readership generally but also a probable second life for the novel, including a reissue by the publisher. Like the phoenix, *Billy* would rise out of the ashes.

I was summoned to a meeting at Sony where I sat down with Larry, Jonathan, and a television writer named Richard Kramer. All of them were enthusiastic about making the movie, and Kramer was retained by Larry to write the screenplay. Again, what could possibly go wrong?

Despite the stars seeming to be aligned, bad luck and misfortune continued to dog *Billy*. Months passed and Kramer failed to produce a script. He eventually admitted to suffering from emotional problems that had immobilized him. After about two years of stalling, he finally presented an incoherent product which Larry and I quickly rejected. Apparently, Hollywood also has a conveyor belt, and Larry had moved on to other things, including producing that year's Oscar ceremony.

In a move similar to regaining control of the courtroom in a trial, I decided to write my own screenplay adaptation. It was immediately optioned by a Hollywood producer named Jonathan Krane. This option initiated a tortuous three-year period of prevarication, fabrication, vacillation, negotiation, and confusion by numerous prospective coproducers and financiers, climaxing on the movie set of *Father of Invention* in New Orleans in what has been described as a near fistfight between Krane and Kevin Spacey, the star of the film. I had been told *Billy Strobe* would be filmed by the *Father of Invention* crew as a means of minimizing expenses, but Krane claimed Spacey wanted producer credit on the *Strobe* movie, and a heated argument ensued between the two men. Blows were averted, but the breach between them was decisive and permanent, thus ending any hope of a New Orleans filming of *Billy Strobe*. When Jonathan's option expired—despite his pleas—I refused to renew it.

## Jailhouse Lawyer

While I was attempting to accumulate sufficient common sense to walk away from Jonathan Krane Productions and his rotating cadre of cohorts, somebody else saw an opening. I received a shocking email from a good friend, Randy Wulff, who told me his connections in Hollywood had sent him a screenplay that looked very much like the plot of my own *Billy Strobe* script. It was entitled *Jailhouse Lawyer* and was a direct rip-off that included a sympathetic prison inmate who gained a law degree by correspondence while incarcerated. The scripts had identical settings, mood and pacing, and similar dialogue and themes, plus closely matching character and plot development.

I was able to learn from the IMDbPro website that the film was in preproduction at Paramount with Mark Gordon as its producer and actor Samuel L. Jackson as an older, blacker version of Billy Strobe. But that wasn't the worst of it. My shock turned to anger when I saw that the agent representing the plagiarizing screenwriter was none other than my own former book-to-movie agent, Angela Cheng Caplan, who had originally sold the option to Sony.

My telephone conversation with her, witnessed and overheard by my literary agent, Fred Hill, nearly melted the receivers. This was a woman who, acting in her fiduciary capacity as my agent, had only months before counseled me in an email, to "Wait until Friday to hear back from Larry Mark. At that point, *we pull the plug and move on with our lives*."

As I put the chronology together, it became clear why she wanted me to "move on." I was unaware that months before this email, Caplan's most notable client, the screenwriter Will Rokos, had been hired to write the final version of a script they called *Jailhouse Lawyer.*

My experience as a trial lawyer told me I had a clear winner, but I also realized my judgment was clouded by anger and bitterness, on top of which I had no knowledge of entertainment law. The lawyer was about to become a client.

I contacted Paul Meyer and Tony Murray, entertainment lawyers in Los Angeles County and friends I knew from the American College of Trial Lawyers and told each of them I needed to interview the three best and meanest entertainment lawyers in Hollywood. I then traveled with Bonnie to Los Angeles for scheduled meetings with three highly recommended firms. It was interesting for the first time to be on the client side of a litigation beauty contest. I was impressed with all three firms but mostly with a lawyer named Larry Stein, known in Los Angeles as "Mr. Hollywood," who, as I would soon learn, would live up to the hype.

## "Mr. Hollywood"

Stanton "Larry" Stein was indeed impressive. As we entered his building, I tried not to be influenced by the affluence reflected in every square inch of the firm's palatial office.

"I hope we don't like this guy, Bonnie," I said. "We obviously can't afford him."

I was only half joking. Notwithstanding my success in the courtroom, my "day job" had not produced wealth—and you know what happened to *Billy Strobe*, the novel.

I had transmitted to Larry a chronology of events and a letter I'd previously sent to Caplan, and he quickly evidenced a solid grasp of the relevant facts. He gave me a reality check by listing some well-known examples of failed efforts to block a movie on the grounds of plagiarism: *Wife Swap* vs. *Trading Spouses*, *Star Wars* vs. *Battlestar Galactica*, and so on. He pointed out that, to establish an infringement of copyright, the plaintiff must prove ownership of the infringed copyright, the defendant's access to his work, and "substantial similarity" between the defendant's work and the allegedly infringed original creation.

I explained that we could easily pass all three tests, including the all-important "substantial similarity." Larry listened patiently, and then offered an interesting alternative approach. He reported that the film was well on its way to production at Paramount and would soon be at the point of acquiring insurance. Once that investment was made, Paramount would be very reluctant to stop production, because the insurance money is nonrefundable. At that point they would be very amenable to a cash settlement with someone who had a solid claim of infringement.

I told him the cash would be nice, but I wanted my book and film rights back. I had written my own screenplay adaptation and was eager to see *Billy Strobe* on the big screen the way it was originally conceived. In other words, I wanted him to go after the bastards, especially Mark Gordon, the producer, and Caplan, the double agent, and try to stop production of the infringing film.

He listened to my story and quickly perused the incriminated Rokos screenplay. After sending his two associates out of the room, he leaned forward and told me the chairman and CEO of Paramount Pictures, Brad Grey, and he played poker together every Thursday night. Larry suggested I authorize him to informally visit the subject with Grey, and I enthusiastically did so.

He stood up, signaling the end of the meeting, and made no mention of fees or the engagement letter required by law. Bonnie and I allowed ourselves to be escorted out with the promise that Larry would call me on Friday, after his Thursday night poker game.

True to his word, he called me that Friday morning.

"Paramount Pictures," Larry said, without preamble, "has decided to cancel production of *Jailhouse Lawyer*."

I was stunned, but managed to say, "How in the hell did you do that, Larry?"

"We just had a friendly conversation," Larry said, with pride in his voice and a grin I could picture. "*Jailhouse Lawyer* is dead."

*Friendly conversation?* Did Larry have steamy pictures of Brad Grey with farm animals? This script had gone all the way through development and was nearly in production! How would Grey explain to the screenwriters—and to Samuel L. Jackson—that he was scrapping a movie about to be filmed? Was I going to be expected to make compensation to Paramount?

"What did you tell him, Larry? How did you convince him to shelve a production so far along?"

"Very simple. I told him about your day job. You know, Mondavi, the *Chronicle*, and so on."

I waited, but his silence seemed to say he was finished.

"Okay," I said, "so he knows I'm a successful trial lawyer, but the head of Paramount would have access to the biggest firms in Los Angeles. You must have had something else."

He hesitated, then I could imagine him smiling again. "Okay, I did," he said at last. "I told him that of all the trial lawyers in the world, John Martel was the last guy he'd want to fuck with."

Now it was my turn to smile. I thanked him and told him to bill me, but he just laughed and said he had enjoyed seeing the look on Brad's face. When I next looked for *Jailhouse Lawyer* on IMDbPro, it was gone without a trace. I never received a bill from Mr. Hollywood.

## The American Lawyer

I stewed over *Billy*'s abuse at the hands of Hollywood agents, lawyers, and producers for several years before sitting down at my computer again to write what would become my fifth novel, *The American Lawyer*—one of my best, according to some of my fans. I had been awakened from my self-pitying literary lethargy by a conversation with my sister Mary's husband, Don Eggleston, who told us at dinner one night about the rampant murders and kidnappings taking place in Guatemala. A member of Don's family had been a victim.

Don's father was a US Air Force attaché in Guatemala during the bloody revolution launched in 1954 by the CIA, so Don and his sister were raised there. His sister never left, having married Enrique Font, the largest corn miller in Guatemala. This would turn out to be a good break for me.

I had never written an international thriller, so in 2009 I decided it was time. I imagined a story about young Jesse Stone, an associate in a Montgomery Street San Francisco law firm, sent to Guatemala to help the son of the law firm's biggest client, who's been charged with the murder of a popular human rights activist named Marisa Andrade. Jesse is eventually joined in the quest by an unlikely individual, Teo Andrade, the victim's elderly husband who, ironically, had originally been a prime suspect in her murder.

In summary, *The American Lawyer* is a story about political corruption, runaway ambition, murder, redemption, and a four-hundred-year-old letter that could change the history of Central America and young Jesse Stone's life.

I realized Guatemala's tragic thirty-six-year civil war and colorful Mayan history would give the book a powerful sense of place. I hit the library for some preliminary research, including the State Department's current *Travel Advisory* on Guatemala, and confirmed that the country continued to seethe with violence—kidnapping, drug trafficking, and rampant murder— making it a perfect place for my hero to confront, and perhaps overcome, obstacles fraught with danger.

I continued my research, but one can only learn so much in the library or on the internet. Without having been there, how would I accurately describe Guatemala City, where most of the action would take place? I would have to go.

Don volunteered to travel with me as my interpreter and—hopefully—keep me out of danger. When my wife, Bonnie, expressed the desire to go with me, I told her she couldn't.

"It's even worse there than we thought," I said, and read her an excerpt from the then-current *Travel Advisory*:

> A peace accord, signed in 1996, ended a 36-year armed conflict. Violent crime, however, is a serious and growing concern due to endemic poverty, an abundance of weapons, a legacy of societal violence, and a dysfunctional judicial system. While violent criminal activity has been a problem in Guatemala for years, there has been a substantial increase in criminal violence . . . including numerous murders, rapes, and armed assaults against foreigners.

"They're heavy into kidnapping and killing Americans," I added, citing a *New York Times* article I had found that listed the names of seven American citizens, all victims of unsolved murders in Guatemala.

"It would be far more dangerous for you," Bonnie said through narrowed eyes, "to try to get out of town without me."

"But if you don't stay here, Honey," I argued, "who will ransom me if I'm kidnapped?"

"Very funny," Bonnie said, "but I have a better idea that will solve the problem."

"Let's hear it."

"How about a book called *Jesse Stone Goes to Paris*?

We laughed, but I was set on Guatemala. As somebody said, writers don't pick their subjects; their subjects pick *them*.

So off we went—Bonnie, me, Don, and his adult daughter, Nicole—to Guatemala, hoping for the best.

Bonnie and I boarded a flight out of San Jose. Eleven hours later, we stumbled bleary-eyed through Guatemalan immigration, then entered the fluorescent-lit lobby of La Aurora International Airport in Guatemala City. There, we were welcomed by nine teenaged, uniformed guards holding machine guns, and three German Shepherds the size of small horses.

"Are they there to protect us from violence, or to shoot us?" Bonnie asked.

"We haven't had time to break any laws yet," I said, "so I guess they're protecting us."

She looked tired as she said, "Then I wish they looked less like the Vienna Boys Choir."

— — —

Soon after our arrival in Guatemala, I asked our host and Don's brother-in-law, Enrique ("Quique") Font, to show me the perfect location for a hideout for my novel's fictional villain—a former guerrilla chieftain-turned-drug lord. After thinking about it for two days, he told us to prepare to leave for Rio Dulce at six the next morning. I felt a stirring of anxiety, recalling a State Department warning that the Rio Dulce area was a central reception point for drugs from Colombia and other cocaine and heroin sources. Quique assured us we would be okay.

Our destination was a six-hour drive from Guatemala City to the Bay of Honduras, followed by a short boat ride from Rio Dulce to the proposed location of my drug lord's fictional headquarters, located in a forested area fifteen minutes further up the Bay from the main dock. It sounded perfect. However, upon our arrival by boat to the mouth of the bay, the waters were growing treacherous, and we returned to a nearby village to deposit Bonnie, Don, and Nicole. Quique, his wife, and I got back in the boat in a flurry, while the others waited and worried on the dock for our return.

We were unable to reach the shore at our destination because of a sudden squall, and on the way back to the dock, Quique's small boat lost power when the outboard motor was swamped with saltwater. We had neither life jackets nor bailing buckets on board and it appeared we might sink in the suddenly rough waters of the Bay. I looked longingly at the distant shore, as we all tried to bail water out of the boat with our hands. But it was coming in faster than we could bail it. *This could get ugly.*

Luckily, the squall passed in about twenty minutes, and Quique was able to restart the outboard motor. We eventually made it back to the dock, where we found that Bonnie's valuable camera had been washed overboard. I was exhausted but excited that I'd found the "hideout" I had come looking for, and survived a squall. Eager to get back to Guatemala City, I decided to scratch this mission and use my imagination to write about this scene. We proceeded back to our automobiles.

The sun blasted our windshield as we drove away from the dusty village of Rio Dulce. Dee Dee Font, Don's sister and Quique's wife, was the driver of her new Mercedes sedan. Don occupied the front passenger seat, and Bonnie and I were the back. Quique, with Nicole, would lead the way again in his convertible sports car, which he did until the weather turned cold and he pulled over to raise its top. Dee Dee threw her husband a teasing wave as we passed him by.

I was looking forward to Guatemala City's more hospitable climate (thanks to its five-thousand-foot elevation), but uneasy about the speed at which Dee Dee was driving now that she was in the lead, especially on such a narrow and twisting two-lane highway. Along the route, roadside stands selling pineapple and plantains stood next to tiny shack houses cobbled together with scrap wood and tree limbs, surrounded by cattle so thin they looked like goats. Police in their little Opels were ignored as usual, there being no room to pull someone over even if they could catch them.

We sped again past Lago de Izabal, Guatemala's largest body of water, where centuries before, Cortés and his soldiers had crossed in canoes, many losing their lives in the violent waters. I had just rested my head against my wife's shoulder in the rear passenger seat when something caught my eye. Was some fool intending to pass us? *Crazy bastard*, I thought, as a large white van did indeed pass us at well over 100 kmph. He then tucked in directly in front of us. Soon thereafter, a second van came up close behind. Though Bonnie had commented on the sudden heavy traffic, neither of us thought more about it.

I had read that executive kidnapping was a common income-producing event in Guatemala. Before 1996, during the thirty-six-year civil war, Guatemalan guerrillas had been the first in the world to employ "economic kidnapping," using ransoming to finance their guns and bullets. Now, motivated by greed, not reform, the practice continued. We also knew seemingly rich Americans in an expensive silver Mercedes sedan were obvious targets. It never occurred to us, however, that this two-van gambit was the kidnappers' currently favored mode of operation.

We had much to learn about Guatemala.

I quickly forgot about the crazed van driver now in front of us and began to drift off again, but Quique, finally catching up with us from behind, read something else into the maneuver—particularly when he observed that a second van had moved up and tucked in directly behind us.

Quique later recounted that he knew exactly what would come next: the two trucks would ease us over to the side of the road, like two bouncers escorting an unwanted patron out to the sidewalk, and we would then be forced at gunpoint to drive the Mercedes up into the cargo area of the first van. They would then sell the car and ransom us as hostages, a two-for-one bounty.

But Quique had other ideas. Our niece, Nicole Eggleston, still riding in Quique's passenger seat, must have held her breath as Quique, despite the threat of oncoming traffic, began pulling his sports car tight alongside the following van, which swerved evasively, trying to block him or even run him off the narrow road.

Then, a new complication: another car was coming toward us on the narrow two-lane roadway. The oncoming car tried to slow down, but it seemed too late. Luckily, Quique swerved back into our northbound lane at the last minute, and the two cars passed safely within inches.

All four northbound vehicles—the two vans and our two cars—were locked in a deadly race as Quique began another pass at the second van. For Nicole, it must have felt like being in an action film, but these were not stunt drivers, and there was no director shouting "Cut!" if things got too dicey. Finally, Quique maneuvered alongside the second van.

Nicole's head dropped out of sight in the passenger seat and in her place appeared Quique's .45 automatic, retrieved from under his seat, and now pointed at the second van driver's head. Nicole recalls that Quique looked as calm as if he were pointing out a rare bird, smiling as the stunned, would-be carjacker-kidnapper signaled surrender and contacted his confederate by cell phone. Both trucks braked and pulled over, allowing us to safely pass, and we never saw them again.

I realized later that if Quique had not fortuitously pulled over to raise his convertible top when he did, he would have been in his usual position three or four cars ahead of us and would not have seen the kidnapping attempt until it was too late. We might have been doing up-close book research at a *real* bandit's hideout, hoping to hear from a representative of the fastest growing business in Central America: the ransom negotiator.

Back in our hotel, I had mixed emotions about the day's adventure. I was critical of Quique for putting us in jeopardy but had to reckon with my own dereliction in remaining silent about traveling in a known dangerous area in a target vehicle, which was obviously a bad idea. My criticism of Quique was further offset by a heroic rescue we would never forget, and Bonnie never complained about either Quique or me.

We flew out of Guatemala on July 3, 2002, climbing through low-lying stratocumulus clouds embracing the volcanoes at the perimeter of the city. Our sadness at leaving was tempered by a sense of immense relief and satisfaction. Relief, because we were alive and safe—as safe as one can feel aboard the nerve-racking Mexicana Airlines—and satisfaction, because I could now accurately represent the places where my protagonist would get in and out of trouble, vividly describe the courtroom (we'd visited during a murder trial) in which his client would be tried, and evoke the grim despair of the prison (which Quique got me into) in which he'd be held. I would paint a word picture of my hero's ill-fated boat trip to Arturo Gomez's secret hideout. And, while learning how trials work—or fail to work—in Guatemala, I'd found my fictional prosecutor—a courageous, real-life female Guatemalan prosecutor—who'd also be my protagonist's love interest.

Within a week of our return, Guate gangs kidnapped a Guatemalan judge, snatched from the same courthouse steps where my wife had photographed me for a possible book jacket a few days earlier. They gunned down another judge that same week in exactly the same place. All seven murders of American citizens named in the *New York Times* article of June 18, 2002, remain unsolved to date, and a high percentage of the country's indigenous people will continue to go to sleep hungry. Guatemala is a hard country with a tortured past and an uncertain future. It had drained us both, but we will never forget its dark, brooding beauty.

One thing was certain: If this book failed, it wouldn't be for lack of research. I had no idea writing suspense fiction could turn out to be so dangerous. With the hard work done, the book wrote itself in a little more than a year, and I was proud of the result.

I was persuaded by my agent to allow a brand-new imprint called Vantage Point to publish *The American Lawyer,* and I agreed to a modest advance. My agent, Doug Grad, structured the deal so I'd take a much larger than usual percentage of the royalties and more than make it up there. He also had high praise for the editor in chief, Joe Pittman. Unfortunately, Pittman left the company only weeks after I signed the contract, and Vantage Point printed only a small number of copies of the novel on November 1, 2012—the company's last act before entering bankruptcy. The few copies that made it to a single local bookstore were sold immediately, but the number was very small. There was neither promotion nor advance copies sent to reviewers, so no reviews, and—technically—no publication. I was crushed. The handful of people who read the book said it was terrific, one of my best. What hurts the most is that most of my fans wouldn't get to read the book—wouldn't even know it existed. Heartbreaking.

# Chapter 23

# Women in My Life: In Search of *The One*

I'll never know why you had to be
Too busy being my perfect lover to be friends with me.
Can't you see
That the yearning won't last
If we let it start burning too fast?
I know it's hard to let a romance take its time
But Baby, take your time.
—"Take Your Time" (1975)

My therapist said that my narcissism causes me to
misread social situations.
I'm pretty sure she was hitting on me.
—Anonymous

THE MAN'S BRAIN IS said to be preoccupied with hundreds of sexual thoughts throughout the day. This may or may not be true, but in my case, the preoccupation wasn't just about sex, but about the quest for the perfect partner. This pursuit began for me as a preadolescent, strongly influenced by my love affair with the cinema. Thus, the image of my ideal woman was forged largely in the furtive darkness of four Modesto movie theaters—the State, the Strand, the Lyric, and the Princess—while sucking on Milk Duds and red licorice.

The perfect woman began to form in my young mind in the 1940s and '50s, a composite of Lana Turner, Rita Hayworth, Betty Grable, Cyd Charisse, Gene Tierney, Hedy Lamarr, Brigitte Bardot, Elizabeth Taylor, and Grace Kelly. She was, of course, also smart, funny, committed, caring, and faithful. Thus, the woman I searched for was doomed from the beginning to be a fantasy, formed and imprisoned within my youthful imagination.

But the congenital romantic is not easily discouraged and the search proceeded in accordance with my driven nature. In addition to marriages to Ann Moore and Susan Spalding, and before meeting Bonnie Laird, the love of my life, I engaged in an even dozen "meaningful relationships" that usually lasted twelve to fifteen months and in rare cases, a little longer. Predictably, none of these women turned out to be The One, but I will profile some of them below because each of the relationships was indeed "meaningful," by which I mean it lasted at least one year and I often learned something without doing serious damage to the other person.

These connections were called, in the lexicon of the seventies and eighties, "serial monogamy." The term "monogamous" implies the absence of "cheating" and this part came easily for me. Sexual relations were important to me (too important, as you will see), but as a novelist, musician, athlete, and lawyer, I rarely had the time or energy to pursue multiple sexual partners.

Another factor in my search for The One was the psychic damage caused by the Holy Roman Catholic Church, compelling me to look at each relationship as a marriage possibility. For me, "All roads lead to Rome" meant that all relationships should ideally lead to marriage. This set the bar unfairly high for these women, for as soon as a romantic partner failed to live up to my unrealistic and unreasonably high expectations, there was no point in continuing the relationship. In most cases, if not all, I was the one who terminated it, often over a relatively frivolous "last straw": *Did she really end that sentence with "I" instead of "me"? Would it kill her to turn off the TV for an hour? The John Birch Society? You've got to be kidding me!*

I feel some guilt about being the one who usually broke the connection, but I think it can be said that I hardly ever took much more than a year of a woman's time and that I gave as much as I took. In the case of Sylvia (discussed in greater detail below), I left her with the house I had purchased for us, despite the fact that I caught her cheating on me (the "last straw" in that case).

Revealing the shallowness of my question, the women I'm about to describe were physically attractive. But the resemblance among them ended there, and over time I began to realize two things: First, good looks are relatively unimportant compared to other attributes. Second, I was mainly seeking in each new relationship that which I had found most lacking in the previous one: e.g., a gorgeous nutcase typically followed by a somewhat boring good citizen, followed by a stimulating but erratic intellectual, and so on. It's obvious now, looking back, that this was a disastrous method of finding a mate, and helps to explain my recidivism. I was definitely in the slow reading group in terms of the mate selection process.

Sex is like air. It's not that important unless you aren't getting any.
—John Callahan

Another thing the women discussed below had in common was that they all moved me physically ("turned me on") at the start. I still believe it's foolish to begin a relationship without that certain spark, although granted, in my case, it often blinded me to more important personality traits. Fortunately, I only entered into marriage with one such woman, Susan.

At the beginning of this memoir, I posited the hope that the exercise of writing it would reveal the person or persons responsible for my compulsive drive for achievement and recognition. I don't suppose I can name Hollywood as a suspect, although the cinema convinced me that a poor boy from Modesto would not likely win the hand of the fair princess unless he was capable of slaying the dragon. The contemporary form of dragon-slaying is revealed in the flippant comments of many rock musicians and athletes who say the main reason they perform on the stage or on the field is to "get the girls." I agree, and it does not stretch credulity to suppose that in my mind, to make myself worthy of the fair princess, I would have to be not only an athlete and a singer-songwriter, but also an author, a pilot, and a trial lawyer.

So, here's a look at some of those women I cared about, if only briefly. I will employ pseudonyms for most of them, and alter locations and time periods in order to prevent embarrassment—and to honor my entertainment lawyer's advice regarding my exposure to breach-of-privacy lawsuits. The other salient facts I attribute to each relationship, however, are entirely accurate, as any number of people close to me will attest.

## Julie

> Grant me chastity and continence, Lord, but not yet.
> —St. Augustine

I met Julie in 1951 when I was twenty years old, after I'd had a few sexual experiences. I was stationed at Perrin Air Force Base in Sherman-Denison, Texas, awaiting my appointment to the Aviation Cadet pilot training class.

Julie was attractive and probably ten or fifteen years older. Our relationship was purely and mutually sexual, with Julie my teacher and I her clumsy but eager student. I could drop in to her apartment at any hour without warning and she would always make herself available. Oddly, during our time together, she seemed to have no other lover—or even another relationship.

To my shame, I selfishly took advantage of her kindness. On one occasion, I recall thoughtlessly arriving without warning around eleven at night during a drinking spree with an Air Force buddy. She graciously welcomed my friend to sleep on her couch in the living room and made us both breakfast in the morning. She never complained about anything, and her skill level and wantonness were of Olympian quality. It wasn't unusual, for example, for Julie to disappear out of sight while I was driving us through crowded city streets, forcing me to negotiate heavy traffic with blood rushing southward out of my brain.

Julie made no demands on me. When my transfer orders came, we said goodbye without tears, each knowing there would be no calls or letters. I soon forgot her last name and I'm sure she forgot mine.

I doubt Julie is still alive, and in later years, I have regretted there was no way I could locate her to thank her for her kindness and generosity. Every young man should be so fortunate as to have such a woman in his life.

Thank you, Julie.

## Rhonda

> Don't worry about avoiding temptation.
> As you grow older, it will avoid you.
> —Joey Adams

I met Rhonda Dexter when she was a senior in high school, eighteen years old, and I was a twenty-two-year-old Air Force pilot. Her parents were wealthy socialites in San Antonio, and you can guess how happy they were to have their beautiful, young, virginal daughter in love with an "older serviceman." I was in love, too, and about to learn the power of parents in the life of a young daughter.

We met at a large party, and before we were introduced, we'd already exchanged glances full of promise across the crowded room, lacking only the sound of violins. Rhonda was a straight A student, mature for her age, and somewhat willful, particularly about maintaining her virginity until marriage—not surprising in the culture of the fifties. Accordingly, over the next three years, we did, as they used to say in those days, "everything but."

I was concerned she might lose interest in me once she stepped into sorority life at a college conveniently located near the base where I was stationed, but such was not the case, and our relationship deepened. We began to talk about our future together. My role in it would be to finish my tour of duty, return to complete my college education, hopefully in two summer sessions, get a job, and after we were married in her hometown, return to California to live. Her parents still had not accepted me, but she visited mine in Modesto while I was home on leave, and my parents were as smitten as I was.

After those years of "everything but," followed by my discharge and return to Berkeley and the University of California, everything went according to plan for the first few months when suddenly my letters began to go unanswered. I eventually called her and she broke the news that she'd become engaged to the son of a San Antonio millionaire—a friend of her parents. At the time I called Rhonda, I was visiting my own parents in Modesto and can clearly remember where I was sitting when I got the news—in my boyhood chair at the family kitchen table. I couldn't have felt smaller. I'm sure it had been a couple of decades since my parents had seen me cry. I'm also certain my father was disgusted.

This wasn't my first heartbreak, but it was definitely the worst. I learned several months later from a mutual friend that Rhonda's marriage had been short-lived, but I took no pleasure in the knowledge.

When I returned to San Antonio about a dozen years later, visiting old friends I'd made while in the military, I called Rhonda. She had remarried but her husband was out of town on business, and we met for dinner. She was still beautiful and was now chief financial officer of a major aeronautical company. She'd heard of my success as a trial lawyer and said she wished her parents were still alive to see how wrong they'd been about me.

*You were wrong, too, Rhonda*, I thought.

She was unhappy in her marriage and as we drank too much at dinner, we laughed at how determined she'd been in her youth to protect her virginity—and how frustrating it had been for both of us. We decided there was unfinished business in our relationship and proceeded to finish it.

We said goodbye late that night—this time for good—and I walked her to her car. I suspect both of us felt our long-awaited, much anticipated sexual union had been a bit disappointing. Even though I was single and unattached, I felt uncomfortable about what we had done and surprisingly relieved it hadn't been better. It had been so much more exciting when we were two young people frantically rolling around the floor of her parents' living room, bringing each other satisfaction without despoiling her sacred virginity. Conclusion: sex is more satisfying without guilt.

## Sylvia

> You treat me like an unwanted child
> A weight that makes you hate me hanging around.
> You can't escape me when you're feeling wild
> When you want to go to town.
> —"Unwanted Child" (1975)

After my disappointment with Rhonda and my eleven-year first marriage to Ann, I met Sylvia at a taxi stand. It took just one look, and we fell into casual conversation. She had a spectacular figure, a pretty face, and a mane of flowing black hair. I asked for her telephone number, which she readily provided.

We began dating. Sylvia had an enthusiastic smile and an earthy quality about her, which, combined with her physical virtues and sexual enthusiasm, made her irresistible. Within two months, I asked her to move into my rental house with me, and two months later, I purchased a house in both our names. Unfortunately, other men found her irresistible as well, and I grew suspicious that she was finding at least one of her admirers equally hard to resist. The relationship ended badly when I caught her in a male friend's apartment. They weren't expecting me, and the front door had no peephole; when her friend opened it, there she stood behind him, in a bathrobe, with a whiff of flagrante delicto in the air. In a panic, she claimed she and her friend were on a volleyball team and had just come there to shower.

Although I was angry, I mainly felt vindication and relief that my suspicions had been justified and I knew the truth. She wept for hours, but I was ready to say goodbye to Sylvia without bitterness and even signed "our house" over to her. (Her "volleyball" friend moved in with her soon after I was gone.)

Sylvia was a wild child who could not be contained by any one man, at least not by me. She had provided a bridge relationship back to the single world after the dissolution of my marriage, and I remain today more grateful than angry. Sadly, as will be seen from what follows, I learned nothing from the experience.

## Aubon

Those who cannot remember the past are condemned to repeat it.
—George Santayana

I first saw Aubon while teaching at a seminar in Boston, Massachu-setts. She was a lawyer, practicing there. I was speaking on the subject of minority shareholders rights. At the noon recess following my pre-sentation, Aubon and others approached with questions. I'd noticed her in the audience—you couldn't miss her—and our eyes had locked fre-quently throughout my presentation. I no longer remember her actual question, but it took me so long to answer it that others in line gave up. I concluded by offering to get further into the subject at dinner that night.

Thus began a tempestuous relationship that lasted nearly a year, during which Aubon tried to balance her caring for me with sporadic yearnings for her longtime boyfriend whom she had left to join me in San Francisco. There turned out to be another, more serious problem having to do with her emotional stability, which I didn't suspect at first because it was so carefully concealed.

It was a traumatic year for me—and probably for her other suitor, as well—but nobody suffered more than Aubon, constantly in tears and immobilized by indecision, guilt, and an unbalanced mind. Finally, when she could bear it no longer, she returned to Boston (and, I supposed, back into the arms of her former boyfriend). I was both disappointed and relieved. The triangle nearly ended in tragedy, however, when Aubon called me late one night when I was hosting a new friend for dinner in my apartment. I realized I was being interrogated, and when Aubon found that my guest was female, she said goodbye with a finality that set off an alarm bell in my head.

My instinct was regrettably correct, as I learned an hour or two later when I was called again, this time by a girlfriend of Aubon's whom I knew from my time in Boston. She, too, had received a strangely ominous late-night call and was equally worried. She and her husband ultimately went to Aubon's home and knocked on the door but received no answer. Deeply concerned, they broke into the house and found her unconscious on the floor next to an empty bottle of pills.

"She is still comatose here in Boston General Hospital, John," said the friend, "and the doctors say she may not make it. I thought you should know."

I was scheduled to start a trial the next day. My opponent was Marv Morgenstein (his real name and an actual case), a fine trial lawyer and, fortunately, a friend. He agreed to go to the judge in the morning and seek a continuance on the basis of my "family emergency." (Incidentally, when we finally tried the case ten days later, I displayed no gratitude toward Marvin by beating him in a hotly contested jury trial that resulted in an important, reported case in the field of construction litigation: *Allied Properties v. John A. Blume and Associates*.)

After securing Marv's agreement to delay the trial, I caught a red-eye, arrived in Boston the next morning, and found Aubon in the hospital. She had just regained consciousness and, according to a nurse, had had a very close call with death. The "other man" (Robert) was at her side, and I stood next to him, feeling awkward and confused. Aubon looked at me through red-rimmed eyes, thanked me for coming, and apologized for her "ludicrous and impulsive behavior." Her complexion was the color of the bedsheets. She reached out a trembling, cold hand, and I took it. She then turned to Robert.

"Thank you, Bob, for all you have done." Bob understood that with these words, Aubon had at last made her decision. She had chosen me. I couldn't help but feel victorious after months of competition with Bob. Aubon had finally made her choice.

At his request, I followed Robert out into the corridor and offered him a no-hard-feelings handshake. He couldn't resist uttering the father of all clichés: "Take good care of her, John," he said. I nodded and reentered Aubon's room, where the drama was just beginning.

"You have to get me out of here, John," she said, color returning to her face. "If the papers find out about this, I'll be crucified." I understood. Aubon was up for an appointment to a judgeship in the local superior court. News of an attempted suicide would probably cause the governor to withdraw her name.

"We can't just walk out of here, even if you were capable," I said. "There are bills to pay, and I don't see your clothes anywhere."

"My credit is good anywhere in Boston, John. You know that."

I nodded in agreement.

"They won't complain if I disappear, and it's up to you to disappear me."

I recalled that Aubon's room was next to a fire escape, and that my rental car was in the parking lot below. I assumed the hospital had her financial information on file, so without further discussion, I picked her up, hospital gown and all, and carried her down the fire escape. She probably weighed around one hundred pounds and though I was in decent shape, we barely made it down to my car.

This cinematic episode was not to have a happy ending, however, at least for me. Aubon got her court appointment, but Bob ultimately got the girl when she changed her mind. Again. This on-again off-again drama ended up being another heartbreaking experience for me. Though in retrospect it was predictable, I didn't see this coming and wondered if I would ever find a woman I both wanted and could trust. Despite her emotional problems, Aubon was a very intelligent, quality woman who took me a while to get over. After our final encounter, the United Airlines trip home was painful, aided only slightly by an understanding flight attendant and plenty of vodka on board.

A logical lesson to be learned from this failed relationship was that I should look for a modicum of strong mental health and stability in a potential new partner. What I learned, however, was that there is nothing logical about falling in love.

## Alecia

I'm a gringo desperado captured by his prize.
—Joe Silverhound (1976)

After a therapeutic hiatus from romantic relationships, during which I was busy trying cases and attempting to build a music career, I met

Alecia on a blind date. She was grounded, intelligent, and apparently free of overt neuroses or even neediness. This was a refreshing change from my last relationship, and while Alecia and I were together only one year, she remains a good friend to this day. What we lacked as a couple was the passionate coupling we both longed for.

In our short time together, I realized what attracted me most to Alecia was what my relationship with Aubon had lacked: stability and maturity. Alas, I was soon to learn that such personality traits, though appealing, were, on their own, insufficient grounds for a long-term relationship. There also had to be a spark.

## Sarah

> So I'll keep playing the same old game
> Though I know we both will lose.
> It ain't good, but all the same
> It's all that I can do.
> —"Unwanted Child" (1975)

Yes, I kept "playing the same old game," but finally met my match in Sarah, who played it better than I did.

I was on another Practicing Law Institute speaking trip, this time to Chicago, when I spotted Sarah in a nearby restaurant and she spotted me. She was beautiful and looked to be a professional woman, probably attending the lawyers' conference next door. We met, the mutual attraction was strong, and after two additional trips to Chicago, I proved once again I was in the slow learning group by suggesting she give up her job as a licensed therapist and join me in my Sausalito bachelor's pad. My haste was dictated partly by loneliness and her stunning good looks, but also by the fear that if I didn't act aggressively, I would lose her, for she, like Aubon four years earlier, was in a committed relationship when I met her.

Sarah agreed to move to Sausalito, but unlike Aubon, refused to move directly into my house. She said she would apply for licensing in California and rent her own apartment, then see "how things developed." I was impatient but admired her independence. She was obviously not risk-averse, but neither was she a silly airhead, carelessly putting her life into the hands of a virtual stranger as some women had been willing to do. Sarah's behavior was foreign to me, but not unattractive, particularly since she combined her independence with a kinky sexual proclivity that fascinated me.

The problem with Sarah was that her previous boyfriend still wanted to marry her and had promised her a new Mercedes convertible as an engagement present. Sarah, being typically honest, admitted she sometimes missed him as well. I was troubled by this, of course, but thought it would pass with time. Meanwhile, Sarah's attempt to reestablish a career wasn't going smoothly, and I began to see I was losing ground with her. After only a few months, she packed up her belongings in a U-Haul trailer, with my help, and said goodbye.

My time with Sarah taught me that intelligence in a partner coupled with independence was an aphrodisiac. Could it be I was finally learning something? Perhaps even maturing a bit? Or was I kidding myself and perhaps even heading for danger again?

## Susan

> So goodbye, don't cry Blue Moody Lady
> When I'm out of your sight I'll be out of your mind
> Blue Moody Lady
> I'm an eagle, not a bird in a cage
> I'm going back to the country, start acting my age.
> So you follow your dream and I'll follow mine
> Blue Moody Lady goodbye.
> —"Blue Moody Lady" (1977)

They say timing is everything, and I believe it. When I met Susan Spalding (her real name), my law profession star was on the rise. I'd just chaired the State Committee of the American College of Trial Lawyers and had been teaching Trial Practice at the Hastings College of Advocacy. I was reaching the top rung of the profession, but though I'd been wearing out my tuxedo attending professional functions, I often felt out of place, showing up alone or with a pretty, younger date whom all the men noticed and all their wives regarded as a bimbo.

I'd been single a long time and was feeling the need to grow up, settle down, and be a part of The Club again. In addition, I was tired of the dating game, and ready to join the ranks of the solid, boring, domesticated, card-carrying grownups.

Susan was a former Eileen Ford face model in New York City, and a senior sales executive for Henredon, an upmarket furniture and design company. She had been retained by my law firm to assist with designing and furnishing our expanded office space. It was 1980. I was still riding the public relations renown from the Mondavi case and had just been engaged to defend the *San Francisco Chronicle* and the *Examiner* in a retrial of a dangerous antitrust case.

Being engaged was on Susan's mind as well. I was being stalked and didn't know it, though I should have, since I'd done it enough myself. It started when she called me early in the morning of New Year's Day, ostensibly to wish me a Happy New Year. I thought it rather strange, and not a little presumptuous, to assume I would be alone in bed early on New Year's morning. I wasn't, of course, which made it not only strange, but awkward as well. I was still in bed with Sarah, enjoying our last fling together before she would leave for home in two days, back into the arms of her former fiancé.

"Moving right along are we?" said Sarah, with a wry smile as I hung up the phone. We both understood she was in no position to complain. She had dumped me but was still free to tease me.

To ease my anticipated loneliness with Sarah on her way out the door, I had signed up for a week at John Gardiner's Tennis Ranch in Arizona.

Soon after I arrived there, I was resting in my room after lunch, when there was a knock on the door. I opened it, and there, totally out of the blue, stood Susan Spalding. I must have mentioned my plans during our awkward phone conversation while I was in bed with Sarah.

> You know that tingly little feeling you get when
> you're attracted to somebody?
> That is your common sense leaving your body.
> —Anonymous

There was nothing subtle about Susan and, although I barely knew her, she was soon in my Tennis Ranch bed. She hadn't flown out from San Francisco to discuss tennis strategies. I didn't resist, especially when, after a brief conversation, she exposed a pair of incredible breasts.

In retrospect, I never knew what hit me. In my defense, Susan met all my demanding criteria: she was intelligent (master's degree from Boston University), beautiful, and possessed a dramatic history. Her father had died when she was twelve, and she and her siblings were left in the hands of an alcoholic mother. Susan rose to the task and essentially raised her three younger siblings by herself. How could I not be impressed? The package seemed complete.

> My wife and I were happy for twenty years. Then we met.
> —Anonymous

Earlier, I explained how Susan and I were married on July 26, 1980, beside the Neptune Pool at the Hearst Castle. The wedding was a spectacle, lacking only the presence of my children, Jay and Melissa, who sensed my folly and were gracefully "unavailable" for the occasion.

Susan was thrilled to be married at Hearst Castle. She planned the string quartet, the Gatsby attire for the limited number of guests we were allowed to invite, and an informal reception at a nearby restaurant.

Later, a formal reception was held at the Mondavi winery. As mentioned, these events constituted the high point of the marriage.

Soon after the wedding, Susan told me she had a great idea: computers designed especially for hotel rooms that guests could use to find their way around town, make reservations, arrange a wake-up call, check out of the hotel, and so on. These are common in hotels nowadays, but in 1980, it was Susan's original concept, needing only to be discovered. The problem was that Susan looked to me for financing. I wasn't a wealthy man, but because of my standing in the firm, and the firm's standing in the community, I had an unlimited line of credit with the California Canadian Bank that I used to fund her start-up business.

The first step in her plan was to build a prototype to use as a demonstration model for presentations to financial institutions and hotels, and Susan hired several people to put this together. She started with Dudley Warner, an experienced software design engineer. The second step was to hire a competent chief executive officer. We interviewed several candidates before hiring Don Marro, a mid-level executive from the Sony Corporation. We also hired several programmers and eventually took office space in Silicon Valley when her staff grew to over ten people. Susan quit her job with Henredon and HotelTech International (HTI) was born.

Other than helping with a few sales pitch demonstrations, I wasn't involved, partly because I already had a demanding job (several of them!) and partly because technology wasn't my thing. Moreover, I was in final preparations for the commencement of the second Hearst-*Chronicle* antitrust trial. My role in HTI was solely to provide funding. Susan or my secretary would put a check in front of me and I would sign it. That was my second mistake. You may have guessed by now what my first one was.

Cutting to the chase, we did not acquire the major financing to actually construct the product, and consequently had trouble getting hotel contracts. Finally, my line of credit was mercifully cut off by "Doc" Blanchard, our representative at the California Canadian Bank. HTI, along with my marriage, mercifully died along with it.

Viewing the wreckage, I had lost all my savings and, with unpaid debts, was out over a million dollars, more than several years' earnings. I had agreed to be the personal guarantor on all obligations that HotelTech International acquired, and bills continued to come in long after Susan left for Los Angeles with my blessing—indeed, my encouragement.

Susan and I had made a stab at counseling when things first got rocky, not long after our marriage. But after only two sessions I approached the psychiatrist in a private one-on-one, hoping to skip the psychobabble and get some direct advice about what he thought I should do.

"All right," he said. "Here is my advice. Run! Run as fast and as far as you can!"

I told Susan I wanted no more of her verbal abuse, hot temper, and relentless greed. We agreed that a year was enough unhappiness and she moved to Los Angeles where she had no trouble finding employment with an upscale supplier of fine fabric. I learned from our mutual friend, Jan, that within a matter of months, Susan had persuaded her new boss to marry her as soon as I could get our dissolution finalized. She then persuaded him to launch a hostile takeover of the company for which they both worked. Miraculously, but not surprisingly, given Susan's incredible talent and greed, they won control of the company. Their success was short-lived, however, owing to what Jan described as Susan's outrageous demands for a monthly salary so high it soon put their new company out of business. I'm sure she would deny much of this and I only know what Jan told me.

In summary, I see Susan as a woman who left a trail of debt and wreckage in her wake. The last time I saw her was when she showed up at a well-publicized book-launch party at the Century Club in New

York City, hosted by my good friend, Michael Cooper. I had invited the Weschlers (friends from John Gardiner's Tennis Ranch), not realizing they were still in contact with Susan and might bring her with them. I greeted her coldly, so she attached herself to my son for the night. Jay was too nice to give her the cold shoulder.

At the end, I had to accept that I had lived for nearly half a century and still knew nothing about women. An even darker analysis was now unavoidable: the intuitive trial lawyer, who was said to be able to see into the mind of a witness on the stand during cross-examination, was unable to see inside his own head when it came to the opposite sex. It was more than a matter of making poor choices. There was something seriously lacking in me.

I not only had a second failed marriage on my record but was also deeply in debt, saved from bankruptcy only by loans from friends and an understanding banker. It took me several years to dig out.

## Sherry

> You ask me to unmask you
> I know you really want me to
> But I guess I'm just not strong enough
> To save both me and you.
> —"Unwanted Child" (1975)

After Susan, I took a year off from dating before eventually connecting with a woman who appeared to be stable and independent, having raised four boys as a single mother.

Sherry (her real name) and I met at a museum, and, after exchanging a few words, decided to have dinner together the following night. We shared a love of movies and all forms of music and slipped effortlessly into a relationship. She was employed by the Kohl Corporation in their accounting department, but I was able to get her an introduction and, eventually, an improved position, at the Bank of America executive offices.

Although independent, Sherry betrayed early signs of insecurity. She enjoyed sex but it wasn't high on her list of priorities, and we were more friends than lovers, much like my relationship with Alecia. She made few demands, but I began to see that despite her courageous history as a single parent, she was seriously lacking in self-confidence, mainly concerning her appearance. Although I tried to talk her out of it, she insisted, for example, on having her upper thighs liposuctioned at the hands of a San Francisco cosmetic surgeon whose incompetence nearly killed her.

Without telling me, Sherry scheduled the procedure and drove to the doctor's office in her own car, possibly not warned that she should have somebody pick her up afterward. She lost a great deal of blood during the procedure and was nearly unconscious when she called me to come drive her home. She was pale and looked as if she might pass out any minute. I suggested we go to the hospital but she refused. I took her to her home, and several days passed before she regained sufficient strength to get up and return to work. In addition to the trauma she'd suffered, the liposuction had created deep, unsightly grooves, cosmetically destroying her thighs.

I told her I would sue the doctor on her behalf, but I later learned how these doctors worked together to protect themselves. Before her surgery, she was required to sign away her rights to a trial and submit any claims or complaints to a "board of physicians." This procedure essentially required her to accept, as her sole remedy, surgical repair under the supervision of the consortium of doctors to which her doctor belonged. A different, admittedly respectable, surgeon tried to repair the job under proper medical circumstances, but Sherry was never the same, and neither were her legs. Worse, her frail self-confidence about her appearance was further damaged.

Sherry's problems were above my competence, but sympathy compelled my continuing loyalty. We spent another six or seven months together, but it wasn't an easy time for either of us.

Our breakup occurred in Paris, at an American College of Trial Lawyers conference. I had told her how important it was that I appear at the opening cocktail party to "work the tables" on behalf of my law firm, which was bearing the expense of the trip for the two of us. When it came time to dress for the party, however, she kept stalling, apparently obsessing over her appearance. I finally had to go to the cocktail party alone, and I realized that this would be my life with Sherry. She didn't want the relationship to continue either, and we tearfully parted as friends. We drifted apart but stayed loosely in touch for several years. About ten years later, Sherry died of breast cancer. She was a troubled person who gave her young adult life to the care and nurturing of her boys and who deserved better from life than she got. Sherry was a good woman.

## Olivia

> Your words stood there like an undertaker
> At the back door of my pain.
> You're a blue moody lady and I am just a fool
> About to come in out of the rain.
> —"Blue Moody Lady" (1977)

My year with Olivia was well spent. For one thing, she helped me understand at last what had probably been plain to my friends for years and should have been obvious to me. I was being largely motivated in my selection of partners by physical beauty and the promise of great, enduring sex.

Olivia was twenty-eight years old—more than twenty years younger than I—a model, and by anyone's standards, a beautiful woman. She was also a skilled dancer and an athlete who brought her physical dexterity into the bedroom. I sometimes wondered whether I could possibly satisfy her sexual appetite, but I need not have been concerned, for she created in me an equally eager partner. She did this in a variety of ways, employing creativity, physicality, and acting skills. One night early in our relationship, for example, she showed up at my door dressed as a teenage cheerleader, playing the part expertly and staying in character, even when we were in bed: "Oh, Mister, what are you *doing*?"

Two nights later, she might appear in full nurse's regalia, complete with stethoscope.

"Please lie still Mr. Martel, this will just take a minute. Oh, my goodness, *Mr. Martel*!" Over the course of our year together, Olivia tapped into dozens of male sexual fantasies.

Regrettably, the relationship ended badly, mainly because Olivia was pathologically jealous, constantly applying her considerable creativity to imagining mischief I might have been up to whenever we weren't together. Given our age difference, I hardly had the energy—let alone the time—for sex outside the relationship, even if that were my style. Time after time I was able to use my courtroom skills to prove her wrong in her bizarre imaginings, and on each occasion, she would profusely apologize—until the next time. I began to realize that Olivia suffered from a deep insecurity and that our relationship, fatally lacking in trust, could never work.

When I finally faced this reality and told her goodbye, she took my decision as proof I had been cheating on her all along, looking for an "older, more suitable marriage partner." She was only partly wrong, of course, and our parting was deeply sad for both of us. Yet, as I look back, I'm exceedingly grateful for the year I had with Olivia, who, despite her insecurity, had a good heart and a generous nature. And, as I said about Julie—my companion when I was a young man in the Air Force—every man should be fortunate enough to have an Olivia in his life at least once.

## Postscript: Lauren Bacall

Betty Joan Perske (Lauren's friends called her Betty) was born on September 16, 1924. Although I never came close to dating her, Lauren Bacall deserves mention here because she was one of the most fascinating women I've ever met.

I came to know Betty by virtue of my friendship with Dave Amis. You may recall that I met Dave in the Air Force, and we remained close friends till the day he died. I was best man in Dave and Susan's wedding, and one of their children grew up to be the actress, Suzy Amis.

In 1986, Suzy Amis married Sam Robards, son of Jason Robards and Lauren Bacall. As an unofficial member of the Amis family, I attended the wedding, the rehearsal dinner, and the reception. Lauren had, by that time, divorced Jason, but both were in attendance, and she and I were put up in the same hotel by the Amis family, three days before the wedding. My first direct contact with her was when we were waiting together outside the hotel for a van sent to pick up the two of us and one other hotel guest and drive us to the rehearsal dinner.

Lauren and I introduced ourselves—she called herself Betty, which I took as permission to do the same—and began awaiting the arrival of the third dinner guest, who was scheduled to ride with us. If I was expecting Betty to be glamorous and likeable, I would be disappointed. Instead, I learned a bit about her irascible nature when the van arrived. As soon as we were seated, she instructed the driver to leave.

"But there's another guest coming, Betty," I objected. "We should wait for him."

"Here's what I say about waiting," she pronounced in her theatrical manner. "I say, *fuck it!*"

She then turned toward the driver and said, "Drive, dammit."

He drove. Betty was in her fifties when I first met her. She had not lost her smoldering beauty and could be totally charming and witty or incredibly bleak and mean-spirited. Here's an example: We were together again in the late eighties in New York at a party at her suite at the famous Dakota Building. I was going with Sherry at the time and, along with friends Dave and Susan Amis, we met the unescorted Betty for dinner. Sherry was relatively young and very attractive with her long and lush red hair—and Betty instantly disliked her. She picked on Sherry throughout one of the most awkward dinners I've ever failed to enjoy. Whenever Sherry dared to speak up, Betty found a way to put her down, using phrases such as, "Oh, Sherry, wake up and come to the *pahty.*" I tried in vain to defend Sherry and to control Betty, but that would have taken a Humphrey Bogart, and I was clearly no Bogey.

Her petulant nature aside, Betty could be incredibly charming and carried with her a cinematic history that she wore with the charming arrogance of royalty. Having grown up on "Bogey and Bacall" movies, this kid from Modesto was always a little bit in awe and had trouble staying angry with Betty. I wish I had been able to tell her goodbye.

Betty Joan Perske died in her Dakota apartment on August 12, 2014.

— — —

Summing up, I eventually learned that, like a dog running in circles chasing his tail, I was getting nowhere toward satisfying my impossible criteria and was mainly seeking in every new relationship that which I had found most lacking in the previous one. And then, despite my clumsy efforts, I was about to get lucky.

## Chapter 24

## Finding *The One* at Last—Bonnie Laird Martel

> She . . . slayed the dragons always chasin' after me
> Said our souls would always blend, we'd be together
> to the end.
> —"Bonnie's Song" (2016)

ONCE AGAIN, TIMING IS everything, and nowhere is this more important than in the quest for a permanent loving relationship. For a truly successful coupling to work, both partners have to be "ready," and this implies several considerations.

In my case, I had to be prepared and willing to candidly present myself to another person as I was, which required achieving a certain degree of self-awareness and introspection. I also had to be able to see and accept the other person as they were, not as a corporeal dream fantasy, although that was difficult when it came to beautiful, blue-eyed Bonnie Laird. Finally, readiness was also a function of what I had learned—often the hard way—from previous relationships.

What had I learned? Very little, I'm afraid, as you saw from the series of relationships summarized in the previous chapter. I could blame the Catholic Church or bad luck or growing up in a movie theater with romanticized notions of love, but if you're still with me, you've figured out—well before I did—that I was making the age-old error of mistaking lust for love. Yes, the sex would be good—for a while—but this transitory carnality only temporarily masked the other 80 percent of what it takes to make a relationship work: things like compassion, warmth, empathy, shared interests, a sense of humor, a commitment to growth, a natural curiosity, a mutual enjoyment of travel, a sense of self, and appreciation of the possibility of adventure in even the smallest endeavors—to list just a few.

I finally met a woman with all these virtues (including that lust thing that had hung me up for over thirty years) and the beauty of it was, I didn't even have to look for her.

She found me. I'll explain.

> Fall in love as many times as it takes.
> —John Krasinski

I first met Bonnie Laird in 1987 while having lunch with friends Barbara Horscraft and Chris Shaw at the Crow's Nest restaurant in Santa Cruz. Bonnie was there with friends, seated at a table next to ours. Barbara, Chris, and I were celebrating the completed project titled *Split*, a feature film written by and starring Chris, produced by Barbara, and featuring me and others in lesser roles.

Barbara knew Bonnie and introduced us to each other. We then resumed our private discussions, but I was seated near enough to the other table to overhear that Bonnie was a paralegal, working for Bob Popelka, an acquaintance of mine. I was also close enough to be attracted by her natural beauty and poise. I asked her to give my regards to Bob and handed her my business card. That's as far as it went because I was still in a relationship with Olivia at the time, albeit one that was fading fast, but one to which I still owed loyalty.

## The Nature of Coincidence

Bonnie and I were eventually brought back together by a coincidence. "Coincidence" has been defined as a situation in which unrelated events come together at the same time without planning. It's fashionable for cops and tough private detectives in movies and books to say, "I don't believe in coincidence," but coincidences occur all the time, though we barely notice them unless they have an impact that shakes the foundation of our everyday existence.

I often wonder about the relationship between coincidence and fate (sometimes called "destiny" or "Providence"). Consider this hypothetical: a woman is given a copy of a current legal thriller by her roommate, who assumes she might be interested because the woman is a paralegal. The woman is indeed interested, but not just because the story involves law—rather because several of the characters are cancer victims and the woman is, herself, a recent cancer survivor. She is emotionally moved by the author's portrayal of the victims' suffering. When she reaches the end of the book, she sees the photo of the author and realizes they met in a restaurant a year before, when they were both in other relationships. She takes several months to gather the courage to call the author at his home.

This was a first for me, not to mention a pleasant surprise once I remembered who the caller was, for I, too, was now on my own. I offered to meet for brunch. The woman was Bonnie Laird, of course, and we have been happily married for thirty years.

Was it just a coincidence that the author wrote a book about cancer victims and the woman who read the book was a cancer survivor? Probably so, for coincidence is simply the fortuitous and simultaneous occurrence of unrelated events— in this case, the book's theme and the woman's medical history.

It was fate however, not coincidence, for the couple to meet and end up spending their lives together, because fate is a function of positive action by the people involved, resulting in an event that's relatable to that action. After the initiating coincidence, it was the woman's courage in calling the author at home and the author's openness to meeting with her that brought them together.

The novel in question was my first legal thriller, *Partners.* When you think of your own life, imagine how the slightest alteration in steps you took anywhere along the way could have (and probably did), completely and materially alter your life, your job, or your romantic relationships.

Upon seeing Bonnie in the restaurant at our brunch date the next morning, it all came back to me in a rush—how could I have forgotten those beautiful blue eyes? By the end of brunch, I knew I wanted to know her better. We agreed to meet for lunch the next day at the Crow's Nest, the site of our original encounter, where I learned she was about to leave for Paris with her roommate, Moira. I was both elated and disappointed, for I was smitten and wanted to spend time with her. A lot more time.

Bonnie had mentioned being a friend of Curtis Copple, who was also a friend of mine. Perhaps having learned something about due diligence from the relationships described earlier, I dialed Curt's number, eager to maintain perspective for a change and maybe learn more about this woman before diving in too deep. Curt had nothing but praise for Bonnie, describing her as a quality person. I was ready to take the next step, and the courtship was on.

I scored points by sending roses to Bonnie's hotel room in Paris, and when she returned, it was clear we had missed each other. I persuaded her to spend a day with me at my summer home, River House, in Ben Lomond, an hour and a half south of San Francisco. We sunbathed on the patio, and it became even more obvious that the attraction was mutual. For me, it wasn't just her looks. Bonnie, for example, had raised her son, Jeff, as a single parent, and was never long without a job to ensure their support. That manifest responsibility had always been a major plus for me, and I was pleased to be able to check off independence and self-reliance. Yes, I had a checklist (given my checkered history with women), but my immediate feelings of true attraction to Bonnie, as a whole person, rendered checking a list of attributes unnecessary.

As the sun went down, we both suspected what was about to happen, so Bonnie felt compelled to tell me she was in recent remission from lymphoma. I pointed out the obvious: that I was considerably older, and it was highly unlikely I would outlive her. The duty of full disclosure having been satisfied by both of us, we went upstairs and fell into each other's arms.

I was still working in San Francisco and living in nearby Sausalito. Although I held on to the Sausalito home for three more years (until 2000), the house eventually became nothing more than a crash pad, a place to sleep when I worked at my San Francisco office during the week. I eagerly looked forward to Fridays when I would return to River House and the woman with whom I was falling in love.

Although separated during the week, we got to know each other in a hurry. I learned, for example, that Bonnie was a romantic and a fan of Turner Classic Movies. She has watched every movie starring Cary Grant and Katharine Hepburn at least three times, and particularly enjoyed musical comedies and romances from the forties. She will hate me for revealing this, but she will also go to an animated fairy tale movie by herself if she can't find a grandchild to accompany her. Our own fairy-tale romance came true when the beautiful princess kissed a frog.

Within two weeks, I was deeply in love, and I invited Bonnie to fly to Santa Barbara with me for a Masters Track & Field meet. The trip proved to be disastrous and fortuitous at the same time. Disastrous because I crushed my foot during warm-up, and fortuitous because I was able to use my injury to persuade Bonnie to move in with me to provide care until I could walk again. She rapidly converted River House into a home.

## Our Wedding

It's challenging to be humble when describing our wedding on February 12, 1994. The ceremony took place in the Presbyterian church in Sausalito, a fairy-tale setting in the hills overlooking San Francisco Bay. The church was packed with guests, a substantial number of whom have told us it was the best wedding they ever attended. Episcopal minister William "Buzz" Nern, whom I met while serving on the board of the Homeless Sanctuary he presided over, was our officiant. We were able to rent the famous Alta Mira ballroom across the street for dinner and a reception.

The theme of our wedding was love and music. Bonnie's son, Jeff, was her "maid of honor," and my son and daughter, Jay and Melissa, were my "best men." Bonnie's mother and father were bursting with happiness in the front row, but my mother was in a home in Modesto and too ill to travel. My father was too dead to caution me that I needed another marriage like I needed water in my shoes, and he wasn't missed. I persuaded three background singers from my earlier recording days to sing some romantic tunes during the ceremony. Bonnie looked beautiful in her cream-colored wedding gown, with a crown of roses in her hair, as she sashayed down the aisle to "It Had To Be You," which I sang and recorded for the occasion. Later, I accompanied myself on grand piano and sang my original composition, "The Wedding Song." (Give it a listen on Joe Silverhound's YouTube channel.)

We exchanged our personalized vows and then entered our joyous and loving new life as man and wife. Our love has deepened over the thirty years we've been together. Only our television interests have grown in different directions—I'm a news junkie and Bonnie avoids it—but since we have five television sets in our house, this isn't a problem.

## A Double Bonus

One of the many unique joys that my relationship with Bonnie brings to my life is the total love and acceptance she's earned from my son and daughter, their children, and the entire Martel clan. She loves them all, too, as if they were all her own flesh and blood. The family joke is that she personally clothes not only her husband but his children and grandchildren, as well. No holiday goes by without thoughtful gifts.

Bonnie is the most caring person I've ever known. I wish I had a dollar for every time I've heard her ask a friend or acquaintance, "What can I do to help?" And no matter how busy she is helping other people, she always has time to answer my many needs, particularly now that my balance, coordination, and strength are compromised by Parkinson's, as well as a shoulder and hand weakened by arthritis. Bonnie, without reservation, is here for me with unending love and tenderness. And I'm deeply grateful.

It runs against my macho nature to have to ask my wife to open a bottle for me, help me button a shirt, bring in firewood, or a hundred other tasks I've always considered the role of the husband to perform. It astonishes me that Bonnie has never demonstrated a single instance of resentment at my frequent demands. But even that is not the most amazing thing about my wife. No matter how unworthy I deem myself to be, she constantly demonstrates undying love for her battered and weakened shell of a husband, and she does it in a way that's thoroughly convincing.

Even when I'm hard-pressed at times to love myself, I have never once doubted Bonnie's love for me.

As for my love for her, my words cannot begin to do it justice. I think the best way to describe my love for Bonnie and how she's changed my life is to borrow the lyrics to "Bonnie's Song," which I wrote for her birthday in 2016. I will then reveal a letter I wrote to her on the eve of my brain surgery that she had never seen until she read a draft of this memoir.

First, the lyrics to "Bonnie's Song."

## "Bonnie's Song"

Every now and then I see, all the crazy things I was doin' to me
Too busy playin' to the crowd, always thinkin' out loud
Runnin' too fast to do the things that really mattered
to the people close to me
I couldn't see my soul was scattered
No I couldn't see, I just couldn't see

    That I was driven mostly livin' my life upside down
    Lookin' back at me in the mirror was a sad-eyed clown
    Lookin' for love in painted empty faces
    Like that guy in the song, lookin' in all the wrong places
    Sure I won all of my cases but my brain was nearly toast
    Sure I won a lot of races
    except the one that mattered most (till)

She . . . slayed the dragons always chasin' after me, held me so
tenderly
Even I began to see, that
She . . . slayed the dragons always chasin' after me
Said our souls would always blend, we'd be together to the end

    Yeah, she slayed those dragons like a friendly assassin
    Who saw my years were amassin' and my chances were
    passin'
    She said you can shake all you need to, forsake it if you need
    to
    Break it if you need to
    It won't get us down
    We'll just leave the ground
    At the speed of sound
    And just fly away.

She's strong as steel, yet gentle as a breeze
And her love is real, it brought him to his knees
He reached in his pocket, hoped she'd be pleased
And she took the ring he offered and they made a solemn pact
She said: give me the time you got left and we'll never look back
And we never looked back, no, we never looked back

He saw she's kind and pretty and she's pretty damned smart
And the way she looks at him nearly breaks his heart
And though she's wise and cool, she married that fool whose
life was speeding by in a hazy blur
But he was ready for love, he was ready for her 'cause

She ... slayed the dragons always chasin' after me, held me so
tenderly
Even I began to see, that
She ... slayed the dragons always chasin' after me
Said our souls would always blend, we'd be together to the end

Yeah, that girl would learn to fly, to guide the birds south
She would rescue a dog that was foaming at the mouth
So what d'ya think she would do now, what d'ya think she
would do
For a dog like me?

She's my soul sister nobody can resist her
I'm so glad I didn't miss her, thank God she let me kiss her
She's my best friend, all my troubles she can mend
I'll love her to the end, to the very very end

'Cause she's the one, all my searchin' is done
My very best years, have just begun

321

So what are you gonna do to thank a woman like that now?
What are you gonna do to thank a woman like that?
(Well . . .)
You love her with everything good you got left in your heart,
all day long
You testify to the lady that you'll never part, and you write
her a song
You write her this song ('cause)

She . . .slayed the dragons always chasin' after me
I'll love her endlessly (the way that) She . . .loves . . .me.

An amateurish recording of a rough live performance of this song (I
was five years into Parkinson's at the time), recorded by Bonnie on her
iPhone in our living room, is available on YouTube.

— — —

In closing, here is the letter I wrote to Bonnie the day before I went
into brain surgery for my Parkinson's disease at the age of eighty-six.
I was the oldest person UCSF had dared to perform this operation
on and, according to my surgeon, Dr. Paul Larson, I was probably the
oldest person in the world to receive the surgery. People were naturally
apprehensive—including the surgeon and the patient. Here is the letter,
left where it would—in time—be found.

May 3, 2017

My Dearest Little Honey:

I'll be brief, as you will hopefully never see these words. I am, however, an old dog and one can't be too careful. So, this precautionary note.

Thank you. Thank you for a quarter century of joy and happiness beyond my wildest dreams. I love you more than anyone has ever loved. You are not only the best wife and soulmate in the world, but the best person I have ever been privileged to know. I am unworthy, but grateful for your love and caring.

You are still young and beautiful. Don't grieve long for me. Don't be alone. Seek and find the happiness you deserve.

Love forever,

Your Big Honey

## Chapter 25

## Travels with Bonnie

> I know you like a book from beginning to end
> I am your lover and you know
> I'll always be your friend
> It's good to see you again
> —"Survivor" (1977)

IT's A BIT OF a cliché to say that sharing the experience of travel with friends or family maximizes the joy. Most of my early travels before I met Bonnie were solo, ranging from short trips to Mexico to those wild adventures in Pamplona, Spain; staying in a youth hostel in Mykonos at age forty; and hanging out alone in Paris, the Fiji Islands, and Australia. They were interesting trips, often exciting, but more often lonely.

This chapter is about the magic of traveling with a woman I was getting to know and with whom I was falling in love.

> Venice is like eating an entire box of chocolate liqueurs in one go.
> —Truman Capote

On September 2, 1993, in love and living together but still single, Bonnie and I took our first foreign trip together, destination Italy. Although this is a memoir, not a travelogue, I must dwell on this trip in some detail because of the far-reaching consequences it had on my life.

We agreed to start our trip in Venice, and on the advice of my friend and travel agent, George Lippi, I made reservations at the luxurious Gritti Palace on the Main Canal. Our excitement grew, with maybe also a little anxiety, as we approached our departure date. On the day before, without discussing it, Bonnie took charge of packing for the trip and I was delighted to be relieved of the burden, especially when I saw how efficient she was.

We arrived in Venice after a pleasant flight and were efficiently transferred to a water taxi that took us to the front deck of the Gritti Palace, overlooking the Grand Canal. Later, we took a late afternoon walk around the picturesque Piazza San Marco and enjoyed coffee in one of the outdoor cafés. We soon became hungry and were treated to our first genuine Italian cuisine at the Al Teatro restaurant, where we were serenaded by street music.

After three days of falling in love with Venice and even more in love with each other, we rented a car and drove to Sirmione, Portofino, San Gimignano, Siena, Florence, and, finally, Rome. I had an expert plan each location based on its romantic ambiance. It had been one of those rare trips where absolutely nothing went wrong and everything turned out even better than expected. The highlight of the adventure was a little cliffside village called Positano, soon to become my favorite place in the world (other than River House in Ben Lomond), located on Southern Italy's Amalfi Coast, thirty-seven miles south of Naples, with the Lattari Mountains on one side and the shimmering waters of the Mediterranean on the other. Shops and cafés lined the picturesque streets. We often walked or ran (I was in training) the 560 steps down a steep and narrow stairway from our hotel to enjoy a beautiful white beach. There in Positano, the sun had never felt so bright, and I know now, looking back, that this was probably because Bonnie's love was at my side. In the early evenings, we sat on the same beach, holding hands, listening to live music. I can't remember being more in love.

Yet another virtue of Positano was its proximity (only a short thirty-minute boat ride) to Capri, where Bonnie and I spent a romantic day at a secret beach, its location revealed to me by Jeremiah Tower, an internationally famous chef and owner of Stars, San Francisco's hottest restaurant in the eighties and early nineties. Jeremiah was also a client, and when I told him Bonnie and I were about to leave for Italy, he gave us directions, scrawled on a Stars' napkin, to a clothing-optional beach rendezvous on Capri, known only to a privileged few: dukes, models, movie stars, entertainment executives, ranking politicians, and other glamorous expatriates. He and other insiders wanted to keep it exclusive and he swore us to secrecy.

After several days of enjoying Tuscan cities and Michelangelo's unforgettable *David* in Florence, we reluctantly concluded our first European trip in Rome, where I had been once before. We stayed at the Hotel Gregoriana near the Spanish Steps, and once settled, I had the joy of introducing Bonnie to the Sistine Chapel, the Colosseum, and the Trevi Fountain. As we walked from one historical site to another, I briefly wondered why it felt like I was enjoying the sights of Rome for the first time. One look at Bonnie's wide-open, gorgeous blue eyes made the answer obvious.

After four days, we reluctantly bid goodbye to Rome, but such was our love of the experience we shared that we returned twenty-five years later and stayed at the same small Hotel Gregoriana. Bonnie had brought a photo of herself and the clerk from our first visit, and amazingly had another picture taken with the same clerk who had, after all this time, become the manager. He smiled and upgraded us to the bridal suite.

Mark Twain was correct when he said that traveling with a person is also the best way to find out how you really feel about them, and our trip convinced me I wanted to marry Bonnie and spend the rest of my life with her. Shortly after we settled back home at River House, I took her to dinner at the romantic Shadowbrook Restaurant, followed by a stroll down to the Capitola Wharf, situated on the beautiful Monterey Bay, where I quickly popped the question. Good trial lawyers know you never ask a witness a question without already knowing the answer. Accordingly, I wasn't surprised when she got over her shock and said yes. We were married two months later on February 13, 1994.

Between 1994 and 1998, I served on the Board of Regents of the American College of Trial Lawyers, and it became my solemn duty to frequently travel expense-free with Bonnie for conferences to beautiful places like Rome, Paris, and London. These were all marvelous experiences, meeting bright, interesting people, sometimes seated with dinner mates like Supreme Court Justices O'Connor and Ginsburg. (Bonnie and I agreed that Justice O'Connor was charming and engaging. I couldn't get much out of the taciturn Justice Ginsburg but admired her greatly.)

One of our most memorable experiences occurred during a Mediterranean cruise in 2005. The ship left the port of Sicily (following our second visit to Venice) bound for Barcelona, and at around ten that night, the captain's voice boomed over the loudspeaker.

"I have a special treat for you tonight," he said. "As you can see from the north deck, the volcano on Stromboli is in full eruption. I'm going to get us in as close as I can."

Bonnie and I were already at the rail taking in the dangerous beauty of the flames bursting from Stromboli when the captain's voice was replaced by Plácido Domingo's, singing "Granada"—one of my favorite arias. The combination of sight and sound was overwhelmingly romantic and unforgettable. Just when it couldn't get any better, it did, as Bonnie fell into my arms and we shared our love for one another.

Our ship later stopped at eight ports of call (in addition to Italy and Barcelona), each one so spectacular we returned years later to several of them. Even more important than the destinations was my pleasure in sharing them with Bonnie.

We were destined to take many trips together over the next thirty years, connecting with my Irish heritage in County Mayo, Ireland, in 1996; several trips to Paris with side trips by Eurail to Giverny and Claude Monet's famous Water Garden (proving with each trip that Audrey Hepburn was right when she famously said, "Paris is always a good idea"); a Southeast Asia adventure to Hong Kong, Vietnam, Cambodia and Thailand in 2018; and a tour of the Greek Islands in 2018, followed by our final trip to Rome with visits to the amazing Galleria Borghese and a remarkable performance of *La Tosca* on our last night. I remember glancing unnoticed at Bonnie's sweet face during the opera and thinking to myself I would never have dreamed I would find a love so deep and secure.

Summing up our journeys together, Bonnie was happy to be introduced to foreign travel, and I was happy to have found someone I loved to share it with me. It was clear from our first trip that Bonnie and I were born to travel together, hand in hand, down the road of life.

## Chapter 26

# Another Hurdle—A Senior Citizen Returns to the Cinders

> Kings and priests keep looking for the door
> To Rosetta and her magic stone
> Well guess who got inside one night while dreaming free
> I found her sitting there all alone, watching late TV
> Just like you and me.
> —"Just Like You and Me" (1975)

I'VE ALREADY MENTIONED HOW my plan of participating in the University of Oregon's famous track-and-field program under coach Bill Bowerman was frustrated by the advent of the Korean War. Then, when I was discharged from the Air Force nearly five years later, having only two summer sessions remaining until graduation, I assumed my athletic career, such as it was, was finished.

In my early sixties, however, I began attending weekly open track meets in nearby Los Gatos to watch my daughter Melissa, a star runner, compete in the 1500 meter. I noticed several athletes who appeared to be my age, and Melissa explained that they were participating in an international program called Masters Track & Field.

This intrigued me, so I dusted off an ancient pair of track shoes and the following week ran my first 100 meter hurdle race in nearly forty years. Not surprisingly, I was easily defeated in the 60–65 age group by a man I later came to know as Marion Sanchez, one of the fastest sprinters and hurdlers in our age group. Undaunted by continuing weekly defeats, I was determined to get faster and improve my hurdling technique, and soon began participating in meets all around California, representing the Santa Cruz Track Club.

Though I began to improve, I continued to be defeated by Sanchez and another Masters star, Jim Stookey, whenever we competed together. The defeats taught me I had a long way to go to regain my hurdle form and rhythm, and I began more rigorous training during the next off season—at least two hours a day at nearby Henry Cowell Redwoods State Park. My goal was to someday compete in the US Nationals. My fantasy was to win a medal there.

But hurdling at the age of sixty presented physical challenges—mainly a torn hamstring and strained calf muscles—that proved daunting even for my ingenious massage therapist, Dr. Norm Crandell. In addition, I was also still working full-time at my law firm. Between Norm's good care, however, and the patience of my indulgent girlfriend, Bonnie, I regularly competed throughout the year 1990.

In 1991, however, I suffered a catastrophic injury—a "Lisfranc fracture"—while warming up before a Santa Barbara Masters meet. My foot came down hard on a piece of steel I didn't notice sticking out on the track. The pain was horrific and I was rushed to a doctor. My lead surgeon later explained that the injury was named after Dr. Lisfranc, a French battlefield physician who treated Napoleon's troops during their winter advance on Russia in 1812. Soldiers often suffered dropped cannonballs on their feet in the freezing weather, crushing the metatarsal bones, ligaments, and soft tissue. In the most serious cases, amputation was required.

After a complicated and lengthy surgery, in which a team of doctors rebuilt my foot—reattaching the main tendons to the metatarsal bones and then securing their work with screws—I was told I probably would be able to walk soon and, with luck, be able to jog some day and perhaps even play doubles tennis. Hurdling, they said, was out of the question. But you know me with challenges.

I began physical therapy sessions almost immediately, focusing on the stationary bicycle at first, then later the elliptical trainer. It was during this time that Bonnie moved in to River House and took such loving care of me. After missing two years of competition, I was back on the track in 1993, performing poorly but improving with each race. By 1994, I was running my personal best times again in the 100 meter hurdles, and entered the US Nationals, scheduled to be held at Hayward Field at the University of Oregon in Eugene.

The irony wasn't lost on me. The University at Eugene was where, at the age of twenty, my dream of track stardom had been dashed by the advent of the Korean War. How poetic it would be if the dream were to be rekindled at the same place forty years later. Had my time finally come?

Reality began to set in early in the day when I noticed that my friend and nemesis, Marion Sanchez, was entered. And, although I qualified for the finals, my heat was won not by Sanchez but by Phil Mulkey, a silver medalist at the Pan American Games in 1959 and at the 1960 USA Outdoor Track and Field Championships. Had I once again been guilty of exalting hope over reality? No, dammit, this was going to be my day.

"Come to your marks, get set, GO!"

I had a great start and saw I was running practically side by side with both Sanchez and Mulkey for the first 80 meters, approaching the tenth and final hurdle. But I realized I was coming up short on tired legs and it would be necessary to alternate my lead leg over the last hurdle, taking four steps instead of three between the ninth and tenth barriers. I led with my left foot instead of my usual right and watched both Sanchez and Mulkey surge farther ahead of me. Distracted, I struck the last hurdle and went down hard, then half skidded and crawled the remaining short distance to the finish line, desperately hoping to score a bronze medal for third place.

Sanchez won, the cocky Mulkey took second, and alas, I finished out of the money and instead of a medal, settled for a bucket of ice for a badly sprained ankle.

Later, at the Santa Cruz Track Club's year-end annual banquet, I was nevertheless named the team's Athlete of the Year and presented with the broken top of a real hurdle, inscribed with the words, "Next time, John, get over all ten!"

The following year, 1995, the Masters World Championships were to be held in Buffalo, New York, so I took advantage of the opportunity and registered for both the 100 meter high hurdles and the 400 meter lows. The location also presented an opportunity to spend some time with my son, Jay, who was still living in New York City. The multiple qualifying heats for two hurdle events over a two-day period proved demanding in the hot July weather, but I qualified for the finals in both events. Sadly, I sprained an old hamstring injury on the first hurdle in the finals of the 400 meter hurdles and was therefore forced to withdraw from the finals of the 100 meter highs, which was won by Mulkey in the excellent time of 16.71. At least I got to spend time with my son.

I had promised Bonnie that 1995 would be my last year, but she realized my frustration over New York and graciously granted me another year. The early months of training went well, and I remained injury-free, winning several races around the state. When I learned the USA National Masters Track & Field Championship was to be held in nearby San Jose in 1997, I begged for and was granted another reprieve from Bonnie and commenced cautious, but demanding, training. By June, I was running my personal bests in most of the races I entered. I'd worked hard after my injury to get one more shot at the national gold medal, and I vowed to give it my all.

When the day of the National Championship finally arrived, however, my optimism was challenged when I saw that both Sanchez and Stookey, the 1996 Masters Athlete of the Year, had registered, and that both had qualified for the finals. Sanchez was fresh off successfully defending his world title two weeks before at the World Masters Championships in Durban, South Africa.

Marion and I shook hands at the starting line, which did little to diminish the tension in the air. Even Stookey looked nervous, but I doubted his heart was pounding like mine. It felt like a bird trying to peck its way out of my chest. My bleak thoughts were interrupted by the starter's summons.

"*Gentlemen!* Come to your marks."

His voice awakened me to the reality that it was the last time I would ever hear those words in competition. *So make it a good one*, I told myself.

"Get set . . . *BAM!*"

Was that the gun going off or my heart finally exploding in my chest? It must have been the former, because I recall my legs churning toward the first hurdle. I had a good start, but both my body and brain immediately went on automatic pilot and I was only vaguely aware during the first 50 meters that nobody was in front of me. I was in "the zone" so everything else was a blur, but thanks to a fan with a camera seated in the vicinity of the seventh hurdle, I can piece together where the race stood with less than half the distance and only three hurdles remaining.

The photograph (see center section) shows the race was very close at that point, practically a dead heat. I'm shown in lane six, clearing the seventh hurdle with my lead leg about to return to the track. To my left was Sanchez in lane three, and out of the picture but not out of the race was Stookey, several feet behind me. It was anybody's race and could be mine—if I was just able to do what I'd never done before: maintain my three-step rhythm the rest of the way and, most importantly, get over the last hurdle.

I did both, but I recall having to stretch to clear that final hurdle and then—with the finish line in view—telling myself nobody was going to keep me from crossing it first, neither Sanchez nor Stookey, nor even my foot surgeon telling me "no more hurdling!" Screw all of them. This was my day.

And I was running for my life.

The rest is history—a history of good luck, victory, and redemption, ably captured by a reporter for the monthly *National Masters News* in January 1998:

## John Martel—
## His Biggest Hurdle Was Not on the Track

John Martel of the Santa Cruz Track Club had to defeat 1997 WAVA champion Marion Sanchez and Jim Stookey, 1996 Masters Men's Athlete of the Year, to win the M65 national championship in the 100m hurdles at the 1997 Masters Championships in San Jose. He had never defeated either of them in six years of competition as a masters athlete.

But that's not the story.

In 1991, at the end of his first year of competition as a master, Martel suffered a *LisFranc* foot injury at the Club West Meet in Santa Barbara, Calif. His team of surgeons described the injury as an "exploded foot." It was so shattered that they had to put his left foot under a fluoroscope and then reconstruct his right foot using his left as a model before drilling and inserting metal to hold what was left of his metatarsal bones together and re-attach them to the main major arch tendon. He was told he might be able to jog again, perhaps even play doubles tennis.

## Breaking the "Bad" News

Before he came off crutches seven months later, Martel began work on a stationary bicycle and broke the bad news to his wife that he would be making a comeback after a year of convalescence. Not in doubles tennis, not in racewalking or a throwing event. He would run the high hurdles. Once off the crutches, he began a training program consisting of the stationary bike, Stairmaster, and weights.

In 1993, he did come back, and by 1994 was cruising for a silver medal in the Nationals at Eugene when he hit the last hurdle, badly spraining his left ankle and crawling across the finish line for fourth place. His 1995 and 1996 years were plagued with hamstring and plantar fasciitis injuries, though he was running close to his 1991 personal best of 17.6.

His workout regimen during the '96 season consisted of weights and running in a redwood grove near his home in the Santa Cruz Mountains in California, plus hurdle drills with teammate M40 Don Roberts and workouts with the SCTC. He interspersed 400m "sprints" on soft ground with high-skipping and other plyometric drills.

"Running the hurdles is not so much about speed as it is power and rhythm," says Martel. "I knew that if I could three step at least nine of the ten hurdles I could medal at the Nationals. I thought that if I could do those things *and* run faster than I ever had, I could win the gold."

## How Did He Do That?

Martel won the race on a warm Saturday afternoon, with a 16.69, probably the fastest M65 time in the world in 1997. How did he get faster?

"Ten days before the Nationals, a five-day business trip took me to Hawaii, usually a great place to go but the last place I wanted to be in at that particular time," said Martel. "I asked Coach Marty Kruger what I should do and how I could best avail myself of a nearby golf course."

Kruger surprised him. "Find a gentle downslope and do nothing but run downhill. Run in bursts of 200 meters, walk back and do it over again for about 45 minutes," he told Martel.

The advice surprised Martel, but as an ex-U.S. Air Force pilot (1951–55), he was used to following orders. He credits Kruger's words with improving his "turnover" speed. When he was warming up just before the race in San Jose, he had to check the marks on the track to be sure the hurdles weren't spaced too close together. "I knew at that moment that I might be able to do it," said Martel.

He describes his high school and collegiate athletic career as that of a "decent journeyman athlete, nothing special." He lettered in football, basketball, and track at Modesto Junior College and played basketball at the University of Oregon. His planned 1950 track season at Eugene was interrupted by the Korean War.

## An Accomplished Career

After the service, Martel focused on his studies, which have served him pretty well. He has been described by the National Law Journal as one of the top ten trial lawyers in the U.S. He is a member of the Board of Regents of the American College of Trial Lawyers and has tried 100 jury trials, 96 of them victories.

He is author of the best-selling novel *Partners* (Bantam, 1988) and *Conflicts of Interest* (Pocket Books, 1995). He is currently finishing his third novel, which he considers his best yet.

So, which of his major accomplishments is he most proud of?

"Winning the gold in San Jose, of course. Nothing else is even close."[3]

My goal achieved, I kept my promise to Bonnie and retired from track-and-field that same day. I maintained contact with Marion Sanchez, a good man who'd become a friend over the years. As an example of his character, Marion phoned his local newspaper soon after San Jose to correct a report that his victory in South Africa was the fastest time in the world during 1997, advising the reporter that my time at San Jose was now the fastest in the world for the year. (It was also faster than Phil Mulkey's time winning the 1995 Buffalo World Championship.) In addition, Marion, who took third place in San Jose, was instrumental in coaxing the disgruntled second place finisher, Jim Stookey, to participate in the awards ceremony by taking his place at the lower level of the victory podium.

---

[3] *National Masters News*, January, 1998, 7. Reprinted with permission.

I needed no coaxing to take my place at the top. It was one of the happiest days of my life, and I'll never forget it. My teammates, my sister Mary and her husband Don, and my many other friends in attendance shared my joy. Bonnie was the most ecstatic of all, particularly when I dropped my track shoes in the nearest recycling bin, symbolic of my retirement. I called Jay in Los Angeles and Melissa in Humboldt, where each was working, and thus unable to attend the meet. We shared the excitement together as soon as we could, toasting the event with shots of tequila.

I paused during the celebration to reflect on the apparently flippant response I had given the reporter from *National Masters News* at the end of the interview. He had asked me which of my lifetime accomplishments made me most proud. My answer was, "Winning the gold in San Jose, of course. Nothing else is even close." It struck me on reflection that my frivolous answer had captured the truth. I had been running nonstop all my life in search of self-acceptance, and now I finally felt a sense of inner peace.

# Chapter 27

# Three's a Crowd: Living with Dr. Parkinson

> One for the money, two for the show, three to get ready
> To let it all go.
> Love everything just like it is, and that's all the truth
> You need to know.
> —"On and On" (1973)

**I WAS DIAGNOSED WITH** Parkinson's in 2012, but this will be a short chapter, for although the disease defines nearly all my life's activities now, this is my memoir, so I get to choose how much space it gets. Accordingly, suffice it to say that I represent a textbook example of Parkinson's, experiencing all the classic symptoms: obvious palsy of the right (dominant) hand, difficulty swallowing and speaking, a shuffling walk, difficulty rising from a chair, fatigue, forgetfulness, lost balance, and living in fear of my next fall.

More important is what Parkinson's has *not* taken from me, for I also get to choose the attitude with which I confront these limitations. Isn't this always the case in life? Bad things happen to everybody, but how one reacts to the thing is always more important than the thing itself. No matter how hard the challenge, you can always assume your *attitude* has your back and the way you respond to adversity is the one thing nobody can take away from you.

One way attitude manifests itself in my life is in gratitude. I don't have to look far to see people worse off. Accordingly, I'm grateful, for example, that fate dealt me the Parkinson's hand, rather than, for example, the stage 4 lung cancer hand, for which thirty years of smoking certainly qualified me. Hardly an hour goes by that I'm not grateful my loving Bonnie, to whom I owe everything, entered my life thirty years ago. In short, I've got an attitude of gratitude.

My own version of the disease started at the age of eighty with a barely discernible tremor of my right hand. Alas, that would soon change, and the palsy would exacerbate, eventually depriving me of the ability to legibly write my name, play the piano, or type on a keyboard. (I wrote this book with the aid of speech recognition software created by Nuance called Dragon NaturallySpeaking.) With a steady progression, I feel my body being invaded by an unfriendly alien force. Could it be Dr. Parkinson himself? Who is this guy anyway?

James Parkinson was an English surgeon and social reformer, known primarily for writing antigovernment pamphlets advocating for the people. I probably would have liked the man, but what made him famous—infamous actually—was an essay he wrote in 1817 on what he called paralysis agitans: the "Shaking Palsy." He was the first to publicize the condition that would come to bear his name.

The disease is commonly known as a progressive movement disorder, the accuracy of which I can attest to as I find it a little harder to walk today than it was last month. The problem is that certain nerve cells (neurons) located in the brain are engaging in neurodegeneration, either malfunctioning or dying, so the brain no longer produces dopamine, a chemical messenger essential to normal communication between the brain and the body. Dopamine is called the "feel good" chemical because it serves to mediate the pleasure and reward center of the brain. Dopamine plays a critical role in how we feel about life as we go about such basic functions as remembering, focusing, and movement. It isn't surprising, therefore, that depression is an inevitable symptom of Parkinson's Disease, though it hasn't hit me yet—probably because I've been too busy for it.

Nobody knows why these dopamine-producing neurons fail or how to stop the progressive failure from happening once it starts.

I was going to mention something about the impact of Parkinson's on memory, but it's slipped my mind. My memory's not as sharp as it used to be. Also, my memory's not as sharp as it used to be.

On May 4, 2016, Dr. Paul Larson of UCSF Medical Center, went—like Captain Kirk—where no man has gone before: deep inside my brain. The hope was that the tremor in my right hand would be eliminated or minimized. Because of my advanced years, I was subjected to two days of rigorous physical and mental testing before I got the green light.

Did the surgery work? Only a very little, but every little bit helps with Parkinson's and I was later told the effectiveness of the surgery diminishes inversely with the age of the patient. Still, I have no regrets.


## Coming Attractions Near You

There are a few Parkinson's symptoms I have yet to experience, such as frozen facial features, inability to swallow, serious mental deterioration, hallucinations, and delusions. I choose not to dwell on those. What I want to think about is my good fortune in having been visited with the disease so late in life, having a loving, caring, and competent wife who will stop at nothing to make life continue to be worth living for me, and having the positive attitude to face each day anew. When people offer sympathy to me, I tell them there are worse things, like the cancer that swiftly ended the life of Suzy Katz last year, one of our dearest friends. In summary, I'm a lucky man.

# Chapter 28

# Mystery Solved

> The older I grow, the less I know
> About the man they wanted me to be
> But the more I say goodbye to them
> The more I say hello to me.
> —"On and On" (1973)

**I GAZE OUT FROM** my home office at the San Lorenzo River, as I have done now for forty-five years. Rising up some one hundred feet across the river is one of the most beautiful sheer cliffs I've seen anywhere in the world. Pine boughs and lush ferns cascade down its face toward the river like tears, recording nearly a half-century of personal joy and sorrow, the birth of four grandchildren, five published novels, a happy marriage, and the death of some good friends. I've just turned ninety-three and feel very much alive.

Mallards and wood duck families cruise back and forth on this river, ever alert for the hawk and osprey that coexist with them. A great blue heron soars by in graceful flight, perhaps in search of a mate, or maybe just a meal.

The cliff that majestically rises out of the river is less than the distance of a football field from me, as is the San Lorenzo River itself, its timeless flow moving from east to west. Between my office and the river is a natural white beach that runs a hundred yards along our property line, also visible from the master bedroom, the dining room, and the downstairs guest suite.

Like the cliff, the river has been my friend since 1975, yielding up scores of rainbow trout and seriously threatening my safety only once, in 1982, when it rose nearly thirty feet during a major storm that ultimately took several lives. I was sandbagging my lower patio when the raging waters miraculously crested, then retreated, thankfully without spilling into the guest bedroom below.

The river has traveled past many admirers before me and will continue to flow toward the Monterey Bay long after I'm gone. And although neither the river nor the cliff will long mourn or even note my passing, I'm content to have been able to enjoy both, and to share them with my beloved wife, Bonnie, and other friends and family, especially Jay, Melissa, and their children, all of whom love spending time at River House.

> You know, a man goes through what I've gone through, he's supposed to have learned something. I'm tryin' to figure out what I've learned.
> —Roy, Kevin Costner's character in *Tin Cup*

To my readers: First, thank you for staying with me as I, like Roy, have been "tryin' to figure out what I've learned," so I might hopefully answer the question with which I began this quest over 300 pages ago: Who was responsible for my neurotically driven nature?

Shortly after the publication of his memoir in September 2016, Bruce Springsteen revealed the source of his drive during a conversation with CBS Sunday Morning host Anthony Mason, saying, "I believe every artist has someone who told them that they weren't worth dirt and someone who told them that they were the second coming of baby Jesus, and they believed 'em both. And that's the fuel that starts the fire."

This rang a bell with me, for I had a father telling me I was dirt and a mother who insisted I was Jesus Christ. I suppose I "believed them both."

As for solving the mystery of who or what was most responsible for my driven nature, it's clear at last that the most guilty party was my father, Henry Martel. So, though I am retired from the practice of law, I still have one more case to prosecute. What are the charges I lay against my father? I will list only a few.

First of all, he was guilty of giving me the gift of life, bringing me into a world where anything is possible, where one can have the satisfaction of achievement and the joy of accomplishment, a world in which I have been surrounded by more success than I deserve and a host of supportive friends and loved ones.

He was also guilty of transmitting to me some of his wit and intelligence, and a few of his physical qualities, gifts that have served me well.

Yes, he was also guilty of being harshly demanding and setting impossible standards, especially for an anxious and inept young boy. These standards, however, also set the bar I determined to reach—and exceed—when it was time to face the exacting demands of the real world. I was ready for them. As for fatherly love, I believe Henry Martel was guilty of doing the best he could.

In conclusion, my father needs no forgiveness from me. I have come to understand in the writing of these pages how difficult it must have been for a man of that era to be thrust into fatherhood without a training manual, having lacked a decent role model himself. I certainly struggled with this at times myself.

Perhaps the most you can ever fairly ask of a parent is that they did their best with the tools they were given. The record reflects, however, that were it not for my mother's counteractive and moderating influence, I wouldn't be so accepting now of my father's harsher brand.

Perhaps there is a God.

The road I have traveled in seeking the approval I failed to get from Henry Martel has not always been easy, but despite the occasional ruts and detours, I look back on my audacious journey with appreciation. I took many bold risks, and more often than not, they paid off. I believed, sometimes naively, that I could overcome any obstacle, and this faith in my own abilities caused many obstacles to shrink, even disappear. I understood my limitations but consistently tried to transcend them, with the result of accomplishing more than I ever thought possible. Perhaps most important, I gave my own children the love and encouragement I never received from my father, breaking the cycle of which he was a part.

Finally, in solving the "mystery," I realize that the guilty party, having been dead for over a half-century, has no power now to dictate how I live my life, an insight that will belatedly free me to enjoy my remaining years in peace and tranquility, driven no more.

# Epilogue

I hear my father's stern voice as in a dream. *So, John, what have you done with your life during the past fifty years since that day you saw me off to the Great Unknown?*

I meet his direct gaze, noticing that his eyes seem more gentle than they did before, and say, "Dad, like you, I did the best I could."

# Appendix

## Observations on Our Justice System

The justice system in which I chose to work cannot be blamed for my obsessive behavior or be considered a suspect in my personal investigation. Every vocation or profession has its own system and I would have been neurotically driven in any of them. Whenever I'm asked for my opinion about our justice system, I paraphrase Winston Churchill's comment about democracy: "Our justice system is the worst system in the world except all the others that have been tried."

Although there is indeed much to admire about our system of justice, it isn't without flaws, the worst being its historical failure to consistently provide justice to minorities and the poor. Bryan Stevenson summed it up this way: "We have a criminal justice system that treats you better if you're rich and guilty than if you're poor and innocent."

It's undoubtedly true that wealthy litigants do well in our justice system. We saw in the chapter on the first Menendez case and the Simpson trial how overmatched prosecutors can be overwhelmed by a superior defense team supported by an unlimited budget.

Another problem with our justice system is the average citizen's low opinion of the lawyers who are charged with the responsibility of making it work, combined with a general confusion and distrust about the system's effectiveness. This drawback is aggravated by grossly inaccurate television and movie depictions. The negative results of this distrust are summarized in speeches I gave to plenary sessions of the American College of Trial Lawyers, twice in Florida in 1989 and 1999, once in San Antonio in 1995, and a fourth time to a regional College meeting in Washington state in 1996.

I have included the text of one of these speeches, not because I'm proud of it (although I am), but because of my belief in the importance of the subject. The audience for this particular speech consisted of the top trial lawyers in America, but a lay audience should have no difficulty understanding it, and hopefully will be entertained in the process.

### Justice and the Media: An Address to the ACTL in Florida (1999)

I'd like to speak today about how the current plague of bad legal fiction—books, movies, and television—combined with some current reality in the Clinton impeachment hearings and several high-profile cases, have created a dangerous distrust in our judicial system. Perhaps we should call it "*quasi*-reality," because although we know that events like the O. J. Simpson trial and the Clinton impeachment hearings really happened, they happened for most of us on television, accompanied by talking heads telling us how to think about them. Parenthetically, the "reality" of these particular examples reminds us once again that truth is often stranger than fiction.

I will start my comments with a riddle: What do courtroom fiction, much of the news media, O. J. Simpson, and the President of the United States have in common?

The first thing, of course, is that they all have problems telling the truth. Second, they have all had a profound impact on the justice system and on we professionals charged with protecting its integrity.

I think it not too much to suggest that a war is being waged by a hostile media—especially the entertainment media—on the image of lawyers, and that we've lost nearly every battle to date. An unintended victim of this war has been the justice system. Why is this so and why is it important?

My answer is that the justice system is the foundation of any democracy, and when faith in the existence of justice fades, distrust of the democratically elected government can follow. The public gains or loses faith in institutions because of what it sees and hears, and what the public sees and hears—and therefore learns—is largely what is shown on television, and in movies and books. And what is it that the public learns from these *faux* teachers?

Take the movie version of Grisham's *The Rainmaker*, for example. It opens with a picture of a shark tank and a voiceover that proclaims, "Memphis is infested with lawyers." Later, Danny DeVito tells Matt Damon how to chase ambulances for profit, and the movie closes with Damon—the only lawyer on either side of the featured case who's not an outright criminal—abandoning the practice of law after scoring a $50 million verdict . . . on his very first trial.

Why does he leave the practice? Because, we're told, "*Every* lawyer at least once in *every* case, finds himself crossing the line, and if you cross it enough times it disappears forever and you've become just another lawyer joke—just another shark in the dirty water."

There is an irony here, for as much as the entertainment media—Hollywood, television, and book writers—continue to seem appalled by lawyers and the trial process, they continue to be *fascinated* by the lawyers and the trials they demean.

Judge Alex Kozinski explained this preoccupation with our profession in 1995:

"It's not surprising that lawyers in trials are a perennial subject in movie making. Trials, by their nature, concentrate human conflict. They force a head-on clash of opposing forces."

So why doesn't reality alone provide sufficient excitement to satisfy the demands of fiction, without turning the trial process upside down? As Judge Kozinski suggests, a trial has everything: one-on-one conflict, pressure to win (sometimes against all odds), and that ultimate, heart-stopping moment of suspense: "We, the members of the jury, find the defendant . . ."

I once publicly debated Charles B. Rosenberg, who was a producer of *L.A. Law,* a show described in *Newsweek* as "the TV series that has raised lawyer bashing to a spectator sport." Rosenberg was in charge of legal accuracy for the series, and when I had listed three particularly dangerous procedural and substantive inaccuracies that must have confused the public about the adversary system, his rueful reply was that a day in the life of a lawyer just does not make television drama. "We settle," he said, "for 'reasonably close.'"

So why does the entertainment media feel a need to distort and misrepresent an already-abundant source of suspenseful entertainment? Part of the problem is that most of the professional writers of courtroom fiction are or were merely *amateur* courtroom practitioners. They wouldn't understand this response from blind tenor Andrea Bocelli—who incidentally is a lawyer—when he was asked if experience and repetition made his stage performances easier.

"No," he said. "It gets worse . . . because of the responsibility."

Just out of law school, I recall the level of anxiety with which I approached my first records deposition. My first motion to dismiss under the five-year statute. Then, as a young associate, my first trial. A simple breach of contract case in front of a judge. I was so nervous I could barely state my appearance.

But I did okay, and one morning years later I woke up and found myself a partner and lead counsel in a multimillion-dollar securities fraud case. Does it get easier with experience and repetition? No, *because the responsibility increases correspondingly*!

Like bullfighting and other high-risk professions, jury trials place heavy psychic demands on their practitioners. Picture the courtroom as the *plaza de toros*. Your witness is the bull. The jury's implacable inscrutability pushes you closer to the horns, and you can't shut out Robert Frost's description of a jury as "twelve persons chosen to decide who has the better lawyer." After years of this, some of us begin to feel like a character in my first novel, *Partners*:

> So one day [he says, talking to a younger lawyer] the trial lawyer begins to take full responsibility for whether his client's case is won or lost, the ultimate conceit. Pretty soon he's got himself convinced that the jury is judging him more than the facts of the case. Finally, he wakes up one morning and realizes he's burning himself out. He's begun to fear losing more than feeling the satisfaction of seeing a just result or even the joy of winning. When he does win, he feels only relief he didn't lose.

And here's a piece from my 1994 novel, *Conflicts of Interest*, where my protagonist, who sees that the jury has bought into his opponent's argument, is desperately trying to marshal his thoughts and control his raging emotions as the judge and jury impatiently await his own closing argument. This is a young lawyer and hardly a model for any of us in this room, but his anguish may resonate somewhere in your own past:

> He listened to the familiar courtroom sounds: the clerk's muffled whisper into her telephone, a juror's self-conscious cough, the velvet key-taps of the court reporter's machine catching up on exhibit numbers, and a wheezing noise like a bicycle wheel in need of oil—his own breathing. At least he was breathing again, although it felt like something closer to hyperventilation.
>
> His mouth was dry as asphalt. He wanted to lick his lips, but resisted the impulse, knowing the jury was watching him now as he twisted like an insect on the

end of his adversary's pin, all twelve of them watching
now for the slightest indication of uncertainty, of fear.

He began to resent those jurors with their smoth-
ering eyes all over him, staring at his pock-scarred
cheeks, expecting too much of him. He pictured himself rising to his feet, but instead of delivering his
closing argument, simply wishing his client the best
of luck and then walking out of the courtroom into
the warmth of the late-morning sun.

He didn't walk out, of course, and those of you who read the book—
those of you who I still count as friends—know he won his case by
swallowing a bug in his closing argument, an authentic feat, incidentally,
successfully and legitimately employed in 1963 in a Bakersfield superior
courtroom by a fine defense lawyer, the late Bernard C. Kearns of the
late San Francisco firm of Bronson, Bronson & McKinnon.

The last excerpt I'll read today supports Bocelli's view that the tension
does not ease with time and experience, because the stakes increase and
so does the pressure. The platform from which you dive keeps getting
higher, while the water tank below appears smaller and smaller. Here
are the anguished thoughts of an aging, burnt-out trial lawyer, Barrett
Dickson, from my current novel, *The Alternate*, as *he* faces the jury for
his closing argument:

He had almost forgotten how insatiable jurors could
be in their silent hunger for words that would sway
them, words that would disturb and excite them. In
that passive silence, they demanded more attention
than a division of West Point generals. And given
enough opportunities over enough years, Barrett
knew those twelve silent citizens could suck trial
lawyers dry and turn them into barren husks.

They had done it to him.

Instead of harvesting the lush field of reality offered by the courtroom, nearly all legal fiction writers have distorted what goes on there, including even the most basic procedures. Misrepresentation of the actual workings of a courtroom started with *Perry Mason*, a show that captured the growing cynicism of the sixties by portraying all police as stupid, and the prosecutor—aptly named Hamilton Burger—as a man who managed to charge an innocent person every week. But not to worry. You knew Perry would always bring the perjurers to their knees in tears, blubbering a confession.

Have you *ever* done this, fellow trial lawyers? No? That's why we must take Mason seriously. For a whole generation, *Perry Mason* was the media's primary portrayal of our adversary system and the public's primary source of knowledge about how it worked. And his weekly lesson was that, but for a miracle—a Hail Mary pass in the final minute of play—the criminal justice system was unable to produce fairness and truth.

Moreover, shows like Mason raised unrealistic expectations on the part of clients. Your client may wonder whether you're even a real lawyer if you can't bring the adverse party witness to her knees the way Perry always did—or get up and make an eloquent speech midtrial, like Denzel Washington did in *Philadelphia.* "Hell," your client is probably thinking, "nobody seemed to mind when Denzel did it, so get your ass up there and make a spellbinding speech."

The entertainment media wasn't always this way. As a third-year law student in 1959, I watched Jimmy Stewart and George C. Scott duke it out in *Anatomy of a Murder* and knew I was entering a profession of courage and dignity.

Then there was Harper Lee's inspirational novel *To Kill a Mockingbird* and Gregory Peck's portrayal of the heroic Atticus Finch in the movie version. Peck breathed life into John Henry Wigmore's declaration that "cross-examination is the greatest engine for the discovery of truth ever invented." In the process, Finch exposed bigotry, demonstrated courage, and again convinced me I had made the right career choice—though I was supporting a wife and child that year on $325 a month.

Ah, but that was the past and, to paraphrase Yeats, "In days of great joy, find comfort in the fact that disaster is just around the corner."

Disaster came in the form of movies like *Jagged Edge* (1985), which not only distorted the trial process, but heralded an insidious trend of portraying gross ethical violations by lawyers as commonplace—indeed, necessary to achieving justice. In *Jagged Edge*, Glenn Close struts about the courtroom in sprayed-on skirts that would make a prostitute blush and indulges in a nighttime ex parte visit to the trial judge at his home *during the trial*. Even worse is *Suspect* (1987), in which a victim is found floating in the Potomac River. Defense lawyer Cher, apparently short of her associates' support, enrolls a member of her *jury* to help her track down evidence and do the legal research that wins a verdict for her client. One critic said that the only thing real about *Suspect* is that the Potomac River does indeed flow through Washington, DC.

In *Class Action* (1991), a father and daughter team up at trial to win big for the plaintiffs, then start their own law firm with the fees from the huge class action verdict. Nothing wrong with that, but for the fact that the daughter happened to be lead counsel for the defendant corporation the whole time—which, incidentally, didn't seem to bother anybody in this sterling Hollywood model of family values.

Then there was *Guilty as Sin* (1993), in which Rebecca De Mornay, a successful criminal defense lawyer, decides midtrial that, darn it, her client is guilty as hell, so she breaks into his building and plants evidence that will incriminate him, then anonymously tips off the police.

Perhaps most damaging of all was *The Verdict*, because it was so damned wonderful to watch. It was directed by Sidney Lumet and had a perfect cast, featuring Paul Newman and James Mason, and was adapted from Barry Reed's novel by David Mamet—arguably the best screenwriter around. Given this Hollywood A-Team, one walked out of the theater feeling thoroughly entertained—perhaps even fulfilled—

because, after all, the good guys won. But if we quizzed laypeople the next day as to lessons learned about lawyers and the legal system, I submit they will have gained the following impressions:

1. When sober enough to catch a cab, lawyers attend funerals to pass out business cards (a breach of ethics);
2. An industrious lawyer like Newman will courageously do anything to win for his client, including breaking into an official US mailbox (a federal felony);
3. Good-looking female employees of a big firm will conceal their affiliation with the defense and take their adversary to bed in order to engage in inappropriate physical discovery;
4. Big-firm lawyers like James Mason can simply send unsympathetic medical expert witnesses out of the opposition's reach by treating them to an exotic foreign vacation;
5. Lawyers don't have to convey settlement offers to clients; and,
6. Judges are corrupt and can be bought by big firms.

Would any of you do any of these things for *your* client in the real world? Of course not. As lawyers, we may lament or find laughable the absurd objections made by Mason and sustained by the judge, Mason's failure to ask for a directed verdict, the obvious misuse of the hearsay rule exceptions and the best evidence rule. And yet even most of *us* will suspend disbelief—because it ended up okay.

But it's not okay and here's why:

As I have tried to show, the justice system is at the foundation of any working democracy, and when faith in the machinery of justice fades, anarchy waits in the growing shadows. Sir Edward Coke wrote: "Truth is the mother of justice." Public faith in any justice system, therefore, necessarily depends on the system's *perceived* capacity to discern *truth*. Without the mother, there can be no daughter. Without truth, there can be no justice.

So, to Alexis de Tocqueville's list of conditions that threaten a democracy—egotistical individualism and narcissism—add bad teaching and a failure of public confidence in the justice system.

So you won't think I'm inextricably stuck in the past—a grizzled, jaded anachronism longing for the good old days, contemptuous of all law movies released in the last two decades, and bitter because Hollywood has unaccountably failed to adapt any of my own novels into a movie—I want to leave you with an example of one film that I do think is excellent, a movie that will renew and inspire all of you who treasure our system of justice. I refer, of course, to . . . *My Cousin Vinny* (1992).

Sure, the movie is a farce, but look closely and you'll see that in the end a new lawyer with nothing but wit and guts has successfully refuted the innocently erroneous testimony of three eye witnesses, and then, with the reluctant help of Mona Lisa Vito as expert witness, persuaded the judge, the jury, and even the DA, that an injustice had been done in charging his two clients.

The movie is played for laughs, no harm is done, and all lawyers look honest—if somewhat silly—as the system works to perfection.

My review of current television shows is more optimistic but suffers from the fact that I haven't had much time to watch them lately. I will, however, declare on information and belief—and a handful of episodes—that *The Practice* and *Law & Order* are major improvements on *Perry Mason* and *L.A. Law*. I'm not sure what to make of *Ally McBeal*, which works for me as an entertaining, off-the-wall romantic cartoon, but lamentably veers off course in the direction of *L.A. Law* when it occasionally adopts the solemn pose of legitimate courtroom drama. Perhaps it deserves a *My Cousin Vinny* exemption.

Let's move from make believe to real life for a moment, because as much as fiction has distorted the public's perception of the justice system, the Simpson case and the recent unpleasantness in Washington, DC, suffered by President Bill Clinton—all exhaustively covered by the news media—remind us that life not only imitates art, but sometimes makes it look puritanical and dull by comparison.

Remember, for example, how long the jurors in *Twelve Angry Men* struggled to overcome their prejudices in the interest of finding the truth? Contrast that with the fast-acting relief the jurors afforded themselves at the close of Simpson.

Terms like "jury nullification," "payback," and "judicial affirmative action" were thrown around after the trial, and although we tried to console ourselves by acknowledging centuries of grave injustice cutting the other way against African Americans, the failure of just twelve ordinary citizens to act on the obvious truth first traumatized, then demoralized, most of the nation and engendered a distrust of lawyers and the criminal justice system that continues to this day. Consider, for example, an article from the *San Francisco Chronicle* earlier this year:

> [Citizens are] blowing off invitations to jury duty at a rate as high as 90% in some big cities such as New York and Los Angeles. The reason is simple, say keen observers of the legal scene: It's the O.J. effect, more fallout from the trial of the century. Since O.J., the theory goes, people have lost so much respect for the court system that they believe jury duty is a waste of time. Verdicts come out wrong, and trials are too complex. Better to ignore the summons.

I must repeat that from the Simpson case, the public also learned that we lawyers, the stewards of the system, can be petty, provocative, shrill, lacking in integrity, frequently incompetent, and capable of saying and doing anything to win. We take no prisoners; we shoot the dead; technicalities obstruct facts; much of the real evidence doesn't even get to the jury; and wealth can buy justice. (Eighty percent of people polled by the American Bar Association after the case said that celebrities get more justice than ordinary people.)

And did you read about Bob Enyart, an ordinary citizen (maybe a little strange), who paid $16,000 for O. J. memorabilia, then set it all ablaze on the courthouse steps saying, "We need to let the public know that the criminal justice system is a failure."

The Simpson case even fueled fiction's distortion of the trial process. Joel Schumacher, director of *The Client* and *A Time to Kill*, says "I think after the O. J. trial you can do anything in a movie and people will believe it. People know it is *all* outrageous."

Scott Turow recently said in an interview that it's harder to entertain people because they have seen the Simpson case. Thus, the entertainment bar is raised.

I think that's what may have been plaguing director Steven Zaillian as he undertook the Herculean task of turning Jonathan Harr's novel *A Civil Action* (1998) into a two-hour movie. Here's how *Variety* saw the result: "[a] solid and intelligent legal thriller that may be too complex in its issues, and too . . . unexciting in its style, for today's market demands."

There it is, our dirty little secret out in the open: If you don't give people what they think they want, they won't buy it. Having read Harr's fine book, my own relatively benign quibble with the movie version isn't that it didn't bend enough for commercial acceptance, but that it bent at all. We're not supposed to be dealing in fiction here—*A Civil Action* purports to be a real story about how things really happened—but the movie fudges with reality anyway. Yielding to the demands of "the market" and its cynical expectations, it paints the lawyers as alternately contemptuous of the justice system, and often just plain stupid. Robert Duvall, playing a Harvard Law professor, assures John Travolta's Jan Schlichtmann that the courtroom is "the *last* place you come in search of truth." Travolta, meanwhile, asks the forbidden open-ended "Why" question on cross-examination and gets hammered, then continually overvalues his case and even declines a $20 million settlement offer without telling his clients.

We're left at the finish with the uneasy feeling that righteous outrage, persistence, and even the right cause can't stand up to cunning on one side and lack of experience on the other—or worse, that justice doesn't have a prayer against big money. No wonder people love to quote Shakespeare's "The first thing we do, let's kill all the lawyers." (And never bother to explain the point he was making, which was that for a totalitarian state to arrive, one would have to first "kill all the lawyers"!)

Then there are the politicians and the press, to whom we lawyers should give continuing thanks for trying to make us look good by comparison. God knows a democracy could not function without either, but consider the impact the recent Clinton impeachment hearings had on the public's perception of how our institutions work—or fail to work—thanks in part to the ubiquitous news media.

Regarding modern journalism, incidentally, I give you the assessment of no less esteemed authority than last month's *Rolling Stone* magazine, which includes the article "Columbine: Whose Fault Is It?," written by none other than Marilyn Manson, who the news media (falsely) claimed the killers worshiped and sought to emulate: "Times have not become more violent," Manson says (wrongly). "They have just become more televised." He adds (correctly), about the paparazzi who chased Princess Di: "Disgusting vultures looking for corpses, exploiting, . . . filming and serving it up for our hungry appetites in a gluttonous display of endless human stupidity."

Now, I can hear my fellow writers saying, "Lighten up, Martel. You've had bad-guy lawyers in your own books and, after all, its entertainment, for God's sake! It's okay." Well, first, I *hope* I've shown it's not okay. Second, I'm *not* saying it's improper to write evil fictional lawyers into books or scripts; all thrillers need a bad guy in order to pit good against evil. I'm just asking whether legal fiction writers need to be so *uniformly* hostile. Why must they provide the public with nothing but conniving, foolish, and incompetent lawyers, operating in an inherently vulnerable system that seems incapable of meting out justice without that last-minute Hail Mary pass?

The societal implications of distortion are potentially more danger-ous. Writers of legal thrillers must stop throwing *all* lawyers into the same shark tank. Sure, make your plot as bizarre as you want, but once you put your lawyers into the courtroom, be reasonably accurate concerning those procedural aspects of trial that can—if misrepresented—leave the public thinking there are no courtroom rules to protect them, and, conversely, raising unrealistic expectations on the part of jurors and clients—the kind of expectations that sometimes push good trial lawyers into doing bad things.

As for my own writing, you will be the ultimate judge as to whether I've avoided this distortion without sacrificing page-turning excitement. To be an informed judge of my work, of course, you'll have to acquire and review the evidence—now available in bookstores everywhere!

Can anything really be done about all this? Not easily. As H. L. Mencken said, "Explanations exist; they have existed for all time; there is always a well-known solution to every human problem—neat, plausible, and wrong." Kris Kristofferson put it differently when he said: "I never learned anything that didn't contradict itself." Kristofferson, qua philosopher, is better known for having said, "Never go to bed with anyone crazier than yourself," and "If you can't fix it, fuck it."

But we *must* try to fix it, and certainly we lawyers and judges can do better, both by example and by becoming the primary teachers about how the adversary system *really* works. Lawyer associations like this one have contributed much to encouraging civility among lawyers and educating the public, a function that we cannot continue to abdicate to fiction. We *must* recapture the education process from the media and, to be successful, we must use the media's own weapons.

You can also help by voting with your pocketbook. Continue to pay for assaults on the profession and movie makers and publishers will keep grinding them out. Pay for crap and they'll keep serving it up. I once heard an adman say to a client with a software idea, "It's a great product; I think I can get the dogs to eat it." Tom Wolfe calls this, in his novel *A Man in Full*, "sloppin' the pigs." *He's talking about us, the consumers.*

Oscar Wilde said in *Lady Windermere's Fan*, "We are all in the gutter, but some of us are looking at stars." Publishers look at the best-seller list and conclude that most of the public seems to *want* its writers of legal fiction in the gutter. So, it's ultimately up to those of us who write courtroom fiction to take more time and more care, and to recognize the power of words to do ill as they entertain.

As for my own modest aspirations, I will continue to try to look at the stars, but perhaps all I can hope for is to have said of me what Huck Finn said of his creator, Mark Twain, in Chapter 1 of *Huckleberry Finn*: "There was things which he stretched, but mainly he told the truth."

Thank you.